OXFORD ESSAYS IN JURISPRUDENCE

THIRD SERIES

OXFORD ESSAYS IN JURISPRUDENCE

THIRD SERIES

EDITED BY

JOHN EEKELAAR

AND

JOHN BELL

CLARENDON PRESS · OXFORD

1987

Oxford University Press, Walton Street, Oxford OX2 6DP
Oxford New York Toronto
Delhi Bombay Calcutta Madras Karachi
Petaling Jaya Singapore Hong Kong Tokyo
Nairobi Dar es Salaam Cape Town
Melbourne Auckland
and associated companies in
Beirut Berlin Ibadan Nicosia

Oxford is a trade mark of Oxford University Press

Published in the United States
by Oxford University Press, New York

British Library Cataloguing in Publication Data
Oxford essays in jurisprudence: third series.
1. Jurisprudence
I. Eekelaar, John II. Bell, John, 1953–
340'.1 K230
ISBN 0–19–825507–1

Library of Congress Cataloging-in-Publication Data
Oxford essays in jurisprudence, third series.
1. Jurisprudence. I. Eekelaar, John. II. Bell, John (John S.)
K235.093 1987 340.1 86-33302
ISBN 0–19–825507–1

Set by Wyvern Typesetting Ltd, Bristol
Printed in Great Britain
at the Alden Press, Oxford

PREFACE

THE first volume of *Oxford Essays*, published in 1961, collected together essays on jurisprudential topics by writers who were, or were recently, teaching in Oxford. A second followed in 1973. The present collection might therefore be considered to reflect the direction taken in the jurisprudential interests of many of the successors of those essayists in the following decade. Given the number of persons engaged in the subject and the wide variety of their interests, this volume has not attempted to be fully representative of current activity in jurisprudence at Oxford. The editors did not impose a specific structure on the collection, other than to express the wish that the general orientation of the volume would be towards the exploration of how far legal theory or theories might illuminate particular areas of practical law, and, conversely, how far the experience of practical law might contribute to a fuller evaluation of theory. The result, it seems, has been to draw the spirit of the contributions closer to that of the 1961 collection than to that of the second volume. But their substance is, we think, very different from either of the preceding books.

Our main task has been the administrative one of assembling the material. Our gratitude, and that of various of the contributors, is owed in full measure to Professor A. M. Honoré, who read most of the submissions in draft and made numerous valuable criticisms from which we all benefited and which will be passed on in unobservable ways to the reader. Professor Honoré will vacate the Chair of Civil Law through retirement at the end of the academic year during which this volume will be published. We hope that his influence will continue to be felt for long after that.

JOHN BELL
JOHN EEKELAAR

CONTENTS

I

Belief, Intent, and Criminal Liability*

ANDREW ASHWORTH

1. CRIMINAL LAW AND CRIMINAL LIABILITY

THE fundamental reason for having a system of criminal law is to provide a framework for the state punishment of wrongdoers, and thereby to preserve an acceptable degree of social order. Without criminal laws and their enforcement, each individual's person, property, and family would be substantially less safe from deliberate violation by others. It would hardly be sufficient to declare that individual members of society have certain rights, to physical integrity, security of property, and so on. It is also necessary *inter alia* to take steps to see that rights are not violated, a first step to which is to declare that individuals have duties not to violate the rights of others. Various branches of the civil law require those who negligently breach a duty to pay compensation to those whose rights were thus violated, and other parts of the civil law provide remedies for some deliberate breaches of duty. The specific technique of the criminal law is to provide for the conviction and punishment of those who culpably breach the more serious duties. Typically, the criminal law will declare which forms of conduct and omissions constitute such a serious breach of duty that they call for prosecution, conviction, and sentence under a special 'criminal' procedure and separately from private disputes among citizens. Attached to that declaration will be a system of enforcement and sentencing which operates, by and large, to influence people not to violate these laws. Even those who adopt a retributivist or rights-based approach to criminal liability and punishment surely cannot maintain a general indifference towards the frequency with which these more serious rights and duties are breached. A major part of the reason for having a system of criminal law and punishment is surely to reduce the frequency of those violations.

When one turns from the justifications for having criminal law to the conditions for criminal liability, the issues are different. The process of prosecution, trial, conviction, and punishment involves prima facie violations of the interests of the individual defendant. Indeed, some punishments (such as fines and imprisonment) are distinct derogations from the freedom of the individual. In what circumstances is it justifiable to punish an individual for a crime? It should first be stated that this essay proceeds on the general assumption that most individuals have sufficient capacity for choice to make it fair to hold them criminally liable when the other requirements of the law are fulfilled, and to regard references to 'choice', 'intention', and so on as meaningful.[1] Those who are consequentialists would justify the threat and the infliction of punishment if and in so far as its effect in deterring the commission of offences by others (general deterrence) and/or the commission of further offences by this offender (individual deterrence) outweighs any detrimental effects it may have. Many consequentialists would, however, qualify this justification by accepting that punishment ought not to be inflicted on an individual unless he has committed a criminal act with the required fault, a qualification which respects the right of an individual, as an autonomous and responsible being, not to be subjected to criminal sanctions unless he can fairly be said to have chosen to commit the crime.[2] The qualification might not be insisted upon for all types of offences, for example crimes of strict liability.

An alternative approach is that of modern retributivism. The punishment of a criminal may be justified if and in so far as it tends to 'restore an order of fairness which was disrupted by the criminal's criminal act'.[3] The criminal law imposes various duties on individuals in order to secure for everyone the benefits of security of person and property. It might therefore be said that, in committing a criminal offence, the offender casts off the burden of self-restraint which other citizens continue to bear. He gains an unfair advantage over the law-abiding citizens, which it is the purpose of criminal punishment to counterbalance.[4] An individual deserves punishment if and to the extent that he has

[1] For an elaboration and defence of this view, see A. Kenny, *Freewill and Responsibility* (London, 1978).

[2] See H. L. A. Hart, *Punishment and Responsibility* (Oxford, 1968), ch. 1; D. A. J. Richards, 'Rights, Utility and Crime', in M. Tonry and N. Morris (eds.), *Crime and Justice*, iii (Chicago, 1981), 247.

[3] J. Finnis, *Fundamentals of Ethics* (Oxford, 1983), 128.

[4] For two slightly different versions of modern retributivism, see J. G. Murphy, 'Marxism and Retribution' (1972–3) 2 *Philosophy and Public Affairs*, 217 and W. Sadurski, 'Distributive Justice and the Theory of Punishment' (1985) 5 *Oxford J. of Legal Studies* 47.

culpably failed to observe the duty of self-restraint imposed upon him by the criminal law,[5] and the punishment is justified as an integral part of the restoration of the distribution of benefits and burdens in society (compensation of the victim is the other part).[6]

Both modern retributivists and those consequentialists who accept the qualifying principle maintain that criminal liability should only be imposed on persons who have broken a reasonably specific law, who had the full capacity and opportunity to conform to the law, and who could reasonably have been expected to know that such a law existed.[7] These requirements are based on the premiss that individuals have a general capacity to choose between alternative courses of action, and are entitled to equal concern and respect in exercising that capacity.[8] On the same view, the quantum of punishment should be regulated by the principle of proportionality between the sanction and the gravity of the offence.

> In this way, each person is guaranteed a greatest liberty, capacity, and opportunity of controlling and predicting the consequences of his or her actions compatible with a like liberty, capacity and opportunity for all ... In general, forms of mental state (intent, knowledge and individualized standards of recklessness and negligence) are required as necessary moral conditions of just punishment because the presence of these mental states ensures that the person may fairly be said to have had the capacity and opportunity to conform his conduct to the law. To the extent that intentional, as opposed to unintentionally negligent, actions involve easier or fuller opportunities to regulate conduct by principles, a higher grade of sanction would, on this view, justly be applied to the former than the latter, other things being equal.[9]

In principle, therefore, the gravity of an offence is not simply, and in some cases not chiefly, determined by the magnitude of the harm inflicted. The content of those duties, breach of which the criminal law penalizes, should consist of the culpable violation of rights or protected interests and not simply any violation of a right or protected interest.[10] In this essay there is to be no discussion of negligence or recklessness as forms of culpability. Intention and knowledge are the mental states

[5] See, for example, Sadurski, 55.

[6] For further discussion of the place of compensation, see A. Ashworth, 'Punishment and Compensation: Victims, Offenders and the State' (1986) 6 *Oxford J. of Legal Studies* 86.

[7] Hart, op. cit. n. 2 above; R. Dworkin, *Taking Rights Seriously* (London, 1977), 8–13.

[8] Richards, op. cit. n. 2 above; Dworkin, 199.

[9] Richards, 274–6, adapting Hart, op. cit.

[10] This leaves open the question whether negligence may be regarded as a form of culpability for this purpose, and also the question of the legitimacy of using 'strict' criminal liability for some offences.

which most clearly supply the basis for culpability, and by thus restricting the analysis it will be possible to explore more fully the relationship between culpability and harm.

Although culpability and harm may be regarded as the central elements of most crimes,[11] there are some classes of offence which cannot be cast so readily into the form of culpable non-self-restraint by one individual and harm to another. First, there are crimes against the state—espionage, disclosure of official secrets, treason, and so forth. These might be accommodated within the analysis by regarding them as crimes against collective interests, or against all citizens and not simply one citizen, but the point will not be developed here. Second, there are the so-called victimless crimes—possession, supply, or importation of dangerous drugs, for example. These are offences which are defined so as not to require any harmful consequences, and/or where the individual harmed has chosen to inflict the harm on himself. The justifications for extending the criminal law to such conduct may be moralistic or paternalistic; whether either justification is sound will not be discussed here. Third, there are preventive offences such as possessing an offensive weapon or behaviour likely to cause a breach of the peace. The point of criminalizing conduct of this kind is to forestall the occurrence of harm. Preventive offences must therefore be justified as an explicit exception to the harm requirement, or at least as an extension of it. The extension might be that the manifestation of a firm intent to cause a substantive harm (in the sense that possessing a weapon betokens an intent to inflict injury) gives rise to such fear and concern among citizens as to amount to a harm in itself, albeit a diluted version of the substantive harm intended.[12] However, the justification for preventive offences is probably better regarded as an exception to the harm requirement, allowing criminalization before the actual occurrence of harm so as to ensure fuller protection for the rights upheld by the

[11] There are weighty arguments in favour of a threefold analysis of harm, unlawfulness, and culpability: see P. H. Robinson, 'A Theory of Justification: Societal Harm as a Prerequisite for Criminal Liability' (1975) 23 *UCLA Law Rev.* 266 and G. P. Fletcher, *Rethinking Criminal Law* (Boston, 1978). However, in the present context nothing turns on whether unlawfulness (absence of justification) is regarded as part of the harm requirement or as a separate element, since the aim is to explore the moral basis for liability and non-liability.

[12] Robinson argues that the harmfulness of inchoate offences is different 'from the harm which might have resulted had the actor's intent been fulfilled'. In explanation, however, he merely asserts that 'the harm is intangible in character, and society is its object' and that it consists of a 'disturbance of the social order' and 'substantial but incomplete impairment of some interest' (269–71).

criminal law. On this view, the proper limits of preventive offences should be set by reference to the closeness to the substantive harm, the firmness of the defendant's intent, and the protection of defendants' rights.[13] It should be noticed that in English law one offence of burglary is now drafted as a preventive offence, criminalizing a person who enters a building as a trespasser with intent to steal (irrespective of what happens thereafter, whether he finds anything to steal or whether there is anything capable of being stolen).[14] The offence of theft in English law also comes close to being a preventive offence, since it may be committed by dishonestly interfering adversely with a right of the owner of property, with intent to deprive him permanently of the property, even though the owner does not lose the property.[15]

Fourth, there are inchoate offences—attempt, conspiracy, and incitement. To a large extent the inchoate offences function as preventive crimes, rendering conduct punishable before the defendant has completed what he set out to do and before the intended harm has been caused. To this extent these 'incomplete attempts' share the rationale of preventive crimes, discussed above, and the same conflicting considerations bear upon the thorny issue of how early in the course of conduct it is proper to regard the *actus reus* of an attempt as fulfilled. However, inchoate offences have a separate function which should not be overlooked: they provide for the criminal liability of persons who complete all the acts they intend to do, and yet who fail to cause the consequences intended ('complete' attempts). Prevention is a relevant consideration in these cases, since the non-punishment of unsuccessful attempts might encourage more people to try (or to try again) and thus lead to more *successful* attempts, but prevention may not be an adequate rationale in all cases. If A shoots at B with intent to kill and misses, and then announces that he has no desire to try again, should he not be liable to conviction? Is it not arguable that he is punishable for his display of non-self-restraint, just as if it had resulted in the harm which he intended? The unavoidable element of chance in human affairs means that a person who commits a 'complete' attempt, as distinct from an 'incomplete' attempt, may be considered as culpable as the person who commits the substantive offence.[16] In terms of non-self-restraint, there is no relevant difference

13 A. Ashworth, 'Punishing Criminal Attempts' (forthcoming).

14 Theft Act 1968, s. 9 (1) (a).

15 Theft Act 1968, ss. 1 (1) and 3 (1), as interpreted by the House of Lords in *Morris* [1984] AC 320.

16 The distinctions between 'complete' and 'incomplete' attempts are explored further below.

between them. The same point applies to cases in which the defendant has done all the acts he intended to do but the intended result fails to follow because in the actual circumstances, unknown to the defendant, the result cannot be achieved by the acts done. On this view conspiracies, incitements, and attempts to do the impossible are rightly regarded as criminal offences, provided that the defendant believed that it was possible to achieve the intended result and acted in accordance with that belief. In terms of non-self-restraint by the defendant, there is no real difference in culpability between an 'impossible attempter' and a 'possible attempter'.

Those inchoate offences in which the defendant did all the acts he intended to do but nevertheless failed to achieve the desired effect, whether through incompetence or because the effect was impossible to achieve in the actual circumstances, may be regarded as embodying a challenge to the 'harm plus culpability' analysis of crimes suggested above. Such offences may be committed without causing harm and in circumstances where no harm could possibly result. A further challenge may be found in the fifth class of cases—those where a person inflicts harm on another but then discovers that, unknown to him, the victim was about to attack him in a way which would justify a violent response. Should such cases be decided according to the culpability requirement alone (ignoring the absence of a legally defined harm, arising from the unknown circumstances of justification), or should there be an insistence on the 'harm' requirement?[17] In English law there is authority for the former approach, apparently dispensing with the 'harm' requirement in such situations.[18] There are, however, strong arguments in favour of impunity in the absence of a legally defined harm and arguments against the criminalization of impossible attempts. One, which is discussed below, is that the criminal law should not diverge greatly from popular sentiments, and that these attribute considerable significance to the occurrence or non-occurrence of harm.[19] A second consideration is that 'public and visible facts' must be required if the criminal law is to have a sound political basis, since they 'assure the

[17] Those who adopt the threefold analysis of the elements of a crime (above, n. 11) would differentiate the fifth class from the others on the ground that it raises the distinct issue of unlawfulness and justification. However, the legal implications of this analysis may be overestimated (see A. T. H. Smith, in P. R. Glazebrook (ed.), *Reshaping the Criminal Law* (London, 1978), 95 and Glanville Williams, 'Offences and Defences' (1982) 2 *Legal Studies* 233, 243–52) and the moral issue remains the same.

[18] The much discussed case of *Dadson* (1850) 3 Car. & Kir. 148: see below, text associated with n. 72.

[19] See below, pp. 18–20.

community's acceptance of the finding of guilt and exempt the political authority from the suspicion of carrying on a private vendetta'.[20] The demise of the harm requirement would, on this view, be convenient for the police and prosecutors in enabling them to bring charges based on confessions of intent and not evidenced by the occurrence of any acts or results which independently confirm the intent. This reasoning contains more than a pragmatic argument. It suggests that the rights of defendants and suspects would be better protected under a system which retained the harm requirement, since it would be impossible to build a case against an individual simply on the basis of his own alleged admissions about his state of mind at the relevant time. To the extent that the culpability requirement is sufficient, there is an opportunity for the police and other investigators to violate a defendant's rights by, for example, forcing or fabricating a confession.

These counter-arguments demonstrate that, even taking rights arguments alone, there will be conflicts which have to be resolved by resort to priorities. However, the case for protecting the rights of persons accused of crime through limitations on the conditions of criminal liability itself can only be assessed once the basic principles of criminal liability have been established. The argument here is that one of those principles is that a person should be liable to criminal conviction only when, and only to the extent that, he or she chose to do a prohibited act or to bring about a prohibited state of affairs or consequence.[21] Thus, respect for individuals as rational choosing beings suggests that in general it is fair to hold them liable for their conduct on the basis of what they believed they were doing, not on the basis of actual facts and circumstances which were not known to them at the time. This will be termed 'the belief principle'. The same approach, it will be argued, suggests that it is fair to hold individuals liable for what they intended to do or to bring about, and not according to whether the intended state of affairs or consequences did occur. This will be termed 'the intent principle'. Both principles tend to reduce the effect of chance on the incidence and degree of criminal liability, and to heighten the relationship between criminal liability and the defendant's choices. The two principles will now be considered in turn.

[20] G. P. Fletcher, 'The Right Deed for the Wrong Reason: A Reply to Mr. Robinson' (1975) 23 *UCLA Law Rev.* 293, 298.

[21] The principle states a morally relevant reason in support of criminal liability, which may sometimes be outweighed by other reasons. It therefore functions similarly to those principles which Feinberg describes as 'liberty-limiting' or 'coercion-legitimizing': J. Feinberg, *Harm to Others* (Oxford, 1984), 9–10.

2. THE BELIEF PRINCIPLE

In deciding the case of *Smith (D.R.)* in 1974,[22] the Court of Appeal adopted a simple, straightforward, and attractive approach to the interpretation of criminal legislation. Section 1 (1) of the Criminal Damage Act 1971 provides that 'a person who without lawful excuse destroys or damages any property belonging to another, intending to destroy or damage any such property or being reckless as to whether any such property would be destroyed or damaged, shall be guilty of an offence'. In this case defendant D had damaged certain panelling which he had purchased and had affixed to the walls of the flat which he was renting. He was charged with criminal damage to the panelling since it had, by operation of law and unknown to the defendant, become the property of the landlady of the flat. His answer to the charge was that he thought the panelling belonged to him. He was convicted, but on reasoning which was fallacious. One cannot assert, as did the trial judge, that the two propositions (i) D intended to damage the property and (ii) the property belonged in law to another yield the conclusion that (iii) D intended to damage property belonging to another. Proposition (iii) does not necessarily follow because it is possible, as in fact occurred in *Smith*, that D believed that the property did not belong to another, in which eventuality it is wrong to describe him as intending to damage property belonging to another. The Court of Appeal recognized the fallacy and propounded the simple approach that the *mens rea* of the offence, that is intention or recklessness, must apply to each of the elements of the offence. 'It follows that in our judgment no offence is committed under this section if a person destroys or causes damage to property belonging to another if he does so in the honest though mistaken belief that the property is his own.'[23]

Although it would detract from the simplicity of this decision, it would be preferable to present the defendant's mental attitude as having two aspects—his belief as to the relevant characteristics of the property in question, and his intention as to his conduct and any relevant consequences of that conduct. The requirement 'D must intend to damage property belonging to another' is ambiguous between 'property which D (correctly) believed belonged to another' and 'property which in fact but contrary to his belief belonged to another'. It is much clearer to say that he intended to damage the property but believed that it belonged to him

[22] [1974] QB 354.
[23] Ibid., 360.

and not to another. Lawyers have sometimes referred to this second aspect of the doctrine of *mens rea* as 'knowledge of circumstances', stating that the mental element in crime consists of foresight of consequences and knowledge of circumstances. It would be more accurate, however, to use the terminology of *belief* when describing the required mental attitude towards facts and circumstances relevant to the definition of a crime. 'Knowledge' might be taken to imply a degree of certainty and verification which simply is not present in many instances. There are surely far more things which we believe to be so (on the basis that they usually are so, or that a normally reliable person informed us), than things which we know to be so (on authority or having verified them ourselves). It may not seem objectionable to refer to someone as *knowing* X when he believes that X is so and in fact it is so, since these beliefs are usually correct. But occasionally the beliefs may turn out to be incorrect, and it is these occasions when belief and knowledge diverge which establish that our mental attitude to relevant facts and circumstances is often, strictly speaking, at the level of belief rather than knowledge.

The point assumes significance in view of what has been described as 'a general principle of morality and the criminal law that people ought to be judged on the facts as they believed them to be'.[24] This is the belief principle. One of its applications in moral philosophy is to support the proposition that a person can never properly be said to be under a moral obligation unless he believes that the circumstances which give rise to that obligation exist. It would generally be unfair to criticize someone for failing to discharge his moral duty if he was unaware that the event giving rise to that duty had occurred.[25] The criminal courts have applied the principle in similar circumstances. In *Harding* v. *Price* (1948)[26] the driver of a lorry was prosecuted for failing to report an accident; his defence was that, owing to the noise made by the trailer of his lorry, he had been unaware that an accident had taken place. In the Divisional Court Lord Goddard CJ held that it would be wrong to convict a defendant in these circumstances. 'Unless a man knows that the event has happened, how can he carry out the duty imposed? . . . Any other

24 Sir Rupert Cross, 'Centenary Reflections on Prince's Case' (1975) 91 *Law Quarterly Rev.* 540.

25 H. A. Prichard, *Moral Obligation* (Oxford, 1949), 18–39. This is not to deny that there are situations where, both in law and in morality, it is proper to impose a duty on a person who carries on a certain activity to take reasonable care in what he is doing, or to find out the true facts of the situation (see the rape example in the text associated with n. 29 below).

26 [1948] 1 KB 695.

view would lead to calling on a man to do the impossible.' Thus, where an offence penalizes an omission to fulfil a legal duty, it would be wrong to convict a defendant unless he knows of the circumstance which gives rise to the duty.

In criminal law the belief principle is better known for its application to cases of mistake. Although lawyers sometimes refer to 'the defence of mistake' in cases where D argues that he was mistaken about certain key facts or circumstances which are relevant to the definition of the crime, it is the prosecution who must establish that D did not have such a belief if they are to prove their case. The decision in *Smith (D.R.)* is one example,[27] and the famous rape case of *Morgan* v. *DPP*[28] is another. The House of Lords held that the prosecution must establish that D believed that the woman was not consenting or was reckless as to whether she was not consenting at the time of the sexual intercourse. If it appeared that the defendant believed that the woman was consenting, he would be entitled to an acquittal. This decision bears testimony to the strength of the belief principle as a ground of exculpation, for sexual intimacy is surely one of the contexts in which it should be outweighed by a duty on the man to establish that the woman is consenting.[29] The belief principle prevailed, however, as it has also done in most cases where D wishes to rely on a 'defence' (such as self-defence, the prevention of crime, or duress) of which the existence of a particular fact or circumstance is an essential part.[30] For example, in *Gladstone Williams* (1984)[31] Lord Lane CJ applied the belief principle in a case where the defendant used force in order to apprehend an offender. D believed that victim V was criminally assaulting a third party and used force in order to apprehend V and stop the assault. It was held that D should be acquitted, even though V had in fact been acting lawfully in an endeavour to arrest the third party for an offence committed against a fourth person, because on the facts as D believed them to be he would have been justified in using force.

The belief principle has not, generally speaking, been applied where the mistake is as to what is permissible under the criminal law. The

[27] Above, n. 22.

[28] [1976] AC 182.

[29] Cf. Celia Wells, 'Swatting the Subjective Bug' [1982] *Crim. LR* 209; Kenny (above, n. 1, 57–63).

[30] It is also accorded priority in recent reform proposals: see Criminal Law Revision Committee, 14th Report, *Offences against the Person* (Cmnd. 7844, 1980), para. 283; Law Commission, *The Mental Element in Crime* (Law Com. No. 89, 1978), 64. For an apparent exception, see *Graham* (1982) 74 Cr. App. R. 235.

[31] (1984) 78 Cr. App. R. 276.

maxim that ignorance of the criminal law should afford no excuse is inconsistent with the principle of equal liberty, capacity, and opportunity, and there are strong arguments for allowing at least reasonable mistake or ignorance of law as an excuse.[32] However, English law has generally allowed the maxim to prevail in order to uphold the importance of ascertaining what the criminal law permits and prohibits and to reinforce the law's function of declaring minimum standards of behaviour. Apart from the occasions when mistake or ignorance about the *civil* law may excuse the defendant,[33] and the doubly subjective definition of the crime of blackmail,[34] a defendant's beliefs about what is permissible are not legally relevant. A person who takes a girl out of the possession of her parents in one of the circumstances specified in sections 18, 19, and 20 of the Sexual Offences Act 1956 is liable to be convicted, even if he had never heard of those prohibitions. As a ground of exculpation, then, the belief principle is generally restricted to beliefs about facts, circumstances, and matters of civil law.

Does the same restriction apply to the belief principle as a ground of inculpation? In *Taaffe*, D was caught bringing a quantity of cannabis into the country. When questioned, he agreed that he had been asked to smuggle prohibited goods into England but said that he believed the goods consisted of currency. There is, however, no prohibition against importing currency. Both the Court of Appeal and the House of Lords were unanimous that D could not be convicted of being knowingly concerned in the fraudulent evasion of a prohibition on importation. (Nor, indeed, could he have been convicted of attempting to commit that offence.) In the Court of Appeal, Lord Lane CJ, stated:

> He is to be judged against the facts as he believed them to be. Had this indeed been currency and not cannabis, no offence would have been committed. Does it make any difference that the appellant thought wrongly that by clandestinely importing currency he was commiting an offence? [Counsel for the Crown] suggests that a man in this situation has to be judged according to the total mistake that he has made, both the mistake with regard to the fact of what he was carrying and also the mistake of law as to the effect of carrying that substance. We think that that submission is wrong. It no doubt made his actions morally reprehensible. It did not, in our judgment turn what he . . . believed to be the importation of currency into the commission of a criminal offence. His views on

[32] Cf. A. J. Ashworth, 'Excusable Mistake of Law' [1974] *Crim. LR* 652; L. Houlgate, 'Ignorantia Iuris: a Plea for Justice' (1967) 78 *Ethics* 32.

[33] e.g. Theft Act 1968, s. 2 (1) (a), Criminal Damage Act 1971, s. 5 (2) (b) (iii).

[34] Theft Act 1968, s. 21, as interpreted in *Harvey* (1981) 72 Cr. App. R. 139.

the law as to the importation of currency were to that extent, in our judgment, irrelevant.[35]

The effect is to recognize a limitation upon the belief principle, parallel to that imposed on its exculpatory effect by the *ignorantia juris* principle. On this view, there can be no criminal conviction for trying to break a non-existent law.[36]

Although in English law the belief principle is outweighed by another principle where a person is mistaken about the criminal law, it does operate as a ground of inculpation when the mistake relates to facts or circumstances. Section 1 of the Criminal Attempts Act 1981 provides that a person is guilty of an attempt to commit an offence 'even though the facts are such that the commission of the offence is impossible'. The question for the court is whether his intention would have been regarded as an intent to commit the offence 'if the facts of the case had been as he believed them to be'. In dealing with such cases, lawyers slip quickly into the language of attempts even though that term is perhaps more apt to deal with cases where an intended consequence fails to flow from an act. Just as in *Smith (D.R.)* it would be more accurate to describe D as intending to damage property in the belief that it did not belong to another,[37] so in cases of attempting the factually impossible it is more accurate to adopt a description such as 'putting a hand in an empty pocket in the mistaken belief that it contained money, intending to steal that money' or 'importing snuff in the mistaken belief that it was cannabis'. The first part of the description shows the actual harmlessness of what was done, but the description of D's belief reveals the basis for holding him liable for a criminal attempt. In general, he should be judged on his view of the facts or circumstances, for better or for worse.[38]

Since liability for attempted crimes involves both the belief principle and the intent principle, detailed discussion is postponed until the next section of the essay. So far as the belief principle is concerned, it will be

[35] (1983) 77 Cr. App. R. 82 at 85–6, affirmed by the House of Lords [1984] AC 539. Lord Scarman held that 'the principle that a man must be judged on the facts as he believes them to be is an accepted principle of the criminal law when the state of a man's mind and his knowledge are ingredients of the offence with which he is charged'.

[36] This is an application of the principle of legality: see J. Hall, *General Principles of Criminal Law* (Indianapolis, 2nd edn., 1960), ch. 2.

[37] Note 22 above, and text thereat.

[38] The qualification, 'in general', serves as a reminder that the belief principle may be outweighed by other principles if the arguments are sufficiently strong: see the reference to *Morgan* above, nn. 28–9, and text thereat.

seen that it operates so as to tie D's liability for his non-self-restraint, and the extent of any liability, to what he believed he was doing. It respects him as a rational, choosing individual by seeking to minimize the effect of chance upon the law's assessment of his behaviour and by basing that assessment on the factual assumptions upon which he was acting.

3. THE INTENT PRINCIPLE

Just as the belief principle argues for criminal liability or non-liability based on the facts or circumstances as D believed them to be, even if they were otherwise, the intent principle argues for criminal liability based on the consequences D tried to cause, even if the actual consequences were different. The principle is not about the justice and fairness of regarding intent as a primary basis for culpability and thus for criminal liability. That is taken for granted. Rather, it concerns the nature of the relationship between the culpability requirement and the harm requirement, the argument being that a proper appreciation of the essence of the culpability requirement makes it possible to dispense with the harm requirement in its traditional terms.

One reason for adopting this approach is that 'things do not always work out as one expects'. What matters is what D intended and tried to do; whether or not the intended harm did result adds nothing significant to the justification for criminal liability or punishment (although some would argue that it should affect the quantum of punishment).[39] In order to sustain the analysis, however, it must be possible to draw a sensible distinction between an act and its consequences, or between the trying and the causing. Is A, who shoots at X intending to kill him but misses because X unexpectedly moves, any less culpable than B, who shoots at Y intending to kill him and does so? If A and B are asked what they are trying to do they will both, if honest, give answers which are materially the same: shoot X, shoot Y. Their intended actions are materially the same even if, after the event, it turns out that the result of B's act fails to fulfil his intention. The moral justification for the intent principle will be considered in section (b) below. First, the problems of drawing a satisfactory analytical distinction will be explored. Would it be proper to say that A's and B's own acts were the same, but the consequences were different?

[39] For discussion of the quantum of punishment, see A. Ashworth, 'Punishing Criminal Attempts', forthcoming.

(*a*) *Trying, acts, and consequences*

Austin's view, briefly put, was that a human act is a muscular contraction preceded and caused by an act of will.[40] One criticism of this is that it begs an explanation of how the act of will occurs and suggests an infinite causal regress.[41] Another is that it misrepresents and exaggerates our awareness of the movements involved in our behaviour.[42] These criticisms have led Hart to propose a definition in the negative form, distinguishing *in*voluntary actions as 'movements of the body which occurred though the agent had no reason for moving his body in that way.'[43] Hart's approach thus avoids temporal and causal assumptions and gives pride of place to the actor's own conception of what he is doing. All movements of his body count as his 'acts' (or, more fully, his 'voluntary acts') except those for which he could give no reason.

An emphasis upon the actor's own beliefs and purposes is also integral to the concept of trying, but there is a linguistic problem to be dealt with when it is sought to distinguish acts of trying from their consequences. Is it proper to describe each of two actors as having tried to do *x* when one failed and the other succeeded? One difficulty, similar to the second criticism of the Austinian analysis, is that it diverges too widely from our ordinary way of describing behaviour. Heath puts the criticism in this way: 'if the performance is simple, easy, direct and costs the agent no trouble, then—as Wittgenstein pointed out—it is just idle to talk of him as trying, or having tried, to do it'.[44] In a general sense this is true. Anyone who referred routinely to 'trying' to do the many straightforward acts one does each day would be regarded as extremely odd. Is it, as Heath maintains, just as idle to talk of someone as *having tried* to do *x* as to talk of him as trying to do *x*? It is true that before the act one would not speak of 'trying' to do *x* unless *x* presented known difficulty or uncertainty of outcome.[45] Equally, the language of trying would not be used by the actor if one were to ask him, in the middle of his behaviour, to describe what he was doing. But if one asked him afterwards, his description would surely depend on what actually

[40] J. Austin, *Lectures on Jurisprudence* (London, 5th edn., 1885), 411–24, elegantly summarized by Hart, 97–8.

[41] A. I. Melden, 'Willing', in A. R. White (ed.), *The Philosophy of Action* (Oxford, 1968), 77.

[42] Hart, 103.

[43] Hart, 255–6, reformulating (in response to criticisms) the passage appearing at Hart 105.

[44] P. Heath, 'Trying and Attempting' (1971) XLV *Proc. Aristotelian Society* 193.

[45] O. R. Jones, 'Trying' (1983) 92 *Mind* 368.

happened. He would say either 'I shot him' or 'I tried to shoot him but he suddenly moved and the shot missed . . .'. Does the use of the concept of 'trying' in the second description suggest that he performed different actions than if he simply shot him? The language of trying is made appropriate by the fact that in the second case there was a failure in result. If failure had been recognized as a possibility at the outset, the language of trying should perhaps have been used throughout, but since this was not the actor's view of what he was doing, the language of trying is used only after the (unexpected) failure. The outcome alters the action-description which is appropriate in ordinary language, reflecting the significance attributed to outcomes in much social life.

There is also, however, a flexibility in ordinary language which makes it difficult to distinguish between acts and outcomes. One could say 'B killed Y' as a description of his act. Alternatively, one could say that B pulled the trigger, in consequence of which the bullet shot into Y's body, in consequence of which Y died. This has been called 'the accordion effect' of language, because 'an act, like the folding musical instrument, can be squeezed down to a minimum or else stretched out'.[46] In the context of trying, the linguistic problem is reduced because the relevant result or state of affairs is specified by the actor's purpose or belief (and, for legal purposes, by the definition of the offence). Both A and B were trying to kill a particular person. The firing of the gun might be regarded as a consequence in purely linguistic terms, but it is irrelevant in the present context because A and B are not charged with firing a gun but with attempted murder and murder respectively. The killing of the victim is the relevant consequence, and all the movements in which A and B engaged in order to produce that consequence may be regarded as the acts of trying. Because of the element of uncertainty about and lack of control over the results of human conduct, the 'trying' or the intended action can be identified as the highest common factor when assessing culpability.[47] The argument below is that this factor should be a primary determinant of criminal liability and punishment.

[46] J. Feinberg, *Doing and Deserving* (Princeton, 1970), 106.

[47] It might be contended that the argument is not taken far enough; the highest common factor which excludes the operation of chance is a person's self-exertion or setting himself to do something. If a person had, without knowing it, become paralysed since the last time he had tried to effect a given type of change, 'his self-exertion, though it would not produce the effect, would obviously be of exactly the same character as it would have been if he had remained unparalysed and it had therefore produced the effect': Sir David Ross, *Foundations of Ethics* (Oxford, 1939), 160. There are two reasons for not

(b) The 'no relevant moral difference' thesis

Is A, who shoots at X intending to kill him but misses because X unexpectedly moves, any less culpable than B, who shoots at Y intending to kill him and does so? An external description of both sets of events would probably not suggest that they have 'done' the same thing, whereas an account which paid more attention to the actor's point of view and to matters which lay within the actor's control would suggest that they both intended and tried, to the same extent, to do the same thing. The argument here is that, because of the element of uncertainty in the outcome of things which we try to do, it would be wrong for assessments of culpability to depend on the occurrence or non-occurrence of the intended consequences. 'Success or failure ... makes no difference at all to [an agent's] moral status in relation to his original act. His original act, strictly considered, was simply his trying and *that* is what moral assessment must concern itself with.'[48] The argument has been more fully developed in relation to the concept of moral obligations; in view of the limits to the individual's control over the effects of his actions, a person cannot be morally obliged to cause a particular consequence but only to *try* to bring it about. The same reasoning should apply to moral blame as to moral obligation. The elements of uncertainty and limited control make it unfair to treat consequences as the determinant of culpability, since these may be affected by occurrences which to him are matters of chance, and moral blame should rather concern itself with what the person was trying to do. This does not amount to punishment for mere intentions: 'what is intended in an act' is the proper object of moral assessment.[49] Moral blame and criminal liability should be based so far as possible on choice and control, on the trying and not on what actually happened thereafter.

What are the reasons for wishing to reduce the influence of chance upon criminal liability? It cannot be doubted that luck plays a considerable part in everyday events. Actual results also play a considerable part in judgments of others, and tend to dominate assessments in such fields as business, sport, and education. Those who try hard but are unsuc-

pursuing the argument to this extent. First, it would place the highest significance on an internal trying or self-exertion, thus threatening individual rights to an unacceptable extent and allowing, in effect, conviction without evidence of public and visible facts (see n. 20 above, and text thereat). Second, the paralysis argument seizes upon a far more remote contingency than the mere unpredictability of human affairs.

[48] P. Winch, *Ethics and Action* (London, 1972), 139, stating the view with which he wished to disagree.

[49] Ross, 160.

cessful often receive less recognition than those who achieve goals (no matter how little effort they put into it). But these are not moral assessments of the individuals or their characters. If one turns to moral and social judgments, it is doubtful whether outcomes should be the proper criteria. It may be desirable overall to have fewer bad outcomes and more good outcomes in society, but that does not lead to the conclusion that moral praise and blame should be allocated solely according to result. Indeed, a bad outcome stemming from a good intent may be a better predictor of good outcomes than a good outcome born of a bad intent. From time to time we may praise someone for producing a good result, even though it was not what he was trying to do, but this is more a reflection of our pleasure at the outcome than an assessment of his conduct and character. If we turn to blaming, is it not unacceptable to blame people for causing results irrespective of whether they were caused intentionally, negligently, or purely accidentally? Blaming is a moral activity which is surely only appropriate where the individual had some choice or control over the matter. For this reason the criminal law should seek to minimize the effect of luck upon the incidence and scale of criminal liability. For the modern retributivist who regards the individual as a rational choosing being, it is right to impose a criminal conviction only if and in so far as the individual chose to bring about a prohibited consequence. The criminal law does not purport to be a complete system of moral accounting. The offender may well have a duty to pay compensation to the victim, but that raises issues of cause and responsibility which differ from those raised by the imposition of a criminal conviction. On a consequentialist view the conclusion would be the same, because the justification for conviction and punishment revolves round the effect on the future conduct of this individual and others. If on this occasion D tried and failed, punishment may deter future trying. If on this occasion D caused serious consequences by accident, punishment is unlikely to serve sufficient purpose. When matters lie outside D's choice and control so that he cannot determine their occurrence or non-occurrence, conviction and punishment are out of place.

What the intent principle involves is that a defendant should be open to conviction for crime if he intends and tries to produce certain prohibited consequences, irrespective of whether those consequences occur in the particular case. On retributive grounds the person who fails to cause the intended result deserves conviction no less than one who succeeded, since those parts of the endeavour which lie within his choice and control—his non-self-restraint—are the same. The consequentialist, looking to future outcomes, would adopt the same reason. That which has come to be accepted as a necessary condition for criminal liability should, in other words, be recognized as a sufficient condition in principle. Some would prefer to reach this conclusion on a reciprocity argument; it would be indefensible to recognize as a ground for exculpation a condition whose reverse one is not prepared to accept as a ground for inculpation. One could not rationally support mistaken belief (when the facts actually fall within the prohibition) as a defence whilst refusing to countenance mistaken belief (when the facts actually fall outside the prohibition) as a ground of liability; nor could one properly support absence of intent (when D causes prohibited consequences) as a defence whilst refusing to accept intent (when D fails to cause the prohibited consequences) as a ground of liability. However, the reciprocity argument is less convincing than a direct application of the premiss that choice and control should form the basis of criminal liability. What are the objections to this approach?

One counter-argument is that this reasoning is too simplistic. Not only does it conflict with widely held assumptions that the occurrence of consequences should be relevant to blame and punishment, but it also overlooks the difference in moral status between B, who committed murder, and A, who committed attempted murder. According to Winch, the key to the distinction is what a person becomes afterwards: a simple equiparation of the cases of A and B fails to take account of the complexities of moral judgment.

> In *doing* something evil one *becomes* something evil . . . What one thus becomes is inseparable from the complex network of relations one enters into with other people which imposes limits on what can and what cannot be intelligibly said of one's subsequent life by way of moral assessment. If a man tries to do something evil and fails, then he does not become what his success would have made him and thereby the possibilities of moral assessment of him are different. It is not that the man who fails has nothing to condemn himself for or to be condemned for; but he does not have that to condemn himself for which he would have had if successful.[50]

This does not really meet the point at issue. Clearly B incurs a greater number of moral obligations than A does, on the basis that a person should pay compensation to those who suffer harm or loss through his intentional acts. B has a duty to pay compensation, whereas A will not (unless for shock or other psychological effects of the attempt). Clearly

[50] Winch, 149–50.

there are also important differences in the world. B may come to be regarded as a killer (which A cannot be),[51] and Y's family may feel a great sense of loss at the death of Y, whereas X and X's family may feel relief at the failure of the attempt and are still able to continue personal relations. Yet these points about moral status, the duty to compensate and the social implications of actual events can be and should be taken separately from the deservedness and proper extent of moral blame.[52] There would be little support either in moral principle or in popular sentiment for an approach which treated as equally culpable two people who caused death, one through a deliberate shooting and the other through a simple push in a street argument, causing the victim to fall backwards, trip over the kerb, and suffer a brain haemorrhage from the head striking the pavement. What was intended in the latter case was a mere assault, and it is this, rather than the unfortunate result, which is the proper object of moral blame (and legal liability).[53] Results may be relevant to other kinds of assessment, but the primary condition of criminal liability should be that 'one cannot be more culpable or estimable for anything than one is for that fraction of it which is under one's control'.[54]

Another counter-argument is that this 'no relevant moral difference' thesis attributes far greater significance to the actor's intentions than is supportable. The assumed relationship between choice and control may be overdone. So much depends on the individual's capacities, temperament, and inclinations, but these are hardly under one's control. Much depends, too, on the kinds of problem and situation one has to face, but this may be largely a matter of luck. The argument is therefore that the controlled element in an individual's conduct is rather low in many cases, and that a thesis which places such weight on the individual's intentional acts in the particular situation may be charged with distorting reality. A compatibilitist reply to this would acknowledge the philosophical paradox and seek a pragmatic solution. The paradox is that it seems wrong to blame someone morally for any matter which lies outside his control, whilst an enquiry into the actuality of individual

[51] See also the argument of H. L. A. Hart and Tony Honoré, *Causation in the Law* (Oxford; 2nd edn., 1985), lxxx–lxxxi.

[52] N. MacCormick, *Legal Right and Social Democracy* (Oxford, 1982), ch. 11; Ashworth, loc. cit. n. 6 above.

[53] As the Criminal Law Revision Committee put it, when recommending the abolition of 'unlawful act manslaughter', 'the offender's fault falls too far short of the unlucky result': op. cit. n. 30 above, para. 120.

[54] T. Nagel, *Mortal Questions* (Cambridge, 1978), 28.

agency and control produces the conclusion that it 'shrinks under this scrutiny to an extensionless point'.[55] The whole possibility of moral judgments of people for their actions is thrown into doubt. The pragmatic solution is that an element of capacity to choose and of control is assumed not only in moral discourse but also in a large proportion of dealings between people. It is quite possible to concede that an individual's control may be reduced in particular circumstances (as indeed is done at the sentencing stage in criminal cases, when considering mitigating factors), whilst maintaining that there is generally speaking sufficient choice and control to form the basis of moral blame and criminal liability. If the time comes when human enquiry establishes that this element of control and choice is illusory or negligible, then not only moral judgment and legal liability but the basis of much social intercourse would have to be rethought. Until then, it is proper to assume that generally individuals have sufficient control over their circumstances and their actions to justify attributions of blame and to seek to reduce the effect of chance upon those attributions.

The argument here is, however, for the intent principle as a fundamental principle and not as an absolute rule. The main aim of the criminal law is to provide for the punishment of the seriously blameworthy and thereby to restore the social order and reduce the frequency of the violation of victims' rights, but each legal system has to operate in a particular social and political context. In certain spheres of criminal law an outcome-orientated 'popular morality' may have such a firm grip that full implementation of the intent principle might undermine respect for the law and co-operation in its enforcement. If this leads to derogations from the intent principle, they should be acknowledged as pragmatic compromises. There may also be other spheres in which the intent or belief principle is outweighed by other principles or policies. The conflict with the principle *ignorantia juris neminem excusat* has already been described. Some conflicts may arise when the intent or belief principle is used for inculpation and not when it is used for exculpation, one example being the threat to defendants' rights from a rule which is such as to allow conviction based solely on an alleged confession. Some argue that different considerations should apply when the outcome is legally justified (rather than merely legally innocuous). It is to some practical applications of the belief and intent principles that we now turn.

[55] Ibid., 35.

4. APPLYING THE PRINCIPLES

Inchoate offences are, as pointed out above, one of the spheres of criminal liability which provide a testing ground for the belief principle and the intent principle, since they involve culpability without harm. It is true that each inchoate offence requires some form of *actus reus*, for example, the agreement in conspiracy and the proximate or 'more than merely preparatory' act in attempt, but these acts bear little relation to the gravamen of the offences, which is to be found in what the defendants intended to do. The infliction of harm, in the traditional sense, is not required for these crimes. What, then, is the justification for imposing criminal liability in these cases? Is the justification sufficiently strong?

Inchoate offences are usually associated with a preventive rationale; one of the principal aims of criminal law is to protect the rights of individuals, and protection is more aptly achieved by intervention before the right is infringed than by waiting until the right has been violated. At what stage is it proper to authorize the intervention of law enforcement officers by holding that an inchoate offence has been committed? The uttering of the incitement and the agreement in cases of conspiracy are more obvious and less controversial than any particular stage in an attempt. There is a range of possible definitions of the *actus reus* of attempts. At one extreme is the view that any overt act accompanied by the intention to commit the substantive crime should be sufficient, for at this stage the individual has gone beyond mere intention and has manifested non-self-restraint. Against that, it might be argued that an individual's rights might be laid open to violation in that wrongful arrests might be more numerous, and the primacy of the mental element might tempt the police to exert pressure in order to obtain a confession. Moreover, there would be less opportunity for the individual to change his mind and to recant if his conduct were criminalized at this early stage.[56] At the opposite extreme lies the 'last act' approach which would not criminalize an attempt until the individual had performed the last act he intended to do. This would reduce the preventive effect of the law of attempts by requiring the police to wait until the substantive offence had almost been committed. Between the two extremes fall several intermediate points: a 'proximate' act, a 'substantial step', or a 'more than

[56] Many European codes allow a defence of abandonment, as does the American Law Institute's Model Penal Code, but English law has never done so: see M. Wasik, 'Abandoning Criminal Intent' [1980] *Crim. LR* 785.

merely preparatory' act. It is not proposed to discuss here the compatibility of the various tests with the protection of rights.[57]

Although the preventive rationale for inchoate offences is widely discussed, there is a second and distinct rationale for criminalizing cases where the individual has done everything he intended to do towards committing a substantive offence but the intended harm has not resulted. These are not cases where the attempt fails because of some interruption in the train of actions upon which the defendant embarked, and so what Hart has termed 'the Interruption Model' of criminal attempts does not apply to them.[58] Thus prevention is not necessarily uppermost in the criminalization of these cases; if, for example, the individual who had made such an attempt declared that he would not try again and this was believed, the justification for criminal liability would remain. He has indulged in just as much non-self-restraint as a person who succeeds in causing the intended harm. The question is not, therefore, whether there is a need to intervene in order to prevent him from repeating his attempt but whether he has not already crossed the threshold of criminality in all material respects. Take the example of an individual who sets up a booby-trap in order to injure V, against whom he has a grudge. V comes along, triggers the booby-trap, but is uninjured. The justification for punishment in this kind of case should not depend on whether the plan failed because of the individual's incompetence in miscalculating the working of the trap, or because V unexpectedly paused to listen to a bird-cry at the crucial time, or because the police had acted so as to immobilize the booby-trap. Indeed, the justification for punishment should be no different if V had suffered the intended injury. In all the examples put, the individual had done, or believed he had done, all the acts normally necessary to produce the intended effect. He had unambiguously traversed the boundary of non-self-restraint.

It is necessary to employ terminology which distinguishes these cases in which the individual has done the physical act(s) he intended to do without producing the intended result;[59] they will be termed 'complete

[57] See further, Law Commission, *Attempt and Impossibility in relation to Attempt, Conspiracy and Incitement* (Law Com. No. 102, 1980), and Ashworth, 'Punishing Criminal Attempts'.

[58] H. L. A. Hart, 'The House of Lords on Attempting the Impossible', in C. Tapper (ed.), *Crime, Proof and Punishment* (London, 1981), ch. 1.

[59] Hart (loc. cit. n. 58 above, 15) warns against 'the incoherence of the statement that in such cases the accused has done *all* he intended to do'. The sentence in the text here is restricted to 'the physical act(s) he intended to do', because the statement '*all* he intended to do' might fairly be thought to incorporate a description of the object of his acts in terms

attempts', as distinct from 'incomplete attempts' where the individual stops or is interrupted at an earlier stage. Further distinctions may be drawn within the category of complete attempts. (i) Some complete attempts fail because, even though D is properly aware of all the facts and surrounding circumstances, his execution of the attempt is incompetent or the intended victim behaves unexpectedly. Whilst there might be an argument that the incompetent attempter deserves less punishment on the ground that he is less psychologically committed than other attempters,[60] there is little reason to doubt the justification for criminal liability in this category. D has indulged in non-self-restraint to a sufficiently full extent. (ii) Some complete attempts fail because of incompetence or luck of another kind: D makes a mistake about the facts or about the circumstances in which he is acting. For example, D stabs a shape in a bed believing that it is his mortal enemy Y, whereas in fact it is a bolster; or D takes possession of a substance believing that it is cannabis, whereas it is dried lettuce.

It might be thought that there is no relevant moral difference between categories (i) and (ii), since both involve cases in which the intended result does not occur. However, lawyers tend to describe category (i) as cases of failure and category (ii) as cases of factual impossibility. And, whilst there is little dispute about the application of the intent principle to the former, some would argue against giving inculpatory effect to the belief principle in the latter. It seems to be assumed that where the crime was impossible in the circumstances, this raises difficulties which are not present in simple cases of failure. However, as Hart has demonstrated, such arguments proceed from the notion that the 'Interruption Model' is the sole rationale for punishing attempts, and the concept of factual impossibility might be applied to many cases of simple failure (for example, it was impossible in the circumstances to kill Z by shooting in the direction in which D fired, because Z moved).[61] The moral and conceptual distinctions between categories (i) and (ii) are therefore negligible, but there remains a practical distinction which may be important. In the former it is often easy to infer from the external events what D was trying to do, whereas in the latter the external events *might* appear innocuous (for instance, possession of lettuce leaves) in the absence of a confession by D about his beliefs in relation to the events.

of a property which he mistakenly believed that object to have (e.g. he intended to smuggle drugs).

[60] See Ashworth, 'Punishing Criminal Attempts'.

[61] Hart, loc. cit. n. 58, 12–14.

Thus category (ii) cases might raise the same doubts about the protection of suspects' rights which are raised by the *actus reus* of attempts, and this should be a matter for practical enquiry. The theoretical issue would then be whether the case for criminalization is outweighed by the possibility of some infringements of suspects' rights which cannot otherwise be prevented.[62] But the case for criminalization is certainly strong. In category (ii) no less than category (i), there has been such non-self-restraint as to make the moral foundation for criminal liability as clear as in the case of the substantive offence. The intended or believed effect does not happen, but that is a matter of chance which should not affect criminal liability.

A third category (iii) consists of cases in which D has done the physical acts he set out to do but the substantive offence has not been committed because an element in the definition of the offence is absent. D believed it was present, but it was not. The usual example is where D buys goods believing that they are stolen when in fact they are not.[63] D has not committed the crime of handling stolen goods: should he be liable to conviction for attempting to handle stolen goods? Now it might be thought that there is no material distinction between this kind of case and those falling within category (ii), since in both cases D has made what may fairly be termed a mistake of fact. There is no question of a mistake of law: it is a mistake of fact which leads to the absence of a legal requirement of the offence.[64] From the moral point of view the two types of case seem indistinguishable, and this was the approach of the Law Commission:

> We think it would generally be accepted that if a man possesses the appropriate mens rea and commits acts which are sufficiently proximate to the actus reus of a criminal offence, he is guilty of attempting to commit that offence. Where, with that intention, he commits acts which, if the facts were as he believed them to be, would have amounted to the actus reus of the full crime or would have been sufficiently proximate to amount to an attempt, we cannot see why his failure to appreciate the true facts should, in principle, relieve him of liability for the

[62] This raises general questions of police accountability and safeguards for suspects' rights such as tape or video recording of interrogation and the right to see a solicitor.

[63] In practice, the prosecution's difficulty is often that it cannot establish where the goods were stolen from, even though D admits that he believed they were stolen.

[64] It is unfortunate that these have come to be known as cases of 'legal impossibility'. That term should be reserved for cases in which D's intended conduct would not have been an offence against English law, as in the case of attempting to 'smuggle' currency (*Taaffe*, above, n. 35).

attempt. We stress that this solution to the problem does not punish people simply for their intentions. The necessity for proof of proximate acts remains.[65]

One of the aims of the Criminal Attempts Act 1981 was to bring such cases within the ambit of the law and, after one decision which held otherwise,[66] the House of Lords has now confirmed that the Act does criminalize these cases within category (iii).[67]

Some of those who have misgivings about convicting persons of so-called 'legally impossible' attempts have invoked the principle of legality.[68] They argue that it is as wrong to convict someone of attempting to commit a non-existent offence as it is to convict someone of committing a non-existent offence. There is no offence known to English law of handling *non*-stolen goods, and we should not countenance a conviction for attempt in these circumstances either. However, this argument seems to commit its proponents to a form of reasoning which was noticed earlier as inadequate:

(1) D is handling goods;
(2) The goods are not stolen;
(3) Therefore D is handling non-stolen goods, which is no offence.

This sequence of reasoning ignores D's intention, which has long been recognized as 'the principal ingredient' of attempts.[69] To begin with the proposition 'D is handling goods' is therefore to base the reasoning on a partial premiss. The complete and accurate proposition would be that 'D is handling goods in the belief that they are stolen'. The second step in the reasoning may remain unchanged, but the third step should become: 'D is handling non-stolen goods in the belief that they are stolen goods'. The principle of legality has no greater reference to this category of case than to category (ii) cases, for what D believes he is doing does amount to a criminal offence.

The Law Commission, in the passage quoted above, treated categories (ii) and (iii) as morally indistinguishable, although they phrased their reasoning in the negative: 'we cannot see why his failure to appreciate the true facts should, in principle, relieve him of liabilility for the attempt'. Cast into positive terms, this is surely an assertion that the

65 Law Com. No. 102, para. 2.96.

66 *Anderton* v. *Ryan* [1985] AC 560.

67 *Shivpuri* [1986] 2 All ER 334, drawing upon Glanville Williams, 'The Lords and Impossible Attempts' [1986] Camb. Law J. 33.

68 Brian Hogan, 'The Criminal Attempts Act and Attempting the Impossible' [1984] *Crim. LR* 584.

69 *Whybrow* (1951) 35 Cr. App. R. 141; see also Hart, loc. cit. n. 58, 15–16.

belief principle should be applied so as to inculpate such persons. There is no relevant moral difference between the person who handles goods believing them to be stolen when in fact they are stolen, and the person who does so when in fact they are not stolen. Indeed, there seems to be no material difference between such cases and the example of someone who shoots at a bolster or pillow in a bed in the belief that it is a human being whom he intends to kill. Although that is sometimes thought to be a case of 'factual' as opposed to 'legal' impossibility,[70] the analysis should be the same. Considered solely from the external point of view, D was shooting at a bolster and there is no offence of shooting at a bolster.[71] There can on that view be no conviction for attempted der, since one of the elements of that crime is that the acts are aimed at a human being. From the internal point of view, however, the crucial fact is that D believed he was aiming at a human being and, if that belief were true, he would have committed the substantive offence. The belief and intent principles support conviction for an attempt, and the concept of legal impossibility should be confined to cases where the offence which D believes he is committing is not known to the law, in which cases the principle of legality should certainly operate to prevent conviction.

A different but related problem is that of the unknown justification, usually discussed in relation to the old case of *Dadson*.[72] D, a constable, shot at a man who was running away from a copse carrying wood and who had failed to stop when requested. D was charged with wounding the man. Under the law as it then stood, it was only justifiable to use this amount of force if the victim was a felon, and theft of wood amounted to a felony only if the thief had two previous convictions for the same offence. Ought D to be convicted if he did not know whether this man had two previous convictions? The judges held that he should be convicted and that the justification, 'being unknown to the prisoner', could not avail him. On the reasoning above, the belief principle would appear to support criminal liability in this type of case. However, there remains the question of what D should be criminally liable *for*. The court in *Dadson* upheld a conviction for the substantive offence of wounding, a ruling which must have been premissed on the proposition that all the justifications for the infliction of what would otherwise be criminal harm require both objective circumstances and a subjective state of mind. Dadson could not take advantage of the defence because

70 See n. 64 above, and text thereat.
71 It could amount to criminal damage, but that is incidental.
72 (1850) 3 Car. & Kir. 148.

he lacked the mental element which is thought to form part of this head of justification.[73] The opposite view is that there cannot be a conviction of the substantive offence in such circumstances because an element is missing. Just as there can be no conviction for handling stolen goods if the goods cannot be proved to be stolen, so there can be no conviction for unlawful wounding if the circumstances of justification were present, since the element of unlawfulness was absent.[74] Old authority may be found for this approach in *The Abby*:

> if a man fires a gun at sea, intending to kill an Englishman, which would be legal murder, and by accident does not kill an Englishman, but an enemy, the moral guilt is the same, but the legal effect is different. The accident has turned up in his favour—the criminal act intended has not been committed, and the man is innocent of the legal offence.[75]

The difference between the two approaches is one of definition or, at the very least, one of middle-range principle rather than deep principle. Fletcher is careful to restrict himself to the question of whether D ought to be convicted of the substantive offence, arguing that the question of conviction for an attempt raises 'difficult issues' which ought to be discussed separately.[76] Glanville Williams, having argued against *Dadson*, concedes that 'the logic of the argument for consummated crimes does not apply to the inchoate crime of attempt, which does not require an evil result ... even Dadson himself could properly have been convicted of an attempt'.[77] The issue here is whether D should be criminally liable, even for an attempt, not merely whether the substantive offence is or is not properly made out.

Would it be proper to convict Dadson of attempted unlawful wounding, or to convict the man referred to in *The Abby* of attempted murder (of an Englishman)? The elements of these cases differ only slightly from the impossible attempts in class (iii) discussed above. They are broadly similar to the cases of attempted handling, where the goods are not stolen but D believes that they are. The only difference is that D's mistaken belief concerns an element in a defence or justification rather than an element in the definition of the offence itself. There are complications in drawing this distinction, as well as the controversy

73 See J. C. Smith and B. Hogan, *Criminal Law* (London, 5th edn., 1983), 33–4.

74 Robinson, loc. cit. n. 11 above.

75 (1804) 5 C Rob. 251, 254; see also the dictum of Holt CJ in *Tooley* (1709) 2 Ld. Raym. 1296 at 1302; '*ignorantia facti* will excuse but never condemn a man'.

76 Fletcher, op. cit. n. 20 above, 296.

77 Glanville Williams, *Criminal Law: The General Part* (London, 2nd edn., 1961), 26–7.

about the incorporation of mental requirements in the justifications,[78] but in principle there seems no logical or analytical reason against judging D on the facts as he believed them to be. Are there arguments of principle or policy to the contrary? Often quoted in this connection is Macaulay's argument that cases of unknown justification ought to be treated differently:

> When an act is of such a description that it would be better that it should not be done, it is quite proper to look at the motives and intentions of the doer, for the purpose of deciding whether he shall be punished or not. But when an act which is really useful to society, an act of a sort which it is desirable to encourage, has been done, it is absurd to inquire into the motives of the doer, for the purpose of punishing him if it shall appear that his motives were bad.[79]

Much of the force of this argument derives from the reference to the *encouragement* of socially useful acts, as legally justified acts of this kind may be classified, but it is hard to tell whether non-liability in cases where the result fortuitously 'turns up in his favour' would have this effect. If it were treated as a guide to future conduct, it might encourage as many socially deleterious acts (wounding innocent citizens) as socially useful acts. The encouragement should indeed lie towards socially useful acts, but that requires people to try to ascertain the facts before they inflict what (in the absence of a legal justification) would be a criminal harm. It certainly does not support a disregard for the mental attitude of the defendant.

A more promising policy argument is that offered by Glanville Williams (although he uses it against conviction for the substantive offence, not against conviction for the attempt): police officers sometimes act on instinct or 'second sight', and it is 'scarcely fair to the police or socially expedient' to make them criminally liable in cases where the instinct turns out to be correct.[80] This policy seems to underlie the provisions of the new English legislation on arrest, which authorize the arrest of 'anyone who is guilty of the [arrestable] offence' and 'anyone whom he has reasonable grounds for suspecting to be guilty of it'.[81] Fairness to the police in carrying out their difficult task is rightly regarded as important, but this proposed policy must be considered in the context of the commitment to individual rights with which this essay began. The issue cannot be argued to its conclusion here, but the

78 Glanville Williams, loc. cit. n. 17 above.

79 Macaulay, *Works* (London, 1898), 552–3.

80 Glanville Williams, op. cit. n. 77 above, 25; loc. cit. n. 17 above, 244–7.

81 Police and Criminal Evidence Act 1984, s. 24 (4) and (5).

practical effect of allowing police officers impunity for intended excesses of power which turn up in their favour might or might not be regarded as a threat to the rights of innocent persons,[82] which is unacceptable, even though it may promote the enforcement of the law and thereby protect the rights of potential victims more successfully. If this policy is allowed to prevail in relation to arrests, it would seem to follow that *Dadson* should be overruled in its application to all the justifications,[83] although cases of consent raise particular difficulties.[84] However, it is enough here to establish the basic proposition that cases of unknown justification ought in principle and subject to the considerations just mentioned to be treated as criminal attempts. The moral force of the belief principle applies directly to these cases and, although the absence of actual unlawfulness should prevent conviction for the substantive offence, there is a strong prima facie argument that a conviction for attempt should follow.

5. CONCLUSIONS

Although the argument above has drawn upon general propositions about the criminal law and criminal liability and upon general conceptions of moral responsibility, its focus is limited to the relationship between two fundamental elements of criminal responsibility: harm and intention or knowledge (belief). The criminal law calls for a certain amount of self-restraint, specifically requiring individuals to restrain themselves from infringing particular protected interests of other citizens and of the state. The general justification for this is to reduce the frequency of violations of those interests. Respect for the rights of each individual as a rational and choosing member of society requires that criminal liability be restricted (most straightforwardly)[85] to cases where D knows what he is doing and intends to produce the prohibited consequence. The corollary is that individuals who lack the required belief or intent should be exculpated. It has been argued here that it is also logical and proper to inculpate those who believe they are doing an

[82] A threat in the sense that it might encourage police officers to act more frequently on 'hunch' rather than evidence, and thus lead to more violations of the rights of the innocent; see the parallel argument against the non-punishment of unsuccessful attempts, above, p. 26.

[83] Law Commission, *Codification of the Criminal Law* (Law Com. No. 143, 1985), para. 13.36.

[84] Fletcher, n. 20 above, 300.

[85] Still leaving recklessness and negligence out of account.

act which is in fact prohibited and those who intend and try to produce a prohibited consequence, since their moral culpability is no different from that of individuals whose beliefs are correct and whose efforts come to fruition.[86] In legal terms they should be liable to conviction, probably for an attempted crime. In moral terms the justifications for inculpation are the same, in that both the successful and the unsuccessful have done their best to implement their intentions to commit the crime, and it would be wrong to allow the irrationality of chance to interpose itself in a way which rendered the one liable to conviction and the other not.[87] 'Anything which is the product of happy or unhappy contingency is no proper object of moral assessment, and no proper determinant of it, either.'[88] Individuals have imperfect knowledge and imperfect control over events, and it is therefore fairer to assess their responsibility on the basis of their beliefs and on what they try to do.

If the belief and intent principles are accepted as prima facie necessary elements in criminal liability, what role is left to the requirement of harm? It would still be for the legislators to decide what conduct and what consequences are so harmful as to justify the criminal sanction. The extension proposed here is to hold that the harm requirement is fulfilled not merely where the prohibited harm actually occurs, but also where the individual believes he is causing it or tries to cause it. This approach does not necessarily lead to a widening of the ambit of the criminal law. That remains a question for the legislators, and there may be good reason for redirecting the law towards inchoate offences of violence and away from minor property offences. The approach might, on the other hand, have wider implications for the form of the criminal law. The whole classification of offences might be changed, so that there might be no murders, only attempted murders; no rapes, only attempted rapes; no thefts, only attempted thefts; and so on. Such a change would ensure that the labels of offences reflected the moral equivalence between substantive offences and 'complete' attempts to commit them. It would, however, be alien to ordinary linguistic usage, would sometimes misrepresent the external events

86 This is not to ignore the special feelings deriving from authorship and causation, or to divorce D from the results of his action, for which, indeed, he might be civilly liable. See Winch's argument on 'doing and becoming' (n. 48 above and text at n. 50) and Bernard Williams on 'agent regret' (*Moral Luck* (Cambridge, 1981), 28–9), neither of which should affect criminal liability.

87 Hart, loc. cit. n. 58 above, 19, adding, for consequentialists, that 'the same considerations of general and individual deterrence apply with equal force'.

88 Bernard Williams, op. cit. n. 86 above, 20, adapting and restating the Kantian position.

which took place, and would in turn blur the distinction between incomplete and complete attempts. This last consideration suggests that on balance it is preferable to retain the labelling distinction between attempts and substantive offences and to classify complete attempts as attempts, even though in terms of moral culpability they are equivalent to substantive offences. Discussion of the relationship of recklessness and negligence to harm has been eschewed here so as to concentrate on the less disputable forms of culpability. The arguments in this essay would suggest that there is no relevant moral difference between two persons who risk certain harm, one actually causing that harm and the other causing none. However, there are strong social reasons against applying the moral argument directly to criminal liability in this sphere. The question warrants separate examination on another occasion.

The concern to establish the moral pedigree of the belief and intent principles should not be taken to suggest that they should always prevail. Grounded, as they are, in respect for the individuals as rational and choosing beings, they may occasionally yield to the protection of other rights which derive from the same source, as has been observed in the discussion above of 'impossible' attempts and the unknown justification. Other principles and policies might also be taken to outweigh the belief and intent principles in certain circumstances. Two examples are the principle of legality and the policy that ignorance of the criminal law should not be allowed as an excuse. The purpose of this essay has been not to weigh the arguments in all cases of conflict, but to establish that the starting point should always be the belief principle, that an individual should be judged on the facts as he believed them to be, and the intent principle, that an individual should be judged on what he was trying to bring about.

2

The Judge as Bureaucrat*

JOHN BELL

SINCE Weber it has been common in continental Europe, and to some extent also in the common-law world, to talk of the liberal legal order as 'bureaucratic' law, and to apply the same label to the work of the officials who run it, including the judges.[1] A bureaucratic structure involves institutions and officials implementing legal rules which effect the purposes of their superiors, the law-givers. Unlike oracular decision-making, so-called 'kadi justice', the emphasis is not simply on reaching just solutions, but on achieving justice according to standards known in advance. Political domination is achieved through these rules and their implementation, rather than simply through the exercise of power, whether by force or by traditional authority. The structure of rules provides a legitimation for the activities of officials and for the power which they exercise. Within a democratic political regime, such a system ensures the implementation of the decisions of democratic institutions and provides the citizens with the rights and benefits which the rule of law is designed to secure.

Applied to the judicial role, this vision of law as a bureaucratic institution focuses attention on the essential instrumentality and the limited creativity of the judicial function, together with characteristics such as impersonality, impartiality, and dedication to the service of the

[1] M. Weber, *Economy and Society*, ed. G. Roth and C. Wittich (Berkeley, 1968), vol. i, esp. ch. 3 and 881–94 (hereafter 'Weber'). For continental works, see especially: A. Arndt, *Das Bild des Richters* (Karlsruhe, 1957); H. Ostermeyer, *Die juristische Zeitbombe* (Munich, 1973), esp. 112 ff.; T. Rasehorn, 'Unabhängige Richter oder Justizburokraten?' [1970] *Juristenzeitung* 574; id., *Im Namen des Volkes?* (Neuwied, 1968), 15–25; R. Wassermann, *Justiz im sozialen Rechtsstaat* (Neuwied, 1974); id., *Justizreform* (Neuwied, 1970), ch. 1; K. Zweigert, 'Zum richterlichen Charisma in einer ethisierten Rechtsordnung', in T. Eschenburg *et al.* (eds.), *Festgabe für Carlo Schmid* (Tubingen, 1962), 299; W. Aantjes *et al.*, *Recht en Politiek* (Aalphen on Rhine, 1978). R. M. Unger uses the notion of 'bureaucratic law' in a more restricted sense to cover rules applied by an identifiable governmental staff, but the characteristics found there carry over into the notion of 'legal order' which is the closest equivalent to Weber's 'bureaucratic' law, and many of the comments made here can apply to it (see *Law in Modern Society* (New York, 1976), 50–7).

law, which are basic to this task. The outcome of a case should not depend on the identity of the judge, nor on the identity of the litigant, but should be determined by the application of known general rules, determinable in advance. The independent and professional skill of the judge is harnessed to the service of the law shaped by the legislator and the legal tradition. Such a characterization is, of course, only an ideal, but it does assign a social function to judges and explains how the power of the judiciary is legitimated.

This essay attempts to analyse the value of this description of the judicial role in the modern liberal state as 'bureaucratic'. Weber's own concern was principally with the structure of legal institutions and the legitimation of their authority. All the same, his analysis depends on a characterization of the functions performed by officials within such a legal order. In considering the 'bureaucratic' character of the judicial role, one is not simply concerned with the appropriateness of particular labels, but with the value of the analysis as an insight into the judicial function and into the attitudinal characteristics associated with it. I shall argue that Weber's description of bureaucratic activity is inadequate in significant respects. But, even if that description is corrected, I shall suggest that judicial functions do not adequately correspond to his notion of bureaucratic authority, neither in the tasks performed nor in the attitudinal features associated with them.

I. 'BUREAUCRACY' AND THE COMMON LAW

The characterization of the judicial role as 'bureaucratic' is one which might come more naturally to Romano-Germanic and Scandinavian lawyers than to common lawyers. For the former, judges are frequently civil servants with a career structure, which though independent, is not dissimilar to that of other state officials. Judgments are frequently collegial and not discursive, reaching an extreme in the brief and deductive French style which merely recites the essential facts and legal reasons for a decision, without any explanation of how these were arrived at. The proceedings are commonly written and are handled by one of the members of the court, so that the unfortunate litigant can be very much in the dark about the progress of his case, as Kafka brilliantly captures in *The Trial*. Such a set of institutions and proceedings does not differ markedly from the administrative allocation of benefits or permits in the way in which a common-law trial does. For this reason, it is not surprising that continental writers, particularly in West Germany, have been quicker than common lawyers in relating judicial and bureaucratic behaviour.

All the same, there are features of the common-law system which conform to the bureaucratic ideal. The ideal is well expressed by Donaldson J. at the inception of the National Industrial Relations Court:[2]

> As should by now be well known, the Industrial Court is a court of law. As such, it is independent of the government and is in no way concerned with its policies. Equally, it is independent of the parties to the disputes and is not concerned to provide tactical advantages for any of them. Like all the courts, it represents the public and does so by upholding the rule of law and applying the law of the land.

The essential subordination to the law, independent of politics or partial interest and deriving authority from the application of that law, fits well within the bureaucratic ideal which Weber described. In this passage, Donaldson J. appealed to the authority to be accorded to an institution which has the job of giving effect to the law, that is to say, the respect due to his office, rather than to his person. The ideas of impartiality and political neutrality are closely connected with this view, as was suggested in another industrial relations case, this time by Lord Diplock:[3]

> It endangers continued public confidence in the political impartiality of the judiciary, which is essential to the continuity of the rule of law, if judges, under the guise of interpretation, provide their own amendments to statutes which experience of their operation has shown to have had consequences that members of the court before whom the matter comes consider to be injurious to the public interest.

The ideal is that rules, rather than the personal preferences of judges, should govern cases and that the legitimate role of the judge is limited to the application of those rules. Such a view of the rule of law suggests that neither the personality of the judge nor the identity of the litigant should determine the outcome of a case. At the same time, the ideal is essentially formal. It concentrates on justice as embodied in rules of law and abstracts from the social impacts of decisions reached according to law (here on industrial relations). Court proceedings, with their bewigged judges, or at least (in such cases as the National Industrial Relations Court and the House of Lords) its formal procedure and the rule-based and abstract character of legal justifications reinforce the impression that it is the law in its majesty which determines the legal result and not

[2] *Secretary of State for Employment* v. *ASLEF* [1972] ICR 7, 14.
[3] *Duport Steels Ltd* v. *Sirs* [1980] 1 WLR 142, 157.

just the officials present in court. Even judicial discretion is not untrammelled, but guided and circumscribed by the law.[4]

There is no doubt that the judge in the common law is individually more identifiable as a decision-maker and personally justifies what is done in a way which the more anonymous continental courts do not. Personalized judgments and contributions to legal development are well recognized, yet this feature is tempered by the notion, current among some judges and writers, that the judge is rather developing the inherent logic of the law than moulding it directly according to his own lights.[5] Such features, among others, made it difficult for Weber to incorporate the common law into his scheme, and make it difficult for the common lawyer in turn to be happy with the bureaucratic ideal as an exhaustive description of the judicial role. All the same, there is sufficient similarity between the bureaucrat and the judge to make the bureaucratic ideal of value as an insight into the judicial role even in the common law.

2. BUREAUCRACY DEFINED

Weber isolated a number of features involved in a bureaucratic organization. Such a structure involved specialization within limited areas under a hierarchy, with a written procedure. The official was to have a skill acquired in the performance of a full-time function. Finally, the official must follow general rules known to him through his technical expertise.[6] The first feature establishes a routine function into which the official fits. His authority is not personal, but functional. The special skill in administration provides the individual with a livelihood and secures to him independence, as well as a special position in the community. Rule-governance provides not merely authority and legitimation for what he does, but also control and predictability.

(i) *Function*

The contrast which Weber saw in legal authority applied by a bureaucracy, as against the charismatic form of domination, is that the authority stems not from the person and his special qualities, but from the occupation of a particular office. In contrast to the traditional form of domination, it is not an office acquired by birth, but by choice. Respect

[4] Ibid., Lord Scarman at 168.

[5] e.g. Viscount Simonds, *Midland Silicones Ltd.* v. *Scruttons Ltd.* [1962] AC at 467–8; R. M. Dworkin, *Taking Rights Seriously* (London, 1978), 106 ff.; K. Larenz, *Methodenlehre der Rechtswissenschaft* (Berlin, 3rd edn., 1975), ch. 5.

[6] Weber, 957–8.

and legitimacy come from both the fact of the office and the exercise of that function according to what is expected of it. When one considers dispute settlement, then the choice of a judge is typically determined by the characteristics associated with an office, while a mediator may frequently be chosen because of his personal qualities. The creation of offices renders possible the regular performance of tasks such as dispute settlement in a complex society. The notion of an office depends on the definition of the purposes for which acts are done. The official acts for the purposes of his function, in that capacity, and for no other. The task he performs is both instrumental and ubiquitous. It is instrumental in that his decisions are made in order to achieve stated objectives, rather than for any purposes of his own. To act for a personal purpose would be seen as an abuse of office. His task is ubiquitous in that the official is supposed to perform it in the same way and with the same vigour whatever the content of his instructions. Thus the judges are supposed to implement socialist legislation with the same vigour as that of conservative governments. It is only by performing the duties of his office that the official can legitimate what he does.

Since authority and legitimation come from the office held, there is a natural concern among officials not to act in such a way as to undermine the respect for the office on which their authority depends. Judges clearly act in this way. For example, a frequently used argument to restrain what is considered excessive judicial activism is that it will bring the judiciary into disrespect and threaten the continuance of the present judicial arrangements.[7] On the other hand, those judges whose skills enable them to achieve results which are both technically sound and nearer to their notions of what is just may seek to force the pace, rather than content themselves with being the instruments of legal tradition and legislative policy.[8] The oath to do 'justice according to law' involves commitments to legal institutions and to values, as well as to justice, which may conflict with the commitments involved in enforcing specific laws.

(ii) *Professionalism*

For Weber, professionalism involved a domination through knowledge gained by acquiring skills in learning and using the rules. The acquisition of knowledge of the rules, or, more accurately, of how to find and

[7] e.g. *Duport Steels*, above n. 3, Lord Keith at 168, Lord Scarman at 169.

[8] e.g. Lord Denning, 'Way of an Iconoclast' (1959) 5 *J. Soc. Public Teachers Law* 77; Lord Edmund-Davies, 'Judicial Activism' [1975] *Current Legal Problems* 1.

manipulate the rules, is a key feature of any bureaucratic or legal training. It is true that such learning of rules and skills is not confined to bureaucratic legal systems but could be found in the traditions of the Roman pontiffs and other such oracular law-pronouncers. All the same, in the bureaucratic system the emphasis on learned skills takes a systematic and institutionalized form. In many ways, it is not so much the training in rules which matters, but rather induction into a professional tradition and its crafts. To the extent that those outside the profession lack the skills to understand and manipulate the rules in the same way as the professionals, this creates a degree of power in the latter. As Weber suggests, once the society becomes complex and differentiated, so the need for experts arises, and the power of the specialist bureaucracy can become great.

Weber seems to infer that the skills possessed within the bureaucracy are specific to it, so that others are at a disadvantage. This may be the result of his emphasis on bureaucratic secrecy which prevents the knowledge being a public good available to all,[9] which is less true when bureaucratic policies are openly declared or for judges who must publicly justify their decisions. The skills can be replicated by those, such as lawyers, who have access to the knowledge about how things are done. The specificity is also reduced to the extent that the skills of bureaucrats are, in any case, skills common to other professions. Since the bureaucratic function is not simply to keep the machinery of government ticking over, but to achieve specific results in the outside world, its effective performance requires the acquisition of knowledge not merely about administration, but also about the various fields over which officials intend to exercise power.[10] Furthermore, activities like the assessment of veracity or predictions of behaviour require non-professional skills. While the exercise of particular skills may identify a particular social practice, it need not have much influence on the authority and power of an official. In the case of the judicial office, its skills may best be considered a subclass of those possessed by trained lawyers, so that the gulf in knowledge, and hence power, is more between legally trained persons and laymen, rather than between officials and the rest.

While the possession of skill may not in itself command respect, the use to which it is put may more easily do so. Bureaucracy and judging are akin to what Murray, Dingwall, and Eekelaar call 'organized service

[9] Weber, 225.

[10] See *Committee on the Civil Service* (Cmnd. 3638, 1968), para. 41.

occupations'.[11] Those authors concentrate on the way doctors and lawyers claim to put their skills at the service of private clients, but the orientation of bureaucrats towards serving the public justifies similar claims to autonomy and respect. While some studies suggest that it may play a limited role as a spur to effective performance, public service may provide a regulative ideal and a source of prestige in the eyes of the outside world.[12] Such an ideal of public services reinforces the values of impartiality and neutrality found in the bureaucratic and judicial models.

However, the shared professional attitudes and commitments to what is considered to be a service to the public may conflict with the instrumental function which bureaucracy and judiciary have in common. As P. Blau points out, there are tendencies within a bureaucracy which both resist and promote change. Change is resisted if positions are threatened or the stability of the organization is under attack. On the other hand, skilled persons may well want new outlets for their talents once they have mastered their normal tasks, and the search for job satisfaction as well as the commitment to the public service may lead officials to strain towards finding new objectives.[13] Weber's analysis may thus need modification to accommodate the way in which the operation of a bureaucracy may be moulded by forces tangential to its instrumental structure and goals. All the same, such a bureaucratic tendency may help to explain the concern for the respect accorded to the courts and the concern, which can be found among some judges, to do justice whatever legal technicalities stand in the way. The mere fact that both perform a professional function does not, in itself, show the similarity between the judiciary and Weber's notion of bureaucracy. It is the notion of rule-governance which is most central to what he sees as peculiar in the bureaucratic role.

(iii) *Rule-governance*

Weber argued that to follow general rules was a central feature of bureaucratic government. The rationality which was thus set up provided for human dominance, but also controllability. 'In principle', he argued, 'a system of rationally debatable "reasons" stands behind every act of bureaucratic administration, namely either subsumption under

[11] 'Solicitors in Local Government', in R. Dingwall and P. Lewis (eds.), *The Sociology of the Professions* (London, 1983), 195, 198–9.

[12] P. Self, *Administrative Theories and Politics* (London, 1972), 228.

[13] *The Dynamics of Bureaucracy* (London, 2nd edn., 1963), 231, 243.

norms, or a weighing of ends and means.'[14] The formal structure of reason-giving and subordination to rules enables justice within the law to be achieved:

Juridical formalism enables the legal system to operate like a technically rational machine. Thus it guarantees to individuals and groups within the system a relative maximum of freedom, and greatly increases for them the possibility of predicting the legal consequences of their actions. Procedure becomes a specific type of pacified contest, bound to fixed and inviolable 'rules of the game'.[15]

The function of the bureaucracy is to abide by the rules and apply them in individual cases. This governance by laws, not men, seems integral to most conceptions of the rule of law. The principal function of such rule-governance is to ensure the effective instrumentality of the officials, to control their power, and to legitimate their activity. This view can, however, be criticized on all three counts.

As Weber clearly saw, subordination to formal rules may well conflict with substantive justice.[16] Rules, however prescient, are unlikely to be able to cope in advance with the variety of situations which may arise. Policies adopted in general terms will require incremental adjustment if they are to achieve desired objectives without many untoward consequences. As a result, the achievement of the substantive goals of the system may require a degree of initiative on the part of the official. Weber also noted that, at least in regard to law, the ideal of subordination to rules would have the effect of reducing lawyers to a 'slot machine' status which they would not accept, and that they would continue to work as a force for judicial creativity.[17] This is equally true of the bureaucracy. The exercise of initiative increases both effectiveness and job-satisfaction on the part of the official. This has been noticed in relation to the modern British bureaucracy. As Sir Douglas Wass put it:

My own experience of civil servants is not that they are a grey, dispirited and negative collection of people, as some popular images have sought to depict. If there is a prototype, it is a person who is conscientiously and indeed enthusiastically seeking to further the interests of his minister, and who sees it very much as his role to initiate and develop ideas within the contextual framework the government has set.[18]

[14] Weber, 979.
[15] Weber, 811.
[16] Weber, 855–6, 979.
[17] Weber, 886.
[18] 'The Public Service in Modern Society' (1983) 61 *Public Administration* 8, 14; also *Committee on the Civil Service*, above n. 10, para. 54.

The ideal depicted by Wass is concerned less with subordination to rules than with a willingness to channel initiative in directions which others have set.

Under the rule-governance theory, the task is satisfactorily completed when all that the rules require has been done. But the bureaucratic role does not fit this picture. A bureaucracy exists to serve purposes and to make use of human skills in specific directions. To use Galanter's terms,[19] its ambitions are both, in following rules, 'legalistic' and, in applying skills to achieve objectives, 'technocratic'. It is true that the institution may be asked to serve different purposes at different times, but this is not to deny its purposive character. It merely indicates that, since the institution has to be open to new objectives, officials must be flexible. To the extent that judges do not mechanically apply rules, but have to adjust them to fit other objectives of the legal system, or are given standards which require to be made more precise, initiative is also expected of them. Whether the 'technocratic' or instrumental activities of judges are of the same kind as those of bureaucrats will be discussed below, but it is clear that their tasks are not simply of the 'legalistic' character which Weber seems to set out.

The mere fact that judicial activity has such a 'technocratic' or instrumental character does not prevent it being 'rational', in Weber's sense, since reasons can be given to justify the means adopted towards a particular end. However, it does demonstrate the limitations of the ideal of control by rules. Furthermore, that ideal presupposes tasks can be defined and allocated with a high degree of precision, so that the ambit for discretion by the official is low. Yet the complexity of rules permits choices among strategies and the characterization of fact-situations in such a way that they fall under one form of regulation, rather than another. For example, the sovereignty of the trial judge over facts enables many significant decisions to be taken which superior courts cannot control. Even those, like K. C. Davis, who favour rule-following as a way of controlling administrative power also indicate the need for 'checking' by superiors and the legal 'structuring' of the decision-making process.[20] Others have argued that for further controls one must look beyond the law to the social and institutional environment within

[19] M. Galanter, 'Legality and its Discontents: A Preliminary Assessment of Current Theories of Legalization and Delegalization' (1980) 6 *Jahrbuch für Rechtssoziologie und Rechtstheorie* 11, 12.

[20] K. C. Davis, *Discretionary Justice* (Urbana, 1969), 27.

which decision-making takes place.[21] The social norms of a profession and the situations within which an official operates may control discretion, limit arbitrariness, and produce predictability more effectively than mere knowledge of the battery of rules which the official is supposed to apply. Indeed, defensively to 'go by the book' may make outcomes less predictable and less satisfactory than to exercise more discretion and yet conform more closely to the expectations of those affected by administration. Professional and institutional influences, such as those noted by Paterson,[22] may better explain the controls on the judiciary than the notion of rule-governance. At best, rules define the limits, rather than the content of the discretion exercised.

For Weber, rule-governance was also a legitimating device: 'every bearer of powers of command is legitimated by that system of rational norms, and his power is legitimated insofar as it corresponds with the norm. Obedience is thus given to the norms rather than to the person.'[23] Yet it must be questioned whether what confers legitimacy is the following of rules rather than keeping within an official function. As has been said, it is his holding of an office, rather than his personal characteristics, which confers authority on a judge. His institutional position provides a reason in itself for accepting a decision, whatever its content and no matter which judge made it. But the reasons for accepting such an authority in the first place will relate to the values it serves and its position among other institutions of government. As Cottrell has argued:

> It can be suggested that legal legitimacy depends ultimately on the belief of individual actors that law promotes, within the limits imposed by its 'essential' nature as a consistent and comprehensive rational *system* of regulation, what is most fundamental among the actor's values of justice and order, thought of not merely as procedural elements in law, but *social* values.[24]

It is the service of substantive values which grounds the legitimacy of bureaucratic authority. This legitimacy does not depend exclusively on adherence to norms unless the very nature of the office is defined as the application of rules alone. If, however, the office is more broadly interpreted, the exercise of initiative within the performance of that office can be legitimate.

[21] See R. Baldwin and K. Hawkins, 'Discretionary Justice: Davis Reconsidered' [1984] *Public Law* 570.

[22] A. Paterson, *The Law Lords* (London, 1982), ch. 2.

[23] Weber, 954.

[24] 'Legality and Political Legitimacy in the Sociology of Max Weber', in D. Sugarman (ed.), *Legality, Ideology and the State* (London, 1983), 69, 87.

(iv) *Hierarchy*

If the function of rule-governance was to legitimate and to control forms of decision-making, it is arguable that it is inadequate to do so. However, Weber's characterization of bureaucracy contains the element of hierarchical structure which is an alternative element of control. The instrumental character of the bureaucratic function requires that it be subordinated to the objectives and rules which have been laid down for the performance of specific tasks. The structure of rules may set down limits, but within the more discretionary areas of activity this will not operate a sufficient control. The exercise of judgment by the official will be controlled principally by his accountability to hierarchical superiors and to political masters, either for specific decisions taken or for the general pattern of behaviour. This check or scrutiny enables wide discretion to be conferred on the official, while some control is retained over what is done. This may include the power to overrule or to approve decisions prior to their implementation, but may be limited to reporting what has been done. Those who set the objectives can check what is being done and can offer supplementary comments and criticisms about the objectives to be achieved.

Judicial institutions are not under the same form of institutional control. Typically they are independent, either institutionally or at least conventionally in the way they go about their work.[25] They may be subject to appeal or review for the way in which their decisions conform to the legal guidelines, but the more discretionary the decision, the less amenable it is to this form of control. At best the courts are accountable in terms of the professional standards mentioned earlier. Judicial interventions have to make sense according to the standards of the reasonably qualified lawyer and, more tenuously perhaps, according to the standards of the competent and knowledgeable person in the field of social life which is subject to judicial intervention. The less structured nature of judicial accountability may serve as an argument for limiting the kinds of task which it is legitimate for judges to perform.

The foregoing discussion suggests that Weber's characterization of 'bureaucratic' activity needs to be modified to accommodate the way in which the bureaucratic service of objectives may lead to innovation and

[25] Institutions like the French Conseil d'État are part of the administration and are staffed by civil servants, and yet control the operations of the administration and defend the rights of citizens. Although such a body is not institutionally independent, it retains a convention of independence from the administration of which it is part when engaged on judicial tasks: see L. N. Brown and J. F. Garner, *French Administrative Law* (London, 3rd edn., 1983), ch. 4, esp. pp. 51–2.

the pursuit of professional interests may conflict with other aims. The judicial model has much in common with a revised 'bureaucratic' model: the notion of function or office, professional behaviour and attitudes, and the instrumental role which lies at the heart of the notion of rule-governance. Nevertheless, the peculiar demands of adjudication for independence may create a greater freedom from hierarchical control, and this characteristic can be further seen in a closer analysis of judicial tasks.

3. JUDICIAL TASKS

Weber's picture of the rule-bound character of bureaucratic decision-making suggests that bureaucratic tasks are primarily instrumental and static. Innovative and dynamic decision-making belongs elsewhere. Even if this has to be modified to accommodate some technocratic activity on the part of officials, the central place of rule-application might appear to make the judicial role 'bureaucratic'. However, I will argue that this would be to take too narrow a view of judicial tasks.

One can divide the judicial function into eight tasks of varying importance in different legal systems and in different branches of the law. They are (1) dispute settlement through adjudication; (2) informal conciliation; (3) determining rules for the settlement of future disputes; (4) enunciating public standards of behaviour; (5) legal authentication; (6) supervision; (7) constitutional control; and (8) social engineering. There is naturally some overlap between the tasks.

1. *Dispute settlement* through adjudication involves the resolution of a conflict between individuals, or between individuals and the state, by findings of fact and the application to them of general rules. Merely to determine facts and apply rules is a task that judges share with the clerk in the DHSS office who deals with a claim for unemployment or supplementary benefit. Indeed, were it not for the complexity of the rules and facts which require judgment in their determination, the task is one which judges would share with a computer. It is the archetypal bureaucratic activity. The judicial or adjudicative element is the resolution of conflict over how this task should be performed. If a criminal pleads guilty, no such dispute exists and the task might be seen as more like that of legal authentication or supervision discussed later. Where a dispute does exist, the judicial function is to apply an impartial mind to the determinations of the rules and fact involved. The line between

'difficulty' and 'dispute' in applying rules or determining facts is often a fine one. It is not without interest that, in a DHSS office, difficult and controversial cases on social security payments are referred to an 'Adjudication Officer', who is a civil servant different from the one who processed the original claim. The notion of adjudication employed in this instance focuses on the processing of difficulty, and thus of potential, if not yet actual, dispute. Given the element of judgment needed to determine and characterize facts and to interpret rules, especially if they refer to open-ended standards, there is no clear-cut line between rule-application and adjudication. Rather there is an essential continuity between them. Both the bureaucrat and the judge are expected to act impartially. All the same, in the presence of actual controversy, the independence of the decision-maker has to be more clearly visible in order to ensure confidence in the dispute-settlement process; and this is marked in the typical structure of judicial institutions.

2. Although the characteristic judicial task may be the formal and authoritative settlement of disputes, the role of the judge as an informal or semi-formal *conciliator* is not unimportant. In plea-bargaining or discussions in chambers during a trial, as well as in pre-trial work by registrars or masters, the judicial function is to encourage a settlement, or at least restrict the range of dispute, through the agreement of the parties and without a full court trial. For example, in divorce work, English courts are encouraged to use adjournments for intervention by a conciliation officer or pre-trial reviews as ways of restricting the extent of a dispute in court.[26] In part, this can be seen as the action of officials to save public money in trial costs.[27] However, it also falls within the judicial function of resolving disputes.

More than other conciliators, the judge relies on the authority of his office to encourage a settlement. While a solution may be agreed by the parties, rather than imposed by the judge, the structure within which such agreement takes place, notably the authority of the person suggesting the solution and the background threat that an overtly authoritative decision will otherwise be imposed, makes the line between the two methods of dispute resolution less clear. To adopt the analysis of Roberts, the judicial function here is not primarily the neutral one of assisting disputants to communicate better with each other, but is 'directive'. It consists in handing down assistance from above, prescrib-

[26] J. Eekelaar, *Family Law and Social Policy* (London, 2nd edn., 1984), 51–3, 57–8.
[27] Ibid., 52.

ing an outcome and guiding the parties towards it.[28] Such authoritative conciliation is not confined to the judicial role, but may be performed by other officials. Whether the task is performed by judges or others, it is the use of a position of power and authority, rather than the application of rules, which is central to the performance of the task.

3. *Rule determination* is an inevitable task when there is a dispute about the content of the rules relevant to a dispute. The rules thus adopted apply to the dispute in hand, but will have an influence, more or less great depending on the legal system, on decisions in future cases and as standards for future behaviour by citizens. Such an influence is inevitable in any decision-making committed to the application of general standards with a concern to be fair to all subject to the rules. The accumulation of past experiences and decisions about the best way to handle problems both eases administration and promotes fairness and generality. It is behaviour shared by judges and administrators alike. In that rules and particularly standards will require judgment in their application to concrete facts, the specificity which accumulated decisions gives to them maintains judges and administrators within a rule-dominated structure. Arbitrariness in the future is guarded against, and predictability secured through conferring a degree of legislative power. To the extent that the rules or standards are required to remain indeterminate or revisable, this innovative element continues. The performance of this task requires attention to future-regarding and consequentialist reasons which make the function programmatic, rather than simply programmed.

4. The *enunciation of public standards* is not confined to the task of determining rules for the future, but may have an important place in authoritative exposition of the law during the course of the judicial task. 'Lectures' given to miscreant criminals or in the finding of civil wrongs are addressed not merely to the persons affected, but to the public as a whole. From the charge to the Assize jury onwards, the judge's authority as a state officer has put him in a position to deliver statements about conduct on behalf of society. As a spokesman for the community, he purports to propound its requirements for particular situations. Some bureaucrats, such as trading standards or environmental health officers, may exercise similar authority with regard to particular sections of the community. With them, the judge shares an official position, but his authority is also based on the functions performed in other tasks and the impartiality associated with them.

[28] 'Mediation in Family Disputes' (1983) 43 *Modern Law Rev.* 537, 550.

5. The task of *legal authentication* brings the judicial and bureaucratic functions closest together. In uncontested divorces, undefended debt actions, or guilty criminal pleas the decision of the judge is a straightforward application of rules to fact, and merely authenticates what is alleged or what the parties have decided. Like the deposit of a will at the Probate registry or the old French practice of registering land transactions with the court office, the court serves as an institution for the public authentication of acts. Indeed, in areas like divorce, some countries have handed over the whole process to bureaucratic officials.

6. One reason for leaving such bureaucratic tasks with the court is that, in some cases, it can exercise a *supervisory* role. Courts are frequently required to approve decisions by public bodies or private individuals, even when there is no dispute. The taking of children into care, the voluntary winding up of a company, or the variation of a trust may appear very similar to legal authentication. However, the supervisory role of the court has an importance. In checking that the requisite conditions are met, the court looks to the interests of the parties and the interests of the public. As such, it has a kind of role as ombudsman, rather than as the settler of disputes.

Where the court is concerned with the interests of the parties, it will be vigilant to ensure that a proposed transaction is not oppressive to the interests of those who cannot defend themselves properly. In the variation of trusts, it will look to the interests of those unable to consent to the transaction and substitute its judgment for theirs.[29] The protection of the interests of the weak is also a feature of the requirement of a court order to expel a tenant from premises.[30] The defence of interests against private power is matched by the frequent use of the court as a protection against public power. The requirement to obtain the court sanctioning of a child being taken into care is designed to ensure that the local authority does not abuse the wide powers which it has.[31] Rather than quash decisions on grounds of abuse of power after the event, stricter control is exercised in advance to ensure that the right decision is reached. This rectifies the balance between the public authority's power and the parents and children whose lives are affected by it.

The supervisory role of the court is also intended to ensure that the interests of the wider public in the transaction are represented. The public interest that trusts are not varied so as to defraud the public

[29] Variation of Trusts Act 1958, s. 1.

[30] See M. Partington, *Landlord and Tenant* (London, 2nd edn., 1980), ch. 8.

[31] P. M. Bromley, *Family Law* (London, 6th edn., 1981), 391–2.

revenue,[32] or that children are looked after primarily by their parents can be secured by giving the court a veto over what the parties before it have agreed.[33] This supervisory function is designed to produce a kind of public accountability for the exercise of power, not unlike that required of the government at public inquiries. In both cases, officials have to adduce evidence which will satisfy an independent person (even at public inquiries frequently a lawyer or a judge). Supervisory controls are often used over police powers. Circuit judges or, more usually, justices of the peace have to authorize warrants for search or arrest as well for detention in custody.[34]

Such supervisory tasks may be performed in or out of court, and are frequently termed 'extra-judicial' functions. Whether such tasks are best called 'judicial' or merely 'tasks performed by those who happen to be judges' depends on the nature of the process and the skills involved. On the one hand, these tasks rely on the impartial and independent position of the judge as a safeguard of individual rights and of the public interest. Court procedures enable evidence to be gathered and judgments to be made within the overall objectives of the law. On the other hand, they are ill adapted to permit a critical evaluation of possible decisions from the point of view of a wide range of social interests. Furthermore, the evaluation of evidence often requires either non-legal professional skills or the common sense of the ordinary citizen, rather than specifically legal skills. The nature of the issue and judgments involved and the suitability of the judicial process to their adequate presentation and discussion limit the appropriateness of supervision by judges rather than by others.

7. It can well be argued that in many systems the judiciary has an important role in exercising *constitutional control* over the power of other organs of government. In most legal systems, there is some kind of check on the exercise of power by the executive and frequently also of the legislature. Whether this is a task performed by the ordinary judiciary or, as in France, by specialist judges more closely linked to the administration or politics, the result is similar—other branches of government are subjected to independent scrutiny and checking in the procedure they adopt and, to some extent, in the ends they pursue.

Such a constitutional role is not simply the instrumental role of

[32] *Re Weston's ST* [1969] 1 Ch 223.

[33] P. M. Bromley, above n. 31, 397–8.

[34] See S. A. de Smith, *Constitutional and Administrative Law* (5th edn. by H. Street and R. Brazier, London, 1985), 463, 466, 478–80.

carrying out settled policies. It involves balancing the objectives set out in basic and often vague principles of administrative or constitutional law, most notably in a constitution or bill of rights, with the autonomy of the administration or the legislature in carrying out their constitutional functions. It operates as a check on the administrative and political process, exercised not on technical grounds, but so as to enable other political actors or citizens as a whole to play a part in the process of government or in limiting its scope. Those who have wished this role upon the judiciary have argued that its independence from the administrative or political process and the limited professional ambitions associated with the judicial role make it the least dangerous branch of government for such a task.[35] The judicial mandate to uphold fundamental freedoms requires a flexible response to new situations, which can never be determined by pre-established rules. General objectives and values may be set, but their precise content remains a matter for flexible judgment. The fire-fighter is given the tools and the guidance, but is expected to use initiative and judgment in responding to the fires which break out. In this way, the judicial function moves away from a narrowly conveived bureaucratic character.

8. The judicial decision-making process may be concerned not merely to determine rules or rights in past situations, but also to further *social engineering* objectives. Well-established jurisdictions such as making children wards of court and determining guardians, with their balance between the interests of children, parents, and relatives, or the sentencing of criminals, where a balance has to be struck between deterrence, retribution, and reform, are illustrations of the way judges may be involved in organizing social situations for the future. The safeguarding of parental rights and children's interests or the changing of criminals and the prevention of future crime entail a degree of social engineering. The distribution of property and the care of children on divorce offer further examples. More widely, in areas like restrictive practices or labour law, judicial involvement in specific areas of social activity has been designed to help achieve changes in social behaviour, whether in the regulation of competition, in the treatment of workers, or in the conduct of industrial disputes.[36] While much of this activity is ancillary to the resolution of disputes, it can, as in restrictive practices or industrial disputes, become the main subject of concern. To the extent

[35] e.g. A. Hamilton, *The Federalist*, 78 (1788).

[36] P. Davies and M. Freedland, *Kahn–Freund's Labour and the Law* (London, 3rd edn., 1983), 360–6; J. Bell, *Policy Arguments in Judicial Decisions* (Oxford, 1983), ch. 5.

that administrators are concerned with developing plans, distributing grants and benefits, and so on, there is a great similarity between the bureaucratic and the judicial performance of social engineering tasks.

Selznick has sought to distinguish judicial and administrative tasks by suggesting that the judicial task is concerned with justice, while the administrator is concerned with achieving certain social goals:

> The administrator (where he is not really a judge) is also interested in diagnosing and classifying the world. But he properly looks to the end in view, the refashioning of human or other resources so that a particular outcome will be achieved. A judge becomes an administrator when his objective is to reform a criminal, avert a strike, or abate a nuisance. For then his aim is not justice but accomplishment, not fairness but therapy.[37]

The suggestion, closely mirrored in the distinction Dworkin draws between decisions of 'principle' and decisions of 'policy',[38] reflects a view that the judicial task should be about the backward-looking application of rules and moral judgments, rather than their manipulation for forward-looking ends. Of course, in many situations the judges are expected to decide according to what is right and fair under the existing law and to disregard adverse social consequences which would more strongly influence an administrator's decision. However, as I have tried to show elsewhere, the distinction cannot be drawn as sharply as Selznick and Dworkin try to do.[39] It would be wrong to see the social function of adjudication only as settling disputes and vindicating rules of law in terms of past events. The state is concerned about the effects of the exercise of power. There may be a need to ensure that legal powers are being properly exercised and that the consequences, in terms of the rules developed and the situations created, are acceptable for society as a whole. Although such considerations may not be given their full force in adjudication institutions, as opposed to the legislature, they are not irrelevant.

All the same, the specificity of the judicial function is determined by the requirements imposed on it by the central function of adjudication. The confidence which litigants need to repose in the independence and impartiality of the decision-maker may cause judicial institutions to

[37] *Law, Society and Industrial Justice* (New York, 1969), 15–16. Cf. J. Mashaw, *Bureaucratic Justice* (New Haven, 1983), 25–37, who distinguishes the determination of individual entitlements ('moral judgment') from simply effecting the legislative will ('bureaucratic rational' decision-making) and the exercise of professional skill ('professional treatment').

[38] Above, n. 5, at 294.

[39] J. Bell, above n. 36, ch. 8.

develop in ways which make them ill suited to many tasks, particularly of a dynamic nature. Attempts to change society incrementally and by experiment may be more easily effectuated and monitored within a hierarchically integrated, rather than through an autonomous institution. Yet the authority and respect possessed by bureaucratic and judicial institutions may have a greater influence on the precise division of tasks between them than a priori talk of the fundamental orientation of such bodies. The mix of tasks may reflect concern for the effective performance of primary tasks and the institutional constraints they impose, but the eventual content is determined by the political and social environment within which the tasks have to be performed.

4. BUREAUCRATIC CHARACTERISTICS AND THE JUDICIAL ROLE

The foregoing discussion of the judicial function and judicial tasks prompts a reconsideration of the 'bureaucratic' characteristics which were identified at the beginning of this paper and how they might properly be understood. The values of impersonality, impartiality, and dedication to the law focused on the essential instrumentality of the judicial function. To the extent that such a function involves the exercise of judgment and innovation typically independent of hierarchical control, these values set ideals against which the judicial performance can be measured. The question of commitments to instrumental and wider values has already been discussed. Other features of the 'bureaucratic' ideal are, however, worth developing. In discussing the common law, the features which came to the fore were impartiality, political neutrality, and the lack of judicial responsibility for the results of judicial decisions, and it is these that I want to develop here.

(i) *Impartiality*

The judicial resolution of disputes is attractive because it is authoritative and independent. Impartiality encourages confidence in the institution from those who might submit cases to it. It also serves the instrumental character of the judicial function, in that the decision is to be taken not according to the personal views of the individual judge, but according to community standards. The content of impartiality has been well explored by Ofstad.[40] It can be summarized as requiring an honest decision, uninfluenced by personal relationships or prejudice, based on general, not unique considerations, and appealing to standards which

[40] H. Ofstad, 'Impartiality', in *Legal Essays: A Tribute to Frede Castberg* (Oslo, 1963), 135.

are representative and which the judge would be willing to apply to similar circumstances in the future. The ideas of honesty, lack of prejudice or personal relationship, and justification by reference to general rather than particular considerations constitute the unbiased attitude to be expected in the professional performance of any function. Lack of bias is tested by lack of personal involvement in the outcome, and by a willingness to repeat the solution in similar circumstances in the future.

The notion of generality shades into that of representativeness: the decision calls for respect because the standards applied are more than just the personal views of the decision-maker. Judges seem to accept this, as the following passage from Sir Wilfred Greene illustrates:

> The judge's sense of justice, must, however, be universalised. He, no less than the juryman, is the reasonable man, his sense of justice is that of the *bonus paterfamilias.* He must avoid idiosyncracies, his views of right and wrong must conform to a practical standard, they must not be governed by mere psychological or ethical theories, however attractive they may be. It is justice as it appears to the reasonable man, the good citizen, that he must administer.[41]

Unlike the absence of bias, this is not a purely formal characteristic and is less easily achieved. One needs to be clear whether the standard refers to representativeness of what people do accept or of what they ought to accept. In a divided or pluralistic society, the choice of either of these standards will be controversial and call for judgment and sensitivity. One person's view of what is representative of basic values may well conflict with another's, especially where multiple values have to be weighed. In that case, impartiality does not command respect unless attention is also paid to the substantive ends which bureaucratic or judicial institutions are meant to serve.

(ii) *Political neutrality*

The element of representativeness within the notion of impartiality is closely connected to the value of political neutrality which is shared by bureaucratic and judicial institutions. It is said to follow from the instrumental role of the official to take decisions and actions on the basis not of his own opinions but of the instructions and objectives which his activity is meant to further and which have been set by political superiors or by the legal tradition. In that these instructions can vary with changes in the political scene, the official is meant to be willing and able to

[41] *The Judicial Office* (Birmingham, 1938), 7.

change tack as required, whatever his personal preferences and views.

The difficulty with this perception is that it concentrates on a kind of *passive* neutrality, of being the conduit-pipe for changes in political values between political masters and citizens. But the earlier analysis of both the bureaucratic and the judicial roles has emphasized the commitment necessary to implement and promote the values of the framework within which the official has to operate. This need to realize objectives requires an active co-operation on the part of officials, a zeal which is, even at an ideal level, an *active* neutrality. It involves taking responsible decisions, exercising discretion, and making value-judgments which are the product of the creative use of skills by the official. Of course the official might have preferred to start from other premisses, if he had been given a free hand, but he still exercises power to some extent depending on the discretion and judgment required by the task at hand.

Taking decisions from a particular point of view involves commitments both to the institutions which one serves and to the task at hand. As state officials with a general commitment to a particular role, the bureaucrat and the judge are dedicated to certain values associated with their role, both in its professional character and in its social function. Such commitments to values like the rule of law or constitutional principles are political commitments which shape the performance of the particular tasks of applying, making specific, and interrelating particular rules or standards. This general political commitment promotes and limits the ideal of active neutrality. The way in which this general commitment is perceived by judges, as well as their value judgments in interpreting particular legal rules, must be subjected to scrutiny and criticism.[42] The active dedication required for the effective performance of official tasks may come into conflict with the flexibility involved in the instrumental role of officials, and so the personal rather than the institutional element may come to the fore. Where the political neutrality of the judiciary may differ most from that of the bureaucrat is in the area of constitutional control. The institutional independence enjoyed by judges enables them to promote values which it is their special task to refine and balance against other legal objectives. This task is marked more by its independence from the political process than by its lack of political content.

(iii) *Responsibility*

The notion of the 'bureaucratic' nature of law suggests that the judge is

[42] See J. A. G. Griffith, *The Politics of the Judiciary* (London, 3rd edn., 1985).

not personally responsible for the results of the decisions he makes, since it is the law which decides what is permitted. On this analysis, the judge is merely a mechanism to transmit superior orders. While attractive in some ways, the suggestion belies the fundamental creativity and responsibility of the judge. Given that discretion and dynamism form part of the judicial task, the rules cannot dictate a solution which is not the judge's responsibility. In carrying out policies and making value-choices, the values and perspectives of the individual decision-maker are deployed.

At the level of the individual decision, the responsibility of the judge will depend on the degree and nature of the choice he exercises. In characterizing facts, in choosing the appropriate rule, and in making precise the requirements of that rule, there may be an element of individual judgment and choice. This area is extended where the applicable standard is unclear, or leaves much to the initiative of the decision-maker, as with tests of 'reasonableness', 'public interest', and so on. While tasks of legal authentication may involve little initiative, those involving supervision and social engineering as well as constitutional control may involve a great deal. In that judicial action will frequently be circumscribed rather than determined by rules, it involves significant responsibility. In such situations, the office alone may not secure acceptance and legitimation for decisions, unless the individual occupant is also seen to promote the values which it is expected to serve. This places on the individual decision-maker an obligation to ensure that the decision he reaches and the justifications he offers will encourage acceptance and respect.

At the institutional level, in that the bureaucracy and the law are of value not in themselves but as a means for securing social objectives, their legitimacy depends in no small measure on their success in achieving those objectives. As front-line institutions attempting to achieve those objectives in individual cases, the respect accorded to them will depend on the way they meet the expectations of fairness, justice, and so on which individuals have of them, rather than on their mere efficiency in implementing superior orders.[43] Such respect may not wholly depend on individual decisions, but these often have an impact. Indeed the concern of judges to maintain the prestige of the judiciary is a recognition of this. If bad decisions can harm that prestige and respect, good decisions can promote them. The responsibility of the

[43] A. Arndt, above n. 1, 15; F.-J. Säcker, 'Zur demokratischen Legitimation des Richter- und Gewohnheitsrechts' [1971] *Zeitschrift für Rechtspolitik* 145, 149.

judge is thus not merely to those affected by a decision, but also to the good functioning of the institution which may be indirectly affected thereby.

The two facets of responsibility, towards individuals and towards the institution, may lead to decisions by judges and bureaucrats which do not achieve the objectives which a particular set of rules or objectives was designed to secure. Such 'bureaucratic' activity is not an abnegation of responsibility, but a particular version of it. In that judicial decisions are often authoritative, final, and not subject to control by a hierarchical superior, it could be argued that the judicial role typically carries more responsibility than the bureaucratic role.

5. CONCLUSION

This discussion of the judicial role has revealed many similarities in the structure and tasks performed by judges with those performed by 'bureaucrats', as they might properly be called. As state officials and subordinates in the political process, both fulfil offices which are importantly instrumental. However, in contrast with Weber's presentation, this instrumentality involves not the emptying of the individual personality, but its harnessing in a zeal for implementing objectives which may well require further refinement, harmonization, and concretization by the official. Since both derive authority from an office and perform tasks with certain characteristic attitudes, this overlap is inevitable to the extent that the functions of the institutions are broadly similar. However, it is where the functions differ that the greater responsibility of the judiciary lies. Here, the characterization of it as 'bureaucratic' is at its most inadequate.

In those judicial tasks where independence is most integral to their successful performance, the judge is an instrument not so much of the will of the legislator or precedent-setter, as of the general legal values which determine how supervision or constitutional control should operate, or what is the notion of justice which adjudication should serve. Unlike bureaucrats, judges themselves are typically guardians of these values, which they often have to defend against interpretations placed on them by other organs of government and power-holders in society. On the one hand, their very function and the values which they must develop and interpret are in themselves political. Their dedication to the law involves a voluntary orientation in the exercise of that political power, rather than the absence of such power. In this activity, the personality of the decision-maker and his individual responsibility come to the fore in a way which is not adequately captured by Weber's 'bureaucratic' ideal. The legitimacy of decisions cannot rely totally on the office held and the rules applied, but also takes into account the values served by the judges.

Seen in this way, law is not just a bureaucratic set of regulations, but a structure of institutions exercising political power. Weber acknowledged this, but his presentation places undue emphasis on the formal, rule-applying tasks which the law as a social institution involves. In relation to many tasks, judicial authority is more than simply the kind of formal, bureaucratic authority which Weber described. It is true that, even when sitting alone, a judge does not depend for his authority on just his personal qualities, but on the reputation of the judiciary as a whole. But this does not entail that the authority of judicial institutions is purely bureaucratic. Both individually and collectively, the judges gain their authority and legitimacy from the substantive values which their decisions and procedures promote, especially where judgment and discretion are involved. It is only in having regard to the substantive opinions and beliefs of judges, rather than simply to their technical, rule-applying proficiency, that the legitimate authority of the judiciary in the exercise of its political power can be sustained and promoted.

3

Public Law and Private Law: A Study of the Analysis and Use of a Legal Concept*

PETER CANE

THE distinction between public law and private law is one (or a subset) of a complex set of distinctions concerned with demarcating the public and private spheres of life. To discuss the public–private distinction in the context of all the areas of the law to which it is relevant would be a mammoth task and in this essay I shall concentrate on English administrative law. Law is one, but only one, of the techniques which can be used to establish the boundary between the public and the private spheres. The use of law (as of other techniques) to this end has two complementary aspects, one negative the other positive: by way of coercion, legal rules are used to restrain one person (or the state) from interfering with the activities of others; positively, legal rules are used to create certain spaces within which the individual (as against his fellows or the state) is free to express his individuality in choice and action.

TWO VERSIONS OF INDIVIDUALISM

The public–private distinction is commonly associated with liberal political theory. In varying degrees liberals emphasize individual choice and freedom from external control and this leads to a concern to strike a proper balance between the private sphere in which the individual is allowed to pursue his own ends in his own way and the public sphere in which his freedom is subject to restriction for the benefit or protection of the freedom and welfare of others. It should not be thought, however, that the public–private distinction finds a place only in the views of those who would popularly be called 'liberals'. Although a society in which *no* aspect of the lives of individuals was under their exclusive control is theoretically possible, no mainstream western political philosphy espouses such a social arrangement as its goal. Different theories tend to disagree over the appropriate areas (such as economic activity, sexual behaviour, education, medicine) and the appropriate amount of individual freedom rather than over the desirability of individual freedom as such.

However, different theories also disagree about what constitutes the most desirable form of human self-expression and fulfilment. Some would argue, for example, that the model of the competitive market in which individuals give expression to their choices is the best paradigm for many areas of human activity. Others would argue that individuals often derive greater fulfilment from collective and co-operative action than from isolated and competitive activity. These and other views generate important differences of opinion about the proper role and functions of government.

Two versions of individualism, it seems to me, have been particularly influential amongst legal writers. The first is what might be called 'developmental individualism'. This version sees the essence of individual self-fulfilment in terms of self-improvement and self-development. It is partly a reaction to a view which sees man as essentially a consumer or appropriator of goods.[1] Translated into political terms developmental individualism is often thought to require that individuals should be allowed to *participate* directly and effectively in the making of decisions which affect them. The essence of 'participation theory' lies in its assertion of the desirability of involvement in particular forms of decision-making such as discussion, negotiation, compromise, and agreement. Such forms of decision-making give participants the chance to develop their political ideas and skills, to be creative and to have a direct impact on the decision.[2] 'Participation theory' would tend to devalue the adversary technique of dispute settlement because the latter is based on the idea that the truth is most likely to emerge from a *contest* between conflicting views and claims. It would prefer 'participatory analogues' of adjudication such as mediation and conciliation in which the task of the third party is to promote discussion, compromise, and agreement. The nub of 'participation' in this context is, then, co-operation as opposed to conflict and contest.

Participation theory has been very influential amongst certain critics of administrative law theory and of the role of the courts in relation to administrative law. For these writers participatory modes of decision-

[1] C. B. Macpherson, *The Life and Times of Liberal Democracy* (Oxford, 1977).
[2] J. Finnis, *Natural Law and Natural Rights* (Oxford, 1980), 146–7.

making have technical advantages—they are better suited than adjudication to solving complex polycentric conflicts of interests;[3] and political advantages—they allow individuals to be more directly involved in decision-making than do representative modes which encourage political inactivity.[4] Although consultation of interest groups by government and even the delegation to them of governmental functions are common in Britain, and although informal agreement is an important alternative to legislation as a means of government regulation of social and economic activity, much of the participation literature operates on the level of aspiration rather than description, in that its authors wish to see many more opportunities than exist at present for ordinary people to be involved in community decision-making. From this point of view political inactivity is a disease caused by insufficient participation, a pathological state bred of disillusionment with representative democracy as it functions in Britain.

From another point of view, however, political inactivity might be argued to be the natural reaction of most people most of the time. According to what I shall call 'passive individualism' the essence of individual freedom is being left alone to go about one's business. Let the government get on with the business of governing so long as in doing so it does not exceed or abuse its legal powers or encroach upon the fundamental rights and interests of individuals.[5] Passive individualists believe in representative democracy of the traditional Burkeian kind in which representatives, once elected, are free until the next election to act in what they perceive to be the public interest. Passive individualism is important in the legal context because it seems to describe well the attitude of many judges and of some leading legal writers, namely that the role of administrative law and of the courts in relation to administrative activity is to protect the rights and interests of individuals from *undue* encroachment by government, that is, from abuse or excess of government power. From this point of view the function of law in relation to the administration is an essentially reactive and negative one

[3] G. Ganz, *Administrative Procedures* (London, 1974).

[4] C. Harlow and R. Rawlings, *Law and Administration* (London, 1984), 46–7; J. P. McAuslan, *The Ideologies of Planning Law* (Oxford, 1980), 269. As with McAuslan, a commitment to participatory democracy is often accompanied by a commitment to a package of 'anti-capitalist' policies. By contrast, some extreme market capitalists think that government policy-making should be far less subject to the influence of pressure groups and political parties than it is now: see D. Heald, *Public Expenditure* (Oxford, 1983), 167–8.

[5] John Bell suggests that this view can be contrasted with a more continental European account of passivity which views the government as a 'skilled cadre of technocrats' to whom one can safely commit the running of the country.

of *checking* and *controlling* the exercise of power and of settling disputes between citizen and government, whereas participation theorists put much more emphasis on positive action designed to avoid disputes between citizens and government by involving citizens in the making of decisions which affect them. This checking or controlling function is performed within a constitutional framework of parliamentary sovereignty, ministerial responsibility, and the separation of judicial from legislative and administrative (that is, political) functions. These constitutional doctrines constitute a system of checks and balances which, by and large, keep the system in equilibrium. Of course, there are defects in our political and constitutional arrangements, but the way of correcting them is to strengthen the representative element[6] rather than, for example, to inject a significant new element of citizen participation.[7]

Passive individualism, then, provides a good explanation of what is now often called the traditional approach which sees the role of administrative law as being to protect the individual within the context of representative Westminster-style democracy. Developmental individualism, as we have seen, underpins participation theory which, amongst legal writers, has become an important competitor to the traditional approach to administrative law. Whereas traditional theory casts administrative law in an essentially negative protective role, participation theory seeks for it a much more positive role in promoting the realization of the full potential of individuals as members of society.

INDIVIDUALISM AND THE PUBLIC–PRIVATE DISTINCTION

There are significant conceptual links between the different versions of individualism and views about the public–private distinction. For passive individualism there is a protected area of individual rights and interests which government must respect; but passive individualists are often quite tolerant of government power. According to developmental individualism the good life is promoted by individual participation in *communal* (public) decision-making activity. Because communal activity is important for the realization of individuality, the distinction between the public sphere and the private sphere is not as clear and straight-

[6] In the continental account of passivity mentioned in the previous note, representation is not so important a check.

[7] H. W. R. Wade, *Constitutional Fundamentals* (London, 1980), esp. ch. 2.

forward for the developmental individualist as for the passive individualist. It does not follow, however, that the former thinks the public–private distinction to be of no importance. After all, the leading light of developmental individualism, J. S. Mill, also provides inspiration for those who argue that there is a sphere of private activity which is 'none of the community's business'. Conversely, passive individualism is often quite tolerant of public regulation of and even public participation in 'the private sector'. Indeed, passive individualism is to some extent neutral as between more or less active government: it seeks primarily to protect a defined area of individual freedom rather than to extend and maximize that area. Nevertheless, developmental individualists do tend to celebrate the virtues of communal activity as a means of individual expression and development whereas passive individualists see the public and private spheres as separate and occasionally in conflict, although mostly in happy coexistence.

THE INFLUENCE OF DICEY

From what has been said so far we might expect legal writers who espouse developmental individualism to consider the public–private distinction to be less important than do judges and writers who adopt passive individualist premisses. But the approach of legal writers to the distinction is complicated by another very important influence, namely the constitutional writings of A. V. Dicey. His rejection of the distinction seems to have rested, in turn, on a thorough rejection of the idea of the state or the government as a corporate entity in a way which is alien to both the versions of individualism discussed above. Three features of Dicey's approach have been particularly important. First is his idea that as far as possible the individual citizen and government officials ought to be equal before the law and treated alike in like circumstances.[8] Modern scholars who adopt this approach stress the similarities and analogies between governmental and private activity and play down the public–private distinction:[9] what matters for questions of legal liability is the nature of the activity, not the identity of the person or body conducting it; and since activities are not by their nature either public or private, the distinction is irrelevant to the regulation and control of human activity.

[8] Dicey seems, as already noted, to have perceived the government as a collection of individual agents of the public rather than as a corporate entity.

[9] C. Harlow, '"Public" and "Private" Law: Definition without Distinction' (1980) 43 *Modern Law Rev.* 241.

Approaches which play down the distinction I shall refer to as 'integrationist'.

Secondly, Dicey emphasized the role of courts and judicial processes in controlling government activity and making government officials accountable to those over whom they wielded power. Adjudication is the paradigm *private-law* dispute-settling mechanism[10] and so, in accordance with the principle of equality before the law, ought to be used to settle citizen–government disputes as well. This approach has been developed by later writers in two quite different directions. On the one hand, writers sympathetic to Dicey's basic argument have stressed the value of judicial and adversarial processes both in administration (whether within departments and local authorities, before tribunals, or at public inquiries) and in the settling of disputes between citizen and government.[11] This line of reasoning is integrationist in relation to procedure; but its proponents, who are often passive individualists, are not necessarily integrationist in relation to activities—they do not necessarily reject the notion that some activities are peculiarly public or governmental.[12]

On the other hand, writers who have reacted against Dicey's basic premiss have utilized the public–private distinction by distinguishing sharply between judicial, adversarial processes of decision-making and dispute settlement on the one hand, and non-adversarial techniques such as negotiation, agreement, mediation, and conciliation on the other. They also distinguish between 'legal' (and rule-based) processes on the one hand and 'political' (and policy-based) processes on the other. Non-adversarial techniques are seen as particularly appropriate to much government decision-making; and political methods of securing accountability and control are seen as particularly appropriate in relation to activities of public importance (public activities). Such analysis is sometimes taken one step further by the suggestion that more attention be paid to managerial techniques of decision-making and dispute settlement.[13] Systems analysis, budget control, and the establishment of strong internal lines of responsibility within organiza-

[10] Even though the rules of natural justice are based on the adjudicatory model of decision-making, they are often treated as essentially *public-law* rules. The point seems to be twofold: first, that certain bodies can in certain circumstances be under an *obligation* to comply with the rules; and second, that in a public-law context the rules often apply to the initial decision-making process and not just to the *ex post facto* dispute-settling process.

[11] e.g. H. W. R. Wade, *Administrative Law* (Oxford, 5th edn., 1982).

[12] Wade, op cit., n. 7 above, 46–49; 'Procedure and Prerogative in Public Law' (1985) 101 *Law Quarterly Rev.* 180, 197–8.

[13] P. P. Craig, *Administrative Law* (London, 1983), ch. 6.

tions are seen as particularly important in controlling the activities of public bodies which are not subject to market pressures (private); but where public bodies are subject to market pressures a delicate balance has to be struck between public (political) and private (market) forms of accountability.[14]

Dicey's third influential point concerned the best way of protecting individual rights. In his view, guaranteeing specific individual rights by constitutional entrenchment was unnecessary and undesirable. For him the sphere of individual freedom was properly the whole out of which specific restrictions on freedom could be carved. Modern writers who have less faith that our law-making institutions are committed to personal freedom (as they interpret it), and who see value in explicitly stating the rights of individuals against government, have reacted in one of two ways. Most have called for an entrenched Bill of Rights. But another approach looks to the common law to provide at least some protection for the individual against governmental power. Ironically, this approach utilizes the public–private distinction to argue both that governments ought not too readily to be conceded the same rights as individuals; and also that governments ought to be seen, by virtue of their power, as having certain special responsibilities to the citizen which could generate citizen rights against the government (for example, to disobey the law in certain circumstances).[15]

Administrative law writers, therefore, can be divided into two more or less well-defined camps—those who either explicitly or implicitly accept the public–private distinction and those who reject it more or less strongly. In the former camp are those who see the role of administrative law (whether used in a narrow sense to refer to legislation and common law or in a broader sense to encompass all techniques for organizing and regulating administrative activity) as being to strike a proper balance (or equilibrium) between private freedom and public action, between private rights and interests on the one hand and 'the public interest' on

[14] Often linked with the distinction between different techniques of decision-making and accountability is the idea that Dicey's approach encouraged an attitude to administrative law which places excessive emphasis on dispute settlement as opposed to forward planning and dispute avoidance. This point is sometimes associated with advocacy of managerial techniques; but it seems to have little to do with the public–private distinction—the same point has been made in relation to 'traditional' court-centred contract scholarship. Indeed, the point is more properly seen as an anti-formalist one to the effect that legal rules and judicial processes are of marginal importance in facilitating and regulating human and social intercourse generally.

[15] G. Samuel, 'Public and Private Law: A Private Lawyer's Response' (1983) 46 *Modern Law Rev.* 558.

the other.[16] This approach I have associated with passive individualism. Writers in this camp do not necessarily presume in favour of individual liberty and rights—they may be 'more administration-minded than the administration'. They tend to interpret 'the public interest' in terms of the freedom of the administration to do what it perceives to be in the public interest as efficiently and as quickly as possible. By contrast, two strands of thought—developmental individualism and Diceyan integrationism—have influenced writers in the other camp. It is now necessary to analyse the attack on the public–private distinction in more detail.

CRITICISMS OF THE PUBLIC–PRIVATE DISTINCTION

The descriptive attack

Critics of the public–private distinction attack it on a number of grounds. First an attack is made on descriptive grounds: to analyse the relationship between those who wield power and those who are subject to it in terms of the distinction is to misrepresent the world. Take activities and functions: 'No activity is typically governmental in character nor wholly without parallels in private law.'[17] For example, housing for the poor is provided both by local authorities and by voluntary (private) housing associations;[18] the Rowntree Trust administers the Family Fund which provides financial assistance (social welfare benefits) to the families of severely handicapped children;[19] private security companies perform many traditional policing functions;[20] in the United States increasing numbers of prisons are run by private companies. Then consider bodies and organizations: the paradigm of a public body is the department of central government or the local authority. Some non-departmental organizations are clearly public—the NHS, for example. But what about the BBC or a trading corporation wholly owned by the state or in which the state has a controlling interest? Equally problematic are non-governmental bodies to which the government delegates administrative functions (such as the Law Society administering the Legal Aid Scheme) or even powers of making

[16] Wade, op. cit. n. 11 above, 5; D. C. M. Yardley, *Principles of Administrative Law* (London, 1981), 2–4; J. F. Garner, *Administrative Law* (6th edn., ed. Garner and Jones, London, 1985), 79.

[17] Harlow, 43 *Modern Law Review* 241, 257.

[18] See Noble, in M. Adler and S. Asquith (eds.), *Discretion and Welfare* (London, 1981), ch. 8.

[19] See Bradshaw in Adler and Asquith, op. cit., ch. 6.

[20] H. Draper, *Private Police* (Hassocks, 1978).

delegated legislation.[21] The growth of the mixed economy and the so-called 'corporate state',[22] so it is said, render the public–private distinction anachronistic and inaccurate. The real picture is one of interpenetration and integration, a partnership (or at least a division of labour) between the government on the one hand and private individuals and institutions on the other to achieve shared social goals.[23]

The descriptive attack is, however, flawed in a fundamental way. The terms 'public' and 'private' are, in a very important sense, not descriptive terms. To say of some body or activity that it is 'public' or 'private' is not to say that it possesses some 'brute' characteristic but rather that, according to some norm or set of norms, the term 'public' or 'private' is appropriately applied to that body.[24] For example, we might say that waging war is a public function because private standing armies are undesirable; or that the National Greyhound Racing Board is a private body because relations between it and its members depend solely on contractual agreement.[25] Of course, either type of statement can be made from either an 'observational' or a 'committed' point of view: one might personally consider standing private armies to be undesirable or merely observe that this is a normative reason given by some for classifying the waging of war as a public function; and one might merely observe that for certain purposes the law treats the National Greyhound Racing Board as a private body or accept that it is right to do so.

So the descriptive attack on the public–private distinction might be made by critics who say one of three things. They might say that modern social life is characterized by a haphazard distribution of functions having the normative characteristics of publicness amongst bodies some of which have the normative characteristics of publicness and others of which have the normative characteristics of privateness and yet others of which have some of the normative characteristics of publicness and some of the normative characteristics of privateness (and vice versa). But this observation, while undoubtedly correct, does not call into question the relevance or accuracy of the public–private distinction. Indeed, it reveals it as a potentially powerful tool of analysis and

[21] G. Alderman, *Pressure Groups and Government in Great Britain* (New York, 1984), 83.

[22] See e.g. J. T. Winkler, 'Law, State and Economy: The Industry Act 1975 in Context' (1975) 2 *British J. of Law and Society* 103; N. Lewis, Review Article (1985) 12 *J. of Law and Society* 87.

[23] See e.g. *Reform of Social Security*, Cmnd. 9517 (1985), vol. i, para. 1.5.

[24] S. I. Benn and G. R. Gaus, in Benn and Gaus (eds.), *Public and Private in Social Life* (1983), 11–13.

[25] *Law* v. *National Greyhound Racing Board* [1983] 1 WLR 1302.

criticism. Second, the critic might be saying that the set of norms which currently governs the use of the terms 'public' and 'private' is the wrong set or that it is too vague or too variable from context to context and case to case. But this argument invites normative redefinition of the distinction rather than its abandonment. Third, and most plausibly, the critic might be saying that the normative ordering of society which the terms 'public' and 'private' achieve is undesirable no matter to which activities or bodies the terms are applied, and that a new way of organizing and regulating relations between governmental and non-governmental entities is needed. The thrust of this argument is not descriptive but prescriptive.

Prescriptive attacks

In contrast with descriptive attacks, then, there are attacks on the public–private distinction made on prescriptive (or ideological) grounds. Such attacks take a number of different forms.

(i) *Immunities and privileges* First, it is argued that a common normative implication of the classification of a body or activity as being public is privilege and immunity from various legal imposts and liabilities. Such special treatment, it is said, need not always be wrong, but the criterion for it ought not to be publicness. In fact, no single criterion will do the job—each situation must be considered on its merits. To understand the force of this attack it is necessary to draw a distinction between what might be called the 'dispositive' role of a legal distinction or concept and what might be called its 'explanatory' role. A distinction or concept is used dispositively (in my sense) if it provides the immediate criterion or trigger for a particular legal result; a distinction or concept is used 'explanatorily' (in my sense) if it or some idea it encapsulates either explains or justifies or rationalizes some legal rule or criterion which in turn directly determines legal results.

Now it seems clear that the public–private distinction as used in relation to bodies and activities does, at a more or less general or abstract level, influence much legal reasoning in administrative law cases, as we will see later; but it rarely decides cases. As far as I can see, the only institutionally based distinction which operates dispositively *and unequivocally* as a criterion for the enjoyment of immunities and privileges is that between the Crown and other public bodies; but this is, of course, a distinction within the public category and not between public and private. A second dispositive use of the public body–private body distinction concerns whether a body is amenable to the prerogative orders and hence to an application for judicial review under RSC Order 53. Order 53 procedure has built into it a number of significant special procedural protections. Public bodies are amenable to an application for judicial review, private bodies (defined as those the existence and powers of which derive from contract or, perhaps, custom) are not. But the cases show that, when it is argued that there is a choice between Order 53 procedure and some other procedure, it is not always the public body which favours the former or the litigant suing the public body who opts for the latter.[26] Nor, despite the initial enunciation of the exclusivity principle by Lord Diplock in *O'Reilly* v. *Mackman*,[27] have the courts shown a great willingness to force private litigants to use Order 53 so as to accord public authorities the protections contained therein when such an approach would effectively prevent individuals enforcing and protecting their proprietary, contractual, or tortious rights against the respondent body. So the example is equivocal so far as concerns the use of the public–private distinction as a criterion for the enjoyment of a privilege.

The concept of a public function is used dispositively to subject private bodies performing certain functions to the rules of natural justice, and so does not fall within the terms of the attack under consideration, because having to comply with the rules of natural justice is usually seen as a burden and a disadvantage. The concept was used dispositively in *Hoffman-La Roche* v. *Trade Secretary*[28] (in the form of a distinction between legislative and commercial activities) to justify refusal to require the Crown to give an undertaking as to damages as the price for an interim injunction to restrain Hoffman-La Roche from disobeying price restriction orders. It was also used dispositively in *Swain* v. *Law Society*.[29] The Law Society set up a scheme of professional indemnity insurance on behalf of all its members for the protection of their clients. The society earned brokerage commission on the business generated and the House of Lords held that since, in setting up the scheme, the society was exercising a public function for the benefit of those members of the public who consulted solicitors, it did not have to account to its individual members for the commission but was entitled to apply it for the 'benefit of the profession', provided that in doing so it

[26] Compare, for example, *R.* v. *East Berkshire Health Authority, ex parte Walsh* [1985] QB 152, with *Wandsworth LBC* v. *Winder* [1985] AC 461.

[27] [1983] 2 AC 237.

[28] [1975] AC 295.

[29] [1983] 1 AC 598.

acted reasonably in the public-law sense. Whether the proponents of the attack on the public–private distinction which we are currently considering would see this as a case of improper privilege or immunity is arguable. But the case does not really fall within the terms of the attack because it *was* decided in the light of its own facts, the notion of public function or duty being used as a conclusion rather than as part of the argument.

The proper conclusion to draw from the foregoing seems to be that although the public–private distinction can be used to accord public authorities privileges and immunities, it is not invariably used in this way. The truth is rather more complex than the attack under consideration allows. This is partly, at least, because the distinction is itself applied differently in different contexts (see further below).

(ii) *Corporatism and the mixed economy* The second type of prescriptive attack on the public–private distinction rests on the distinction between legal and political accountability: government participation in the economy by contractual rather than legislative means, regulation by informal agreement (that is, encouragement of self-regulation), and delegation of administrative functions to private bodies, are all techniques by means of which, it is said, governments seek to depoliticize and remove from political and parliamentary scrutiny important areas of government activity. Furthermore, the use of such techniques is very often effectively protected from judicial scrutiny because of the informality of the techniques (that is, the non-use of legal forms) or by virtue of common-law doctrines such as freedom of contract. Thus, it is sometimes argued that there is a need for new forms of accountability (although what these might be is yet to be specified) or even a revised concept of the rule of law, incorporating ideas of fair procedure and rational discourse relevant to the new forms of government activity.[30] The nub of this attack is, therefore, that the public–private distinction serves to shield much government and government-promoted activity from proper scrutiny and the need to give proper account.

It is not clear that the ultimate concern of those who make either of these first two prescriptive attacks on the distinction is any different from that of those who espouse it. Opinions differ as to whether the institutions of the mixed economy and the corporate state are basically sinister or benign, and as to whether they call for drastic new measures of control or only the adaptation and slight extension of well-tried

[30] Lewis, above n. 22, 87, 92.

techniques. At the end of the day, however, both the proponents and the critics of the public–private distinction seem concerned with regulating, in what they consider to be an acceptable way, relations between those who wield power and those subject to it. The core of the critics' complaint is that, as they see it, those still satisfied with the 'old wisdom' of the distinction are too content with current controls over the exercise of power in society. Unlike people who would prefer to see the state progressively disengage from the economy and from the provision of welfare benefits and services, these critics of the distinction assume the continued existence of something like current patterns of power distribution and seek more effective ways of *controlling* it. At a very fundamental level, therefore, both the 'old guard' and their critics are imbued with traditional lawyerly (rule of law) concerns. They do not seek to landscape the political environment but rather to tend it and keep weeds at bay. But the critics[31] typically argue for greater or more control over government and government-promoted activity than the 'old guard' appear to consider necessary or desirable.

(iii) *Participation theory* The third prescriptive attack comes from participation theorists. As we have seen, participation theorists favour co-operative as opposed to adversary methods of making decisions. In the legal context the commitment to co-operation has effects in two areas: first, these theorists tend to oppose the extension of trial-type adjudication from the traditional courts to tribunals, public inquiries, and day-to-day administrative decision-making; secondly, they look to participation by interested individuals and groups at various stages of the policy-formation, legislative, and administrative processes as a way of overcoming some of the shortcomings in the parliamentary system of representative democracy, and as a way of identifying and giving effect to the wishes of the community (sometimes called 'the public interest'). Unlike proponents of the first two prescriptive attacks which, I have argued, are concerned with the *control* of decision-making power, participation theorists are more concerned with the distribution of decision-making power. They are not so much attacking public–private as a *legal* distinction but rather as a way of defining the respective *political* roles of those who wield power and those subject to it. At the same time, however, their attack does have important legal ramifications because eventually it will lead to arguments for the legislative enactment of

[31] e.g. T. Prosser, 'Towards a Critical Public Law' (1982) 9 *J. of Law and Society* 1, 12–13.

participation rights and to suggestions that the courts should further the cause of participation in their judgments.[32]

The technical attack

The third avenue of attack is technical. If the distinction is to be of any dispositive legal use it needs to be refined, sharpened, and focused so that its use will yield results which are reasonably consistent and predictable. In the case of normative terms such as 'public' and 'private' this means that the normative implications of each term must be made clear and the terms only applied when the relevant normative consequences are appropriate. There are two great difficulties in doing this. First, as we shall see, the law uses the public–private distinction as an explanatory tool in so many different contexts and for so many different purposes that it could not easily, if at all, be turned into a useful and reliable dispositive distinction. Second, it seems likely, in some contexts at least, that what we really want is a mix of the normative consequences of privateness and those of publicness. For example, we might well want a nationalized industry to be subject in some respects to the ordinary law of contract and competition, and in other respects to be subject to forms of public accountability to which private trading corporations are not subject. It would seem impossible, therefore, to fashion the distinction into a useful dispositive distinction with one invariable 'meaning'. This is a strong attack; for while, at the explanatory level, a certain amount of terminological vagueness and flexibility is tolerable and even useful 'as long as it can generate good coherent insights',[33] at the dispositive level precision is much more important. We should not conclude from this, of course, that the best approach is to treat every case on its own merits, since treating every case as unique offers no more guidance than an overworked rule or concept. What we need to do is to unravel the strands which make up the public–private distinction in an attempt to create a set of concepts or distinctions (for which the public–private distinction might provide an explanatory umbrella) which are useful in deciding cases and guiding action.

Conclusion

I have argued that at the heart of the legal debate over the substantive content of the public–private distinction lie two basic issues: control of

[32] See generally McAuslan, op. cit. n. 4 above.

[33] C. D. Stone, 'Corporate Vices and Corporate Virtues: Do Public/Private Distinctions Matter?' (1982) 130 *U. of Pa. Law Rev.* 1441, 1442.

and accountability for decision-making, and modes of involvement of interested individuals and groups in decision-making. In a sense, the arguments over the distinction are mere skirmishes around these central issues which occur because certain approaches to the issues have become identified with commitment or opposition to the distinction as a way of understanding and organizing social life in general and administrative law in particular.

THE PUBLIC–PRIVATE DISTINCTION IN THE COURTS

I suggested earlier that the views of many judges about administrative law seem to owe something to the concept which I called 'passive individualism'. It is now necessary to examine in more detail how the courts have used the public–private distinction and what are the normative issues underlying their use of it.

Choice of forum

By classifying issues as public or private a litigant can be given or denied the right to choose one or other of alternative forums to hear his complaint. The choice may be between a High Court judge assigned to the hearing of cases on the Crown Office List (public) or a judge of the Queen's Bench or Chancery Division (private); a County Court can entertain an action to enforce a local authority's duty to house a homeless family (private), but only the High Court can decide whether the (public) decision on the issue of homelessness (did the applicant make himself intentionally homeless?) was legal.[34] An NHS nurse dismissed for alleged misconduct should complain to an Industrial Tribunal (private) not to the High Court (public);[35] but a prison officer, who is denied the former option by statute, may use the latter.[36] It is not always easy to discern the real motive behind decisions on 'forum shopping', because judicial reaction often depends on the motives of the shopper. But in some cases, at least, there is a genuine and justified desire to channel cases to the forum with the greatest experience and expertise in dealing with cases of that type. This desire springs, at a deeper level, from a concern for the legitimacy of judicial decisions. This concern can be related to the political premisses of passive individualism—in a system of representative democracy the legitimacy

[34] For example, *Cocks* v. *Thanet D.C.* [1983] 2 AC 286.
[35] *R.* v. *East Berks H.A., ex parte Walsh*, n. 26 above.
[36] *R.* v. *Home Secretary, ex parte Benwell* [1984] 3 WLR 843.

of judicial decisions depends on the 'independence' of the judiciary and their expertise in dealing with particular types of issue.

Remedies

Four examples illustrate this usage of the public–private distinction. In one case a drug company challenged the validity of price restriction orders. It was held that the government ought not to be required to give an undertaking as to damages in return for an interim injunction restraining disobedience of the orders—the injunction it sought was not to protect the government's proprietary or private rights but to enforce governmental legislative (public) acts.[37] This is a straightforward use of the distinction to confer an immunity which is justified on the basis that the government (the public) ought not to, and ought not to be required to, compensate those who suffer financial loss by being made to obey a law (which is presumed to be valid) pending final determination of its validity.

Secondly, more general and significant is the principle that in order to obtain damages for loss inflicted by governmental action the plaintiff must show that he has suffered a tort, breach of contract, or other wrong recognized in private law and that no consideration of public policy or rule of public law justifies the act constituting the wrong. It is by no means clear why monetary compensation is not, in theory, available as a common-law remedy at least for loss inflicted by governmental action which is unlawful. It cannot be on account of the constitutional principle against governmental expenditure not approved by Parliament, because this would equally rule out judgments in contract, tort, and so on against the government. It may be because damages are, in private law, available as of right whereas all public-law remedies are discretionary. The usual justification for this discretionary element is that it protects the public interest in administrative efficiency and prevents government bodies being unduly harassed by disgruntled litigants (see further below). There is no apparent reason why damages ought not to be made available as a discretionary public-law remedy. At all events, as things stand, the public–private distinction plays an important part in limiting the remedies available against public bodies.

Thirdly, in relation to the 'enforcement' of statutory duties a distinction is drawn between duties owed to individuals (private) and duties owed to society as an aggregate (public). Public duties are enforceable sometimes by prosecution or by an application for mandamus (provided

[37] Note 28 above.

the respondent is a public body) or for an injunction by the Attorney-General (the legal representative of the public as an aggregate), or by non-judicial means such as a ministerial default power. Private duties are 'enforceable' under certain circumstances by an action for damages in tort or, according to slightly different rules of entitlement, by an application for mandamus or an injunction by a private individual. These rules, it is suggested, rest on separation of powers concerns (see below).

Finally, we have already seen that private bodies are not amenable to the prerogative orders. This is a technical rule explicable in historical terms. Its importance is that it can incidentally dictate the forum (see above) and the procedure (see below) applicable to particular claims.

Separation of powers

The public–private distinction plays an important explanatory part in dividing decision-making powers between the courts and other branches of government. Courts in this context see their role as being to protect individual interests and rights, not public interests or rights (hence the rules considered above about 'enforcing' statutory duties); as being to give effect to rules not policy; as being to decide impartially between competing claims free from the influence of political considerations. Thus, the judicial process is open to individuals (or groups representing individuals) with (at least) a genuine personal grievance, but not to those merely making 'generalized complaints about the way the country is being run'. Hence derives the idea that the conduct of certain uniquely governmental functions (such as waging war) is 'non-justiciable' because a matter for political judgment, not pre-announced rules;[38] (this is also the basis of some cases of the public policy defence to actions for breach of contract; and of some successful class claims of public interest immunity from disclosure of evidence).

Separation of powers concerns also lie behind the principle that administrative bodies ought to be given considerable freedom in deciding how best to exercise their discretionary powers (except the power to decide questions of law and, to some extent, questions of fact). Courts profess restraint in controlling the content and substance of administrative decisions. Hence derive the *Wednesbury*[39] definition of unreasonableness (a public-law definition as contrasted with the

[38] Cf. *Council of Civil Service Unions* v. *Minister for the Civil Service* [1984] 3 WLR 1174, 1203 *per* Lord Roskill.

[39] *APPH* v. *Wednesbury Corporation* [1948] 1 KB 223.

private-law definition of tort law); the distinction between the planning (public policy) level and the operational level (governed by private-law principles of governmental activity); and the requirement of *ultra vires* action (public-law illegality), as a precondition of actionability in tort for private-law wrongfulness, in cases raising important issues of public policy (decisions at the planning/policy level). In these cases the public- and private-law rules are combined to yield a complex test for liability. But in other cases a simple choice is made between one set of rules and the other. Some of the forum shopping cases may fall into this category because different tribunals may apply different sets of rules to the same dispute. In Australia and New Zealand where the rules of judicial review have been enacted in statutory form disputes have arisen as to whether particular cases ought to be decided according to the rules laid down by the judicial review legislation (if the challenged decision was made 'under an enactment') or according to rules of contract law (if the decision was made 'under a contract'). In *Town Investments Ltd* v. *Environment Secretary*[40] it was said that the relationship between 'the Crown' and 'Ministers of the Crown' had to be analysed in public law terms and not by using private law concepts of agency and trust; and a similar point was made about the relationship between the Law Society and its members in relation to the former's statutory powers to organize block professional indemnity insurance in *Swain* v. *Law Society* (see n. 29 above).

In this context the concerns of the courts are comparable to the concerns of those theorists who see an important distinction between public and private forms of accountability for decision-making. The comparison is not exact, however. Theorists tend to categorize judicial review as 'private' (because it is available at the suit of individuals and because courts purport to decide cases according to rules, not political considerations); and for them 'political' modes and standards of control are 'public'. For the courts judicial review is 'public' (because the fact that one of the parties is a public authority is always a factor to be considered), but not 'political'—the 'public' category is subdivided into the 'legal' and the 'political'. The judicial concern with the separation of powers is perfectly understandable on the assumption that many judges accept the political underpinnings of passive individualism, of which the separation of powers is one.

[40] [1978] AC 359.

Administrative efficiency

Many judges undoubtedly see part of their role as being to strike a proper balance between the rights and legitimate interests of the individual on the one hand and the interests of the state in the efficient administration of government programmes (whatever their content) on the other. This view, which I have associated with passive individualism, finds perhaps its clearest expression in Lord Diplock's attempt in *O'Reilly* v. *Mackman*[41] to prevent litigants who wish to sue public bodies from evading the strict time limit and restrictions on fact-finding facilities contained in RSC Order 53, both of which are designed to prevent public programmes being unduly delayed by litigation. Analogous is the willingness of the courts to enforce short statutory time limits on challenges to planning decisions. More recent cases have refused to follow the underlying logic of the *O'Reilly* approach (namely that public bodies need special protection against excessive litigiousness) by interpreting Lord Diplock's 'collateral challenge' exception widely to cover any case in which the litigant seeks to protect his private law rights. Here we have an ideological struggle within the 'private right versus public interest' (or 'passive individualist') view of judicial review: judicial opinions vary as to how large the area of protected individual rights should be. The debate is conducted in terms of private-law rights, public-law rights,[42] the public interest, and matters and actions 'sounding in public law'. But the underlying concern is procedural—a desire not to impede the execution of allegedly illegal government programmes by lengthy court proceedings or to risk their disruption once begun.[43]

Concern for efficiency is also manifested in the distinction drawn between private individuals and public authorities in the context of estoppel. Subject to minor exceptions, public authorities cannot be bound by acts of unauthorized agents (delegates) nor are public authorities necessarily bound not to change their own lawful decisions if the change of direction is in the public interest.

Finally, efficiency concerns seem to underlie the approach of the

41 See n. 27 above and associated text.

42 These are alternatively called 'legitimate expectations'. They are different from public rights: the private right–public right distinction relates to the identity of the right-holder; the private-law right–public-law right distinction relates to the rules governing review of the allegedly right-encroaching action. In terms of the former distinction public-law rights are private because they are possessed by individuals. Public-law rights are, in one sense, correlative to discretionary powers as opposed to duties. But in another sense they are correlative to the *duties* of the holder of a public discretionary power to act in accordance with public-law rules of legality as they relate to the exercise of discretionary powers.

courts to claims for public policy immunity from discovery of documents. The basic idea, of course, is that a certain amount of secrecy and confidentiality is essential to the efficient conduct of some administrative and of many law-enforcement functions. At the same time, there is also said to be a public interest in the proper running of the adversary system, which requires disclosure of relevant evidence; and a public interest in the free flow throughout society of information of concern to the public. Two points deserve to be made. First, in this area of the law the courts have sought to adapt the law to deal with features of the mixed economy and corporatism. Claims for immunity could originally only be made in respect of documents generated by central government departments; but the right to make a claim has gradually been extended to cover documents generated by local authorities, by non-departmental bodies such as the police and the Customs and Excise Commissioners, by 'private' bodies (such as the NSPCC) performing functions of public importance, and even by newspapers engaging in investigative journalism. Not all will agree with the results, but this example does perhaps give some cause to be optimistic about the adaptibility of the common law to the realities of modern government, in the face of legislative inertia.

Second, the language used in this area is interesting. The courts insist that the balancc between confidentiality and disclosure is one between two *public* interests (although the strength of the interest in disclosure is crucially affected in the context of discovery by the strength of the applicant's case on the merits). The interest in disclosure can usually be depicted as an interest in the proper functioning of the judicial system (or, perhaps, of the political system in cases involving, for example, disclosure of committee documents to members of local authorities who are not members of the committee in question).[44] Calling this a public interest may have been perceived by some judges as a way of bolstering it against government claims to secrecy and thus as a way of legitimizing what might otherwise have appeared as disregard for proper separation of powers principles, namely the courts' refusal to accept ministerial certificates of the need for secrecy as conclusive and the assumption by them of the task of assessing the requirements of government confidentiality. It is one thing for the courts to assert their conception of the public interest against the private litigant, but quite another for them to assert it

[43] The confusion in the case law on this topic is largely a product of the dissonance between the dispositive concepts and the underlying concerns.

[44] *Birmingham City DC* v. *O* [1983] 1 AC 578.

against the political branch of government. The courts normally accept the government's interpretation of the requirements of efficiency and call it 'the public interest'. But in this area some judges, at least, have perceived that the interests of the governors and the governed might diverge and have opted for the interests of the latter. In no other area of administrative law is the ambiguity of the term 'the public interest' so clear.

Importantly, too, just as judges seem to disagree significantly over efficiency issues in the context of RSC Order 53, different judges have taken contrasting ideological views on questions of disclosure of official information and of the identity of sources of 'leaked' information.[45] The real issues have not in this context, at least, remained hidden beneath the public–private distinction.

Decision-making procedure

I noted above the role played by the concept of 'public function' in the law of natural justice. The concept gives effect to the public's interest in the regulation of certain activities, by whomever carried on. As already observed, although adjudication is at one level the paradigm private mode of dispute settling, the requirements of natural justice and procedural fairness have traditionally been seen as public-law requirements.[46] Thus they do not apply to 'pure' master–servant situations (private) but they do apply to the dismissal of an officer, that is someone with public duties. More recently, however, standards of fair procedure have been introduced into the law of master and servant via the law of unfair dismissal. This may be seen as an expression of a legitimate public interest in employment matters or it may rest on a recognition of the importance of fair procedure in disputes between parties of unequal strength. One of the classic definitions of the public law–private law distinction rested on the difference between relationships between equals on the one hand (private), and unequals—namely the citizen and the state—on the other (public).[47] But our awareness of the distorting effect of inequality in traditionally 'private' areas of the law is now much greater than it used to be. Indeed, an increased willingness on the part of the common law to compensate for inequalities in relationships might provide a conceptual bridge between the public and the private and encourage the development of new techniques to deal with certain phenomena of the mixed economy and corporatism.

[45] See e.g. *BSC* v. *Granada Television* [1981] AC 1096.

[46] See n. 10 above.

[47] J. W. Jones, *Historical Introduction to the Theory of Law* (Oxford, 1940), 146–7.

A comparison can easily be drawn between the courts' concern in this context and the concerns of critics of the public–private distinction who concentrate on modes of involvement in decision-making. The ideological issue relates to the *mode* of involvement: whether the basic model should be adversary or co-operative. The common law's concern with fair procedure fits in with passive individualism in that, as noted earlier, that approach is not so much concerned with the scope of governmental power and activity but more with ensuring that governmental power is not abused.

CONCLUSION

I began by mentioning the 'complex set of distinctions' between the public and the private. The discussion has shown that the distinction between public law and private law (or between public and private in a legal context) is, indeed, a complex subset of that larger set. It operates at different levels of discourse and serves as a medium for raising a considerable variety of issues. I have suggested that different attitudes to the public–private distinction can be related, at a very abstract level, to different accounts of the role of the individual in political life and hence to different accounts of the nature of democracy and the state. But at a more concrete level, attitudes to the distinction are more complex than the abstract analysis can capture. Much remains to be done by way of analysis of the relationship between the concepts of 'public' and 'private' and the issues underlying them. But it seems clear that, while the preoccupations of theorists concerned with the distinction and of the courts who utilize it overlap, they do not coincide. Furthermore, it seems that it is premature to pronounce the death of the distinction. Not only is it deeply embedded in the law, but most theorists who are critical of the distinction seem at bottom to be arguing that the relationship between the public and the private should be reinterpreted rather than that the distinction should be jettisoned entirely as a tool for analysing, understanding, and organizing social life. A critic may seem to discredit a conceptual distinction by assuming that it has only one face and asserting that it therefore misrepresents multifaceted reality; but his apparent success is specious. Proper understanding and appreciation of the public–private distinction and its use and abuse must begin with a recognition of its multifaceted nature.

4

Against Abstentionism in Labour Law*

HUGH COLLINS†

LEGAL abstentionism has provided the dominant theme of British labour law for most of this century. Legislative initiatives to supersede industrial conflict by a framework of corporatist controls have proved unworkable or have existed only briefly as wartime expedients. The province of the law in industrial relations boils down to a few legal principles aimed half-heartedly at deterring some of the excesses of industrial conflict and at permitting what the law cannot prevent—namely, union organization and collective bargaining. Couched in this rhetoric of pragmatism, the abstentionist tradition conceals its political philosophy. Occasional glimpses of the underlying normative vision flash past in the course of much longer homilies on the virtues and indeed the necessity of adapting law to social reality. Yet this vision exists and serves to buttress the abstentionist tradition against challenges by governments anxious to redirect the patterns of the labour market. This vision comprises a particular point of view on the problem to be solved by the law, a philosophy of social justice which guides and legitimizes the law's solutions, and a theory of agency which prescribes the best way in which the law can achieve the desired result. By restating this underlying vision, often known as industrial pluralism,[1] we can assess its strengths and weaknesses. Here it will be contended that the abstentionist tradition seriously misunderstands the nature of the problem to be addressed and consequently fails to provide adequate solutions and an effective agent to carry them out. In the light of this critique of the abstentionist tradition, the essay concludes with a plea for greater legal intervention in industrial relations.

† The author wishes to thank Mark Freedland, D. D. Prentice, and David Soskice for their comments on an earlier draft.

[1] A. Fox, *Beyond Contract: Work, Power and Trust Relations* (London, 1974), 260–70; K. Stone, 'The Post-War Paradigm in American Labour Law' (1981) 90 *Yale Law J.* 1509.

1. INDUSTRIAL PLURALISM

Labour lawyers traditionally view the central problem of this branch of the law as one of facilitating the continuity of production in the face of disruptions provoked by the inherent conflict of interest between owners of capital, who seek to maximize their return on capital investment, and suppliers of labour, who seek to maximize their income at the expense of profits. In theory, this problem could be solved by prohibiting the suppliers of labour from disrupting production, but for two distinct reasons labour lawyers reject this option. In the first place, pragmatic arguments warn against such drastic restriction. We should doubt the capacity of the state to subdue the social power of organized labour. Laws which forbid workers to combine and prohibit strikes cannot in the long run succeed in overcoming a determined and well-organized union movement. A second reason for rejecting an absolute prohibition against combinations provides an argument of principle to support the apparently inevitable policy resulting from considerations of expediency. The relation between capital and labour necessarily involves inequality of bargaining power. The strength of the parties depends upon their relative resources which include ownership of wealth, access to information and expertise, organizational discipline, and ability to exclude alternative sources of supply. Because most individuals lack these advantages, 'the relation between an employer and an isolated employee or worker is typically between a bearer of power and one who is not a bearer of power'.[2] In order to counter inequality of bargaining power the law should permit combinations of workers. Of course, inequality of bargaining power pervades any free market order; yet for fear of undermining the efficiency of the market as a provider of goods and services we refrain from assisting just any weak trader. Nevertheless, most writers share a political philosophy which justifies legal intervention in the labour market by regarding the employment relation as a special case.

This philosophy of industrial pluralism emerged in many western industrialized societies at the close of the nineteenth century. Its starting-point lies in the resolution of a perceived contradiction in liberal societies. Although the relations between citizen and the state are governed by the principles of self-determination or democracy, the Rule of Law, and later—with the emergence of the Welfare State—fairness,

[2] P. Davies and M. Freedland, *Kahn-Freund's Labour and the Law* (London, 3rd edn., 1983), 18.

these cherished values of liberal society appear to be eclipsed as soon as we enter the workplace. In their place we find a system of autocratic power exercised by management over the work-force, thinly disguised as a contractual exchange between equals. Once inside the factory gates or on the elevator to officedom, the typical employee is classified as a subordinate under a hierarchy of ranks. In exchange for wages, an employee relinquishes his right to self-determination, to equal dignity, and to freedom from arbitrary power. At the beginning of this century the perception that the values espoused in political society contradicted those practised in civil society was widespread and keenly felt.[3] The theory of industrial pluralism fastens upon the institutions of unions and collective bargaining as the agency to resolve this contradiction by introducing democracy, the Rule of Law, and fairness to the workplace.

Industrial pluralists regard collective bargaining as more than a market mechanism to set the price of labour. It is a form of industrial democracy, because it provides employees with a say in how the enterprise should be run. Of course, collective bargaining falls short of pure participative democracy in that employees do not vote on every issue which arises. Instead, collective bargaining imitates a pluralist form of democratic government.[4] In Parliament, interest groups compete with each other and form alliances in order to pass or defeat legislative initiatives. Similarly, collective bargaining represents a struggle for power between competing interest groups within the workplace. Unions provide the representative organization for employees while management espouses the interests of the owners of capital. In short, a collective agreement exactly mirrors a compromise legislative solution worked out between interest groups in Parliament.

In the context of the relation between government and citizen, the Rule of Law requires that all state power should be constituted and controlled by public rules promulgated in advance. Similarly, in the workplace, the ideal of the Rule of Law requires the subjection of the employer's power to the governance of rules announced in advance. Collective bargaining functions like a legal constitution or code which constrains the exercise of managerial prerogative.[5] In this vein,

[3] W.J. Lauck, *Political and Industrial Democracy* (New York, 1926).

[4] H.A. Clegg, *A New Approach to Industrial Democracy* (Oxford, 1960); H.H. Wellington, *Labour and the Legal Process* (New Haven, 1968), 26–7; Clegg, 'Pluralism in Industrial Relations' (1975) 13 *British J. of Industrial Relations* 309.

[5] Davies and Freedland, op. cit. n. 2 above, 154; *United Steelworkers* v. *Warrior & Gulf Navigation Co.*, (1960) 363 US 574 *per* Justice Douglas at 578; A. Cox, 'Some Aspects of the Labor Management Relations Act, 1947', (1947–8) 61 *Harvard Law Rev.* 1.

industrial pluralists frequently distinguish collective bargaining from any form of market transaction, for it is not primarily an exchange of wealth but rather a form of government, a type of 'joint regulation'[6] or 'joint determination'[7] of the enterprise. Also in accordance with the Rule of Law, these rules should be enforced fairly, without bias or taking into account irrelevant considerations,[8] either by means of further agreements (dynamic bargaining) or by reference to an impartial arbitrator (static bargaining).[9]

Industrial pluralism shares with liberal philosophy an uncertain vision of distributive justice. Liberals oscillate between, on the one hand, advocacy of robust individualism expressed through market transactions and, on the other, a paternalist concern to redistribute wealth so that the poorest sections of society may enjoy meaningful experiences in life. Yet industrial pluralists neatly turn the uncertainty of this liberal vision into the virtue of collective bargaining. Given that we are unclear how much each person should receive, collective bargaining provides the best institutional mechanism for settling wages, for it is a fair procedure (since it avoids unequal bargaining power by allowing the suppliers of labour to form combinations),[10] yet it does not require us to regulate the outcome of wage settlements. Collective bargaining provides an impersonal and neutral market mechanism after all.

This scheme of industrial pluralism provides a legitimating ideology for legal intervention in the labour market in order to redress inequality of bargaining power. Nevertheless, it only justifies legislation on a narrow range of issues, which gives rise to the abstentionist tradition. First, each legal system must define the extent of permissible industrial action on the part of organized labour. Although strikes must be allowed, since without threatening strikes the union cannot improve its bargaining power, legal controls on the right to strike must be introduced in order to protect the continuity of production of neutral employers (secondary action),[11] to keep essential services running in cases of urgent national interest, to avert the possibility that unions will enjoy sufficient bargaining power to challenge the rights of owners of

[6] The term coined by Allan Flanders, *Management and Unions: The Theory and Reform of Industrial Relations* (London, 1970), 222.

[7] A. Cox and J. T. Dunlop, 'Regulation of Collective Bargaining by the National Labour Relations Board' (1950) 63 *Harvard Law Rev.* 389, 401.

[8] These additional qualities of the Rule of Law in industrial relations are argued for in Philip Selznick, *Law, Society, and Industrial Justice* (New Brunswick, 1969).

[9] Davies and Freedland, op. cit. n. 2 above, 70.

[10] See Fox, op. cit. n. 1 above, 265–9.

[11] Employment Act 1980, s. 17; National Labor Relations Act s. 8 (b) (4) as amended.

capital to dispose of it at will,[12] and above all to protect the democratic institutions of the state itself from threats posed by political strikes.[13] Second, theories of industrial pluralism also direct attention to the extent to which the law should be used in order to foster the growth of unions and compel the practice of collective bargaining. Legal systems guided by the philosophy of industrial pluralism differ in the degree to which they regard it as advisable to use law to promote collective bargaining. The earlier insight concerning the impotence of the law to control the social forces of capital and organized labour suggests that legal intervention designed to force collective bargaining on unwilling employers will not prove fruitful. Indeed, examples of such legislative initiatives in Britain and the United States of America indicate that the complex legal procedures necessary for creating and policing such a duty to bargain serve as much to frustrate the aspirations of the employees as to impose the pluralist model upon the enterprise.[14] Although the United States retains the legal duty to bargain on certain stringent conditions, in Britain the extreme abstentionist pattern has been restored with minor exceptions such as Wages Councils.

Abstentionism in labour law thus emerges in the normative vision of industrial pluralism at two levels. In the first place, although the philosophy of industrial pluralism justifies legal intervention in the labour market, it confines attention primarily to the legality of strike action and the need to promote collective bargaining. Outside these issues, the message of industrial pluralism is plain: the law should abstain from intervention because nothing more need be done to diminish inequality of bargaining power and resolve the contradiction between the values of political and civil society. Of course, modern statutory rights given to individual employees to deter discrimination, personal injury, and unfair disciplinary action do not fit into this

[12] Achieved in Britain by confining lawful strike action to disputes over terms and conditions of employment: Trade Union and Labour Relations Act 1974 ss. 13, 29 (as amended), though these provisions receive a generous interpretation in *Hadmor Productions Ltd.* v. *Hamilton* [1982] ICR 114 (HL); compare a similar restriction upon mandatory subjects of bargaining under the National Labor Relations Act ss. 8 (d) and 8 (a) (5) (as amended) 29 USC s. 158 as interpreted in *First National Maintenance Corp.* v. *NLRB* 452 US 666, 101 S.Ct. 2573, 69 L.Ed.2d 318 (1981).

[13] Achieved by confining lawful strikes to 'trade disputes' in Trade Union and Labour Relations Act 1974 ss. 13, 29 and a 'labor dispute' under Norris–LaGuardia Act (1932) s. 1.

[14] P. Davies and M. Freedland, *Labour Law* (London, 2nd edn., 1984), 202–5; P. Weiler, 'Promises to Keep: Securing Workers' Rights to Self-Organization Under The NLRA' (1983) 96 *Harvard Law Rev.* 1769; C.W. Summers, 'Industrial Democracy: America's Unfulfilled Promise', (1979) 28 *Cleveland State Law Rev.* 29.

abstentionist framework. Writers within the industrial pluralist tradition thus hive off these apparent anomalies to a peripheral discipline called individual employment law.[15] Secondly, even within the two fields regarded by industrial pluralists as legitimate topics for legal intervention, legal abstentionism based upon the insistence of the impotence of law exerts a powerful influence to discourage legislation designed to promote collective bargaining. In this respect British law has been unusually abstentionist,[16] but this point should not obscure the fundamental unity of the industrial pluralist tradition in advocating abstentionism on both levels.

In the next section we shall consider three criticisms of this abstentionist policy governing labour law. The first questions belief in the impotence of law to change the relations between capital and labour; the second doubts the capacity of collective bargaining to realize the aim of introducing self-determination, the Rule of Law, and fairness in the workplace; and the third argues that the abstentionist traditon misunderstands the nature of the power exercised by management over the work-force by underestimating the importance of bureaucratic power. The third of these criticisms, I shall suggest, is the most telling, for, if accepted, it requires us to redefine the nature of the subject and reconsider the objectives of social policy on the ground that the existing discourse focusing upon inequality of bargaining power obscures some of the most invidious forms of domination in the workplace.

2. CRITIQUE OF ABSTENTIONISM

One support for the policy of legal abstentionism appears in the guise of wise pragmatism. With respect to most legislative proposals, abstentionists object that the initiative will be pointless or even counter-productive. 'The law may aim to mitigate the inequality of bargaining power inherent in the employment relationship, but success is dependent in the first instance on the strength of worker organization.'[17] For example, appeals to history and bitter experience are employed to vindicate arguments which reject statutory wage controls.[18] Similarly, the failure

[15] A. Wilson, 'Contract and Prerogative: A Reconsideration of the Legal Enforcement of Collective Agreements', (1984) 13 *Industrial Law J.* 1, 7–8.

[16] For an explanation of this pattern of abstentionism, see A. Flanders, 'The Tradition of Voluntarism' (1974) 12 *British J. of Industrial Relations* 352.

[17] J. Clark and K. Wedderburn, 'Modern Labour Law: Problems, Functions, and Policies', in Lord Wedderburn, Roy Lewis, and Jon Clark, *Labour Law and Industrial Relations* (Oxford, 1983), 217.

[18] Davies and Freedland, op. cit. n. 2 above, 179.

of the legislative attempt to introduce compulsory recognition of unions in Britain,[19] which was highlighted by the Grunwick dispute,[20] provides evidence for sagacious commentators to nod their heads wisely and observe that the pragmatic wisdom of abstentionism has been vindicated.[21] In this vein Kahn-Freund argued further that most protective legislation designed to ameliorate the conditions of employees directly could only be effective when supported by the social power of a vigorous and prosperous trade union movement.[22] 'The Truck Acts and other protective legislation began to be effectively enforced when membership in trade unions gave the workers the strength to insist on the maintenance of the legal standards . . .'[23] In other words, factory inspectors cannot hope to provide a measure of protection for the bulk of employees comparable to that achieved through assertive collective bargaining and vigilant trade unionism. All these arguments depend on the view that the law cannot compete with the social forces of capital and organized labour and that, therefore, wisdom directs us to abstain from irrelevant and ineffective legislation. Is this the mere truism that it purports to be: that the laws of the state cannot change the laws of economics? Is the absence of legislation designed to impose a detailed pattern of industrial justice upon every employment relation simply the wise, pragmatic response of the liberal state when confronted by its impotence in the face of market forces and organized labour? Have we no reply to Lord Wedderburn's rhetorical question in defence of the policy of abstentionism: 'Where else was there to go?'[24]

In order to expose the inadequacy of the tradition of abstentionism, we must go so far as to excavate its theory of the relation between law and social power. This musty basement of social theory may be unfamiliar territory to labour lawyers, but it greatly influences the abstentionist tradition. Implicit in the abstentionist programme is the contention that the social power of capital and organized labour exist independently of the law and differ in kind because the latter draws its strength from political power. For only when law is separated from social institutions does it make sense to speak of the impotence of law to affect those

[19] Compulsory recognition procedures were introduced by the Employment Protection Act 1975 and repealed by the Employment Act 1980.

[20] See the *Report of a Committee of Inquiry* under Lord Justice Scarman (Cmnd. 6922, 1977) and *Grunwick* v. *ACAS* [1978] AC 655 (HL).

[21] Wedderburn, 'Otto Kahn-Freund and British Labour Law', in Wedderburn, Lewis, and Clark, op. cit. n. 17 above, 55.

[22] Davies and Freedland, op. cit. n. 2 above, 20–1.

[23] Ibid., 19.

[24] Wedderburn, op. cit. n. 21, 54.

institutions. Such a view of the relation between the law and society, indeed that they are separate entities which need to be related by social theory, enjoys the support of a formidable and distinguished historical tradition. This tradition begins with materialist social theories such as those of Adam Smith and Karl Marx which explain how economic conditions and institutions determine the form and content of the law and the state. For example, the Marxist position, which indubitably influenced the abstentionist labour law tradition the most, holds that the productive relations of society are created through social (that is, non-legal) practices and that the law then acts to sustain and protect those relations. Hence the aim ascribed to labour law is one of facilitating the continuity of (social) relations of production. Although materialist accounts of law have become less popular, the image of the separation of law and society persists and especially dominates the sociology of law. Sociologists frequently emphasize the importance of custom in establishing social relations and relegate law and legal institutions to the peripheral role of settling disputes in the event of major breakdowns in the normal patterns of interaction and social solidarity. This suggests that a mature system of industrial relations can be sustained by conventional norms of social interaction or, less pretentiously, custom and practice, and that the law should be kept out of industrial relations except perhaps in emergencies when it may be possible to avert serious disruption by coercive legal intervention. These theories of the relation between law and society infuse and guide the abstentionist labour law tradition, so much so that they are treated as rudimentary truisms, beyond the reach of criticism.

It takes only a few moments of reflection, however, to discover that there are serious flaws in this theory of law and society. Let us examine briefly the nature and origins of the power of the social and economic forces of capital and labour in order to discover what part, if any, law plays in their constitution. Wherein lies the source of the power of capital? It plainly rests upon the capacity of the owners of capital to withdraw their investment or refuse temporarily to enter into productive arrangements with labour. Why do they enjoy this power? Because the law respects a particular concept of private property which gives the owner of capital complete freedom to choose whether or not to put it to productive use. If the law did not respect this privilege, then the power of capital would be radically diminished. We discover, therefore, that the power of capital itself depends upon certain legal rules which guarantee the free disposition of capital by granting the owner the power to choose whether to put it to productive use. A similar analysis explains the source of power of organized labour. Legal rules determine the extent to which workers may combine in order to improve their bargaining position in the market. During the nineteenth century the permissible range of activities of unions was gradually extended as a result of political pressure culminating in the formation of the Labour Party and the enactment of the Trade Disputes Act 1906. It must be admitted that the earlier restrictions upon the actions of organized labour were largely ignored in periods of high employment, but even so, the threat of criminal prosecution and the drumbeats of the local militia persistently dampened the solidarity of the early trade unions. Thus the power of organized labour depends heavily upon the legality of workers' associations and collective action. Hence law contributes greatly to the bargaining power of trade unions. Contrary to the abstentionist philosophies of labour law, law does not just regulate existing social power. It constitutes the labour market and determines the relative power of the actors within it. The law is neither so impotent nor so irrelevant as labour lawyers commonly suppose. Since it is impossible to distinguish the economic relations of production from their legal definition, it makes little sense to speak of the law regulating social power or being separate from capital and labour, for the law determines in the first instance who should hold power, the strength of that power, and to what ends it may be used.

Does this mean that abstentionism is entirely misguided? Certainly not. A simple push on the legislative button cannot change the demands and aspirations of capital and labour overnight. Yet law makes an enormous difference to the relative power of these social forces. For example, even given the extreme abstentionist pattern of British law, statutes settle base-lines for permissible industrial action. Few unions can afford to ignore these; they decisively affect the power of organized labour. The abstentionist tradition misses the point that the reason why protective legislation has often been ineffective is not some inevitable economic force or dominant social norm of 'living law' but because the legal mechanism was too expensive and cumbersome to operate satisfactorily. The fact that the norms of the Truck Acts were ignored with impunity by many employers except where an effective union existed does not prove the inevitable impotence of the law but rather points to a fault in the legal system itself. If cheap and simple procedures had been available and workers had been protected from retaliatory action such as dismissal, then the protective legislation could have worked satisfactorily.[25] Modern legislation giving employees rights which may be vindicated in industrial tribunals moves a long way towards demonstrating that effective legal mechanisms can be created. These developments in the law indicate that the policy of abstentionism, far from being an inevitable product of an intelligent understanding of the function of law in labour relations, depends on a serious misunderstanding of the role of law in constituting society. Labour law cannot avoid influencing the labour market; so the important question is on what principles the law should constitute and regulate it.

At this point we encounter a second criticism of the abstentionist tradition. Under the philosophy of industrial pluralism, legal intervention is designed to introduce in the workplace the values of democracy, the Rule of Law, and fairness. Industrial pluralists believe that collective bargaining realizes these values, so that the creation and legitimation of unions and collective bargaining become the principal goals of their labour law systems. Yet they seriously overestimate the potential of collective bargaining for realizing the ideals of industrial pluralism. Consequently, the prescriptions of the industrial pluralist tradition appear misguided and unfruitful.

Collective bargaining rarely measures up to the ideal of democracy. One must doubt the reality of any sense of self-determination for members of large bureaucratic unions, for the negotiations are conducted in secret and the results either imposed on the work-force or voted upon in a simple affirmative or negative ballot. Attempts on the part of shop-floor workers to generate self-determination are frequently greeted by union officials with hostility. Even industrial pluralists like Kahn-Freund thought that shop-floor democracy took self-determination too far, because it persistently threatened the continuity of production. Of course, the kind of democracy envisaged by industrial pluralists was hardly participative. The ideal which they presented was one of élite groups competing for power to run the enterprise, though, of course, one of the rules of this democracy was that the union was permanently fated to be a loyal opposition.[26] Surely there must be more direct ways of introducing democracy into the workplace than this alliance between representatives of bureaucratic organizations?

By making sure that management keep to the published rules of the

[25] See Goriely, 'Arbitrary Deductions from Pay and the Proposed Repeal of the Truck Acts' (1983) 12 *Industrial Law J.* 236 for a modern use of the Truck Acts by neighbourhood law centres.

[26] P. Blumberg, *Industrial Democracy* (New York, 1976), 145.

organization, collective bargaining takes some steps towards introducing the Rule of Law into the workplace. But collective bargaining has never succeeded in encroaching very far on the exercise of managerial prerogative. Indeed, to some extent law even confines the ambit of collective bargaining. In legal systems which impose on employers a duty to bargain with unions in good faith, such as the United States, the rules usually limit the duty on the assumption that many issues, such as strategic economic decisions, are none of the employees' business.[27] Under British law, though there is no duty to bargain in good faith, the scope of a union's immunity from actions in tort indirectly confines the range of collective bargaining, for demands which fall outside the statutory list of permissible topics render the union liable to actions for an injunction and damages.[28] Yet, even if the law tolerated a broader range of subjects for collective bargaining, it must be doubted whether bargaining would in practice extend this control over managerial prerogative much further. Apart from standard items like wages, manning levels, and physical conditions of work, collective bargaining rarely reaches into the heart of the corporate enterprise to regulate such matters as job specifications, promotion systems, investment policy, pricing policy, environmental effects of production, pensions, sick pay, holiday entitlements, and women's issues.[29]

It may come as a surprise to generations of labour lawyers brought up on the myths of industrial pluralism to discover that collective bargaining does not introduce a system of joint regulation. But a moment's reflection will reveal why collective bargaining falls short of the pluralists' ideal. Any claims put forward in the collective bargaining process must be backed up ultimately with the threat of industrial action. Whilst basic issues like wages and hours can be used as the platform to generate sufficient solidarity to introduce serious threats of industrial action, more diffuse concerns with corporate policy or items of deferred benefits like pensions will not on their own generate industrial action. They only enter into a collective agreement as part of a trade-off with current wages where the corporation perceives an advantage in attaching fringe benefits to jobs, which might be the case, for example, where

[27] Apart from terms and conditions of employment, the National Labor Relations Act s. 8 (d), 29 USC s. 158 (d) treats bargaining issues as merely 'permissive' subjects, which allows an employer to refuse to discuss them without fear of legal sanction: *NLRB* v. *Borg-Warner Corp*., 356 US 342, 78 S.Ct. 718, 2 L.Ed.2d 823 (1958).

[28] Trade Union and Labour Relations Act 1974 ss. 13, 29.

[29] For the scope of collective bargaining for manual workers, see W. W. Daniel and N. Millward, *Workplace Industrial Relations in Britain* (London, 1983), 197–9.

skilled workers are in short supply. In short, unless management chooses otherwise, collective bargaining is normally confined to a narrow range of issues of direct and immediate concern to the work-force. It rarely, if ever, lives up to the ideal of joint regulation. On the contrary, collective bargaining tends to legitimate the reserved area of managerial rights, since in theory this province was a legitimate topic of negotiation if the union had disapproved of the way in which it was being exercised. In so far as the ideal of the Rule of Law has been introduced into the workplace by the principles of industrial pluralism, it constitutes an impoverished interpretation of that ideal, for at its heart lies the legitimation of extensive managerial discretion.

Finally, we should consider the claim of collective bargaining to establish a fair distribution of wealth. One weakness of this claim, exploited by radicals and conservatives alike, is that the fairness of collective bargaining depends upon the establishment of a just equilibrium between the market forces of capital and labour.[30] Yet it is always open to either side to claim that the other enjoys an illegitimate strength in the bargaining process, and that the results of the agreement are therefore bound to be unfair. These arguments correctly challenge the insistence by industrial pluralists that collective bargaining provides a neutral and just procedure for settling disputes.[31] We have seen that initial bargaining strengths depend on the allocation of rights by the law. Thereafter factors such as the level of unemployment and the rate of inflation alter bargaining power on a temporary basis. On close examination, therefore, the collective bargaining system cannot be presented as a neutral procedure for the determination of terms of employment or one which necessarily produces just outcomes. Industrial pluralists need to justify the balance of forces which has been established by reference to the fairness of the outcomes of collective bargaining, yet this they signally fail to do.

Even if industrial pluralists were to become more forthright in their defence of the equilibrium which has been established, recent studies of the labour market cause us to doubt the justice of the policy of promoting collective bargaining. It is surely a striking fact that after half a century or more of official encouragement for collective bargaining, less than half of the work-force in most industrialized countries benefits from collective agreements.[32] The labour market appears irretrievably

[30] Fox, op. cit. n. 1 above, 265.

[31] Clegg, 'Pluralism in Industrial Relations', op. cit. n. 4.

[32] Daniel and Millward, op. cit. n. 29, 18 report that 67 per cent of establishments

divided into two sectors.[33] The first is a primary sector with large-scale oligopolistic enterprises which control their markets so that they can afford high wage settlements and which offer considerable job security. The other is a secondary labour market where the employers comprise small-scale, labour-intensive industries which exercise little market control and can therefore offer little job security because of their susceptibility to market fluctuations and can provide only the lowest rates of pay. The minority who benefit from collective bargaining are located in the primary labour market. There is good reason to doubt whether collective bargaining will ever expand permanently into the secondary labour market. This sobering insight removes one of the crucial planks supporting the tradition of legal abstention, because industrial pluralism presupposes that the problems of inequality of bargaining power and of the contradictory values of liberal society will be resolved for everyone by collective bargaining. Perhaps even more worrying is the suggestion that the improvements in wages achieved by workers through collective bargaining are only gained at the expense of the employees in the secondary labour market where there exists no union organization.[34] Even if the economic case for showing this direct redistributive effect turns out to be unfounded, there can be no doubt that the redistribution takes place indirectly in so far as high wage settlements produce an inflationary effect on prices throughout the economy with a consequent devaluation of wages in real terms in the secondary labour market. For these reasons, the standards of justice envisaged by industrial pluralists must be criticized not only for their incompleteness but also for their unsatisfactory implications for distributive justice.

We therefore discover a surprising gap between the industrial pluralists' ideal which justifies legal intervention in the labour market and their recommendations for labour law. They advocate the legal conditions under which unions and collective bargaining may flourish, yet when we examine the reality of the relations established by these conditions, we discover that they fall far short of the ideals of democracy,

employing more than twenty-five employees recognize a union for some employees, but this figure includes nationalized industries and the civil service where the government accepts a duty to recognize unions, and of course the figure excludes the bulk of the secondary labour market.

[33] Piore, 'Notes for a Theory of Labor Market Stratification', in R. C. Edwards, M. Reich, and D. M. Gordon (eds.), *Labor Market Segmentation* (Lexington, Mass., 1975); C. Craig, J. Rubery, R. Tarling, and F. Wilkinson, *Labour Market Structure, Industrial Organisation and Low Pay* (Cambridge, 1982), ch. 5.

[34] A. L. Friedman, *Industry and Labour* (London, 1977).

the Rule of Law, and fairness, which industrial pluralism was supposed to promote. Of course, industrial pluralists may shrug their shoulders at this point and revert to the thesis that law is relatively impotent to alter essential relations of market power. In that way they may seek to justify their reliance upon collective bargaining. But given our doubts about the validity of their thesis of the impotence of law, even this avenue of escape appears closed.

The third criticism of industrial pluralism serves to identify one important reason for the shortfall in the realization of its aims. Industrial pluralism views the social power which the law must regulate as constituted by conflicting forces in the labour market. Whilst it is true that law fixes the power relations between capital and labour in the market, it is a mistake to see this as the only source of power which should be the subject matter of labour law. Industrial pluralists overlook the importance of bureaucratic power. 'Rather than simply a conflict between capital and labour, the new conflict is between the structures of economic and political decision-making and those who are reduced to dependent participation.'[35] Market power depends upon access to resources and skills, whereas bureaucratic power relies upon the establishment of a system of ranks organized in a hierarchical structure of authority by a system of rules which define the powers of each rank. Market power rests on a belief in the legitimacy of entitlements to the fruits of the use of property and skills, whereas stable bureaucratic power requires a belief in the legitimacy of the authority exercised through the hierarchical structure.[36] In the modern corporation, the dominant legal form of organizations of capital, the power of management derives primarily from the effective exercise of bureaucratic power. Although in the last analysis the authority of management stems from an acceptance that it is legitimate for owners of capital to control their resources through managerial agents, for practical purposes the day-to-day running of the enterprise assumes the form of a conflict between employers exercising bureaucratic power and employees resisting its exercise. This state of affairs results to some extent from the very size and sophistication of modern corporations which make it impossible for a diffuse body of shareholders to control them.[37] Never-

35 A. Touraine, *The Post-Industrial Society* (London, 1974, trans. by L. F. X. Mayhew), 9.

36 H. Collins, 'Market Power, Bureaucratic Power, and the Contract of Employment' (1986) 15 *Industrial Law J.* 1.

37 A. A. Berle and G. C. Means, *The Modern Corporation and Private Property* (New York, 1932); E. S. Herman, *Corporate Control, Corporate Power* (Cambridge, 1981).

theless, the existence of a bureaucratic organization itself provides senior management with the opportunity to seize a tool of power which can be wielded without regard to the ownership of resources.

The theory of industrial pluralism largely ignores this source of managerial power and consequently fails to develop an adequate conception of labour law. Although this omission might once have been excusable, now that we have a century's experience of the growth of corporations and industrial bureaucracies,[38] the ever increasing numbers of persons engaged in office work,[39] and the rise of the personnel manager whose task it is to handle the complexity of the bureaucratic system,[40] the omission is little short of a scandal. If we accept that the purpose of labour law is to resolve the contradiction between the values of democracy, legality, and fairness espoused in political society and the practice of domination in the workplace, a principal focus of the subject must be a review of the exercise of bureaucratic power as a source of domination. The emphasis placed by theories of industrial pluralism upon the labour market ignores the reality that it is not only market power which establishes the practices of domination in the workplace but also the configurations of bureaucratic power.

To a limited extent, it must be admitted, theorists of industrial pluralism have accepted the importance of bureaucratic power in the workplace. But instead of treating it as an independent source of social power within their theoretical framework, they respond to it within their familiar framework and present collective bargaining as the panacea which will remove any trace of illegitimate domination. Subtly twisting the conventional characterization of collective bargaining as a form of joint regulation, Feller portrays it as joint administration of the bureaucratic system by unions and management.[41] Although this description hits the nail on the head, it also reveals how far collective bargaining falls short of the ideals of industrial pluralism. What unions acquire through collective bargaining is a share in the exercise of bureaucratic domination. Moreover, by accepting this description, industrial pluralism justifies the absence of legal regulation of private bureaucratic power on the ground that it is already handled adequately

[38] E. Jaques, *A General Theory of Bureaucracy* (London, 1976); R. Edwards, *Contested Terrain: The Transformation of the Workplace in the Twentieth Century* (New York, 1979).

[39] M. Crozier, *The World of the Office Worker* (Chicago, 1971, trans. by D. Landau).

[40] T. J. Watson, *The Personnel Managers* (London, 1977); Daniel and Millward, op. cit. n. 29 above, ch. 5.

[41] D. E. Feller, 'A General Theory of the Collective Bargaining Agreement' (1973) 61 *California Law Rev.* 663.

by the institution of collective bargaining. Thus, not only does industrial pluralism tend to misunderstand the source of power in the workplace, but it also implicitly legitimates the abstention of the law from any review of the exercise of private bureaucratic power.

To summarize these three criticisms of the abstentionist tradition of labour law scholarship: it rests upon a mistaken belief in the impotence of law to constitute and change the relations between capital and labour; it reposes a misguided faith in the capacity of collective bargaining to realize the aim of introducing self-determination, the Rule of Law, and fairness in the workplace; and by underestimating the importance of bureaucratic power it misunderstands the nature of the power exercised by management over the work-force. Ultimately, the abstentionist tradition fails to come to grips with the practices within relations of production which tolerate unchecked private bureaucratic power and so permit the systematic negation of the values of liberal society.

3. THE REGULATION OF PRIVATE BUREAUCRATIC POWER

The distinction between the market and the bureaucratic aspects of the power relations engendered by employment suggests that labour law addresses two kinds of problem which require radically different solutions. With regard to market power, the problem lies in countering inequality of bargaining power while at the same time ensuring distributive justice throughout the labour market. In contrast, bureaucratic power creates the dual problems of the potential abuse of managerial prerogative and the need to reconcile efficient direction of production with the value of democracy in the workplace. It is tempting to argue that whereas free collective bargaining provides the appropriate technique for solving the problem of market power, judicial review in labour courts is the most apt method for preventing the abuse of private bureaucratic power. But plainly this proposal fails to address the full dimensions of each problem. Free collective bargaining cannot establish acceptable standards of distributive justice, and judicial review of managerial prerogative, even if it avoids unnecessary impediments to efficient direction of production, fails to respond to the value of democratic participation in decisions. Nevertheless, this division of function between collective bargaining and judicial review provides the most useful starting-point from which to devise more complete solutions to these problems.

Collective bargaining has the virtue that it counters inequality of bargaining power, but its coverage of employees remains incomplete and it has the potential to increase wages at a faster rate than it makes improvements in productivity and so to create inflationary pressures. With regard to the incompleteness of collective bargaining, legal intervention in the form of redistributive taxation and social security payments appears to provide the most accurate method for ensuring distributive justice while at the same time avoiding the increase in unemployment which might arise from raising wage levels by means of minimum wage laws. It follows that the fact of being employed should not bar assistance from the state to the low paid. Indubitably the inflationary effect of free collective bargaining presents a more intractible problem.[42] Although changes in the legal rules governing industrial action and higher levels of unemployment may reduce the risk of inflationary wage settlements, the risk never entirely disappears. In this context the pragmatism of the abstentionist tradition is surely warranted. Statutory incomes policies cannot restrain the rate of increase in wages in the long term without the support of unions and employers. Yet the fragmented plant-level bargaining of the British industrial relations system effectively prevents such binding accords between capital and labour. Until the settlement of wages has been removed in practice from the plant level to more centralized bargaining agencies, no imposed legal regime of central arbitration can hope to succeed in tackling the inflationary effect of collective bargaining.

In comparison to the control of market power, the regulation of private bureaucratic power appears more susceptible to precise legal solutions. In the twentieth century, we frequently employ the term 'bureaucratic' in a pejorative sense, signifying inefficient, rigid, secretive, and even irrational. These Kafkaesque resonances should not obscure the underlying virtue of bureaucratic systems of management, which is that the centralization of power helps to solve co-ordination problems in production and administration. In comparison to an infinite series of isolated, contractual exchanges, bureaucratic administration provides a relatively efficient and rational method for ensuring continuity of production.[43] The efficiency of bureaucratic hierarchies stems

[42] S. Davies, 'Incomes and Anti-Inflation Policy', in George Sayers Bain (ed.), *Industrial Relations in Britain* (Oxford, 1983).

[43] The difficulties of defining efficiency in this context are considered by M. McPherson, 'Efficiency and Liberty in the Productive Enterprise: Recent Work in the Economics of Work Organization' (1983) 12 *Philosophy & Public Affairs* 354.

from their capacity to police shirking by workers,[44] their provision of regular avenues for the transmission of reliable information to management,[45] and their reduction of transaction costs through a capacity to adapt to changing market circumstances.[46] Moreover, a product which is technically complicated to devise and produce can only be created by a group of experts. A large corporation can supply from its profits the capital needed for research and development and at the same time bring together a variety of specialists. The bureaucratic form of organization is needed to ensure the accountability and efficiency of such a large-scale economic organization. Given these advantages of bureaucratic organization, it is hard to imagine alternatives which could equal the efficiency and regularity of bureaucratic structures of power. 'Increasingly the material fate of the masses depends upon the continuous and correct functioning of ever more bureaucratic organizations of private capitalism, and the idea of eliminating them becomes more and more utopian.'[47] Even in worker co-operatives, the hierarchical pattern of organization quickly reasserts itself in the interests of efficient production.

Although in view of its efficiency a bureaucratic organization of the workplace appears inescapable, that does not remove the need to subject this hierarchical power to control. The contradiction between the political values of democracy, the Rule of Law, and fairness and the domination found in relations of production merely takes on a new light once civil society is analysed in terms of bureaucratic as well as market power. Would it be possible to devise a system for the control of managerial power? It could be done, I suggest, if we draw upon the analogy of the judicial review of executive governmental power through administrative law in order to ensure that managerial prerogative is exercised in accordance with the Rule of Law and with fair standards of decision-making. This analogy works because most jobs have become 'offices' as a result of the emergence of the bureaucratic organization of the workplace.[48]

44 A. A. Alchian and H. Demsetz, 'Production, Information Costs, and Economic Organization' (1972) 62 *American Economic Rev.* 777; O. E. Williamson, *Markets and Hierarchies* (New York, 1975), ch. 4.

45 K. Arrow, *The Limits of Organization* (New York, 1974).

46 R. H. Coase, 'The Nature of the Firm' (1937) 4 *Economica* 386–405; O. E. Williamson, 'The Vertical Integration of Production: Market Failure Considerations' (1971) 61 *American Economic Rev.* 112.

47 Max Weber, *Economy and Society*, ed. G. Roth and C. Wittich (Berkeley, 1978), ii. 998.

48 M. Walzer, *Spheres of Justice* (Oxford, 1983), 131. See J. Beatson and M. Freedland, 'The Contract of Employment: The Role of Public Law' (1983) 12 *Industrial Law J.* 43; H.

In public law, the courts forge standards of rationality and respect for individual rights on which to test the legitimacy of acts of the executive. These standards reflect a concern for the Rule of Law and for fairness. In the context of private bureaucratic power, standards of rationality should require that the exercise of power be shown to further the economic interests of the organization. Decisions or rules which derogate from the efficiency of the enterprise should be vulnerable to attack. For example, if the employer cannot demonstrate the rational case for a particular policy on job specifications, then the policy should be treated as an abuse of power. With such considerations in mind, a British tribunal recently upheld a woman's claim against indirect discrimination when her employers insisted upon a policy of requiring all employees to work full time.[49] Similarly, disciplinary sanctions such as demotions and dismissals should be tested against a criterion of rationality which requires the employer to demonstrate how the sanction is calculated to improve the efficiency of the enterprise.

Arguments which favour the rights of subordinates in private bureaucratic organizations gravitate towards two principal safeguards. First, the organization should follow a fair procedure including arrangements for consultation before decisions are implemented. Second, considerations of individual liberty should place limits upon the relevant grounds for disciplinary action. In part, procedural requirements promote efficient decisions for they ensure that all relevant information has been gathered before a decision is reached. Ultimately, however, procedural requirements of natural justice or due process rest upon a moral standard which demands respect for the dignity of individuals. Recent statutes in Europe have introduced these procedural standards into disciplinary measures against individual employees. In France the code requires a written charge, a hearing with a right of representation, and a reasoned decision.[50] No final action can be taken until this procedure has been completed, and the whole process is subject to the review of labour courts which may nullify a decision on the ground of procedural irregularity. British legislation provides weaker protection, for where a court finds that the substantive reasons for a dismissal were self-evident and compelling, no procedural requirements need be

Collins, 'Dismissal and Public Law Remedies' (1984) 13 *Industrial Law J.* 174; and M. Stokes, 'Public Law Remedies for Dismissal' (1985) 14 *Industrial Law J.* 117.

[49] *Home Office* v. *Holmes* [1984] IRLR 299 (EAT).

[50] *Code du Travail* Art. L. 122–41.

observed.[51] This interpretation of the law of unfair dismissal clearly rests procedural standards solely on considerations of efficiency and disregards the more important justification that they promote respect for individual dignity.

Respect for individual rights also demands respect for civil liberties. It is inconsistent, for instance, with discrimination against persons on grounds of sex, race, or membership of a trade union. Furthermore, respect for rights prohibits detrimental acts against members of the organization for reason of their political or social activities outside work. For example, punitive action against homosexuals because of their sexual preference should not be permitted. An employer should not be allowed to rely upon arguments of efficiency to overcome such civil liberties, as he was in one British case of unfair dismissal.[52] Similarly, the exercise of the right of free speech should be immune from disciplinary action, except where the employer can demonstrate that a 'whistle blower' has violated an express agreement to keep information confidential. Any lesser protection restores the contradiction between the rights enjoyed in political society and the absence of those rights at the workplace. Nevertheless, the Supreme Court of the United States, though generally an upholder of the right of free speech, allows public employers to impose severe constraints on the exercise of this right.[53]

The public law analogy fails, however, to provide an adequate indication of how the value of democracy might be realized in the context of employment, since judicial review of administrative action normally presupposes that ultimate control of the executive rests in the hands of a democratically elected parliament. Here we can learn from the existing practice of industrial relations. Studies of organizational efficiency suggest that regular consultation with employees through works councils or production units improves productivity.[54] We can surmise that these improvements in efficiency stem at least in part from the increased satisfaction in work arising from fulfilment of the value of self-determination through participation in decision-making and being

[51] *W. & J. Wass Ltd.* v. *Binns* [1982] ICR 486 (CA) and *West Midlands Co-operative Society Ltd.* v. *Tipton* [1986] 2 WLR 306 (HL) interpreting the Employment Protection (Consolidation) Act 1978 s. 57 (3); see H. Collins, 'The Status of Procedural Requirements' (1986) 15 *Industrial Law J.* 113.

[52] *Saunders* v. *Scottish National Camps Association* [1980] IRLR 174 (EAT), [1981] IRLR 277 (CS).

[53] *Connick* v. *Myers* (1983) 103 S.Ct. 1684.

[54] The theoretical underpinning is provided by the concept of alienation: see S. Lukes, *Essays in Social Theory* (London, 1977), ch. 4; R. Blauner, *Alienation and Freedom: The Factory Worker and his Industry* (Chicago, 1964).

kept in the picture. A rational bureaucratic organization therefore contains an element of democratic participation which runs counter to the normal hierarchy of power. Most large enterprises establish consultative committees which serve the dual function of weakening the sense of domination within the organization and at the same time providing avenues by which information may pass up the hierarchy leading to improvements in productivity.[55] Usually these consultative committees pass alongside the system of collective bargaining like ships in the night. Labour law, under the influence of industrial pluralism, provides little assistance to the development of consultative committees. Industrial pluralists generally view them with suspicion as a potential threat to collective bargaining. Yet these committees often bring employees closer than before to the ideal of self-determination which industrial pluralism advocates. Accordingly, a strong case can be made for legal encouragement of consultative groups and work's councils. In Britain, a hesitant first step has been taken with regard to Safety Committees, though even this form of consultation has been unnecessarily restricted in order to prevent any derogation from the ideal of comprehensive collective bargaining.[56] Similarly, once we embrace the aim of infusing democracy into private bureaucracies, proposals for introducing employees onto the board of directors become attractive.[57] In this context, employees can participate in decisions concerning capital investment, pricing and marketing, and other organizational changes. The Bullock Committee responded to the unions' fear that membership of the board would obscure the conflict of interest between capital and labour in the market by recommending that unions should control employee representation.[58] Yet this attempt to approximate employee representation on the board with collective bargaining appears misguided once it is accepted that there exists an independent sphere of bureaucratic power which the law must regulate in the light of the value of democracy.

Yet, can legislation enforced by the ordinary courts prove adequate to the task of regulating private bureaucratic power in accordance with the values of democracy, the Rule of Law, and fairness? The traditions of abstention and neutrality with regard to civil society run so deep in the

[55] Daniel and Millward, op. cit. n. 29 above, ch. 6.

[56] Health and Safety at Work Act 1974 s. 2 (7) leaves the creation of Safety Committees at the initiative of a recognized trade union.

[57] *Industrial Democracy*, Cmnd. 7231 (London, 1978).

[58] *Report of the Committee of Inquiry on Industrial Democracy*, Cmnd. 6706 (London, 1977).

courts that we have reason to doubt their enthusiasm for embarking upon detailed controls of private bureaucratic power.[59] The solution appears to lie in the creation of a mixture of agencies independent of the ordinary courts. For individual grievances, private arbitration might prove most effective.[60] The arbitrator would, however, depart from the North American pattern. He would be appointed by the state to each enterprise or institution of government regardless of the presence of collective bargaining. These arbitrators would be empowered to intervene both on those grounds of review drawn from public law concerning rationality and respect for individual rights and, where appropriate, from standards introduced by relevant collective agreements or consultative groups. For issues of general concern to the work-force, such as the development of safety precautions or capital expenditure, the law could encourage representation of employees on the committees within the enterprise charged with these responsibilities. These localized groups may be more likely to generate workable standards attuned to the exigencies of production than ordinary courts or administrative agencies.[61] At the same time they hold out more promise than alternative institutional schemes to realize the aim of democracy.

4. CONCLUSION

The abstentionist tradition in labour law confuses the problem of market power with that of bureaucratic power. Although the inequality of bargaining power between employer and employee warrants a pragmatic response which involves support for collective bargaining, the exercise of managerial prerogative calls for different measures. Here the law can identify a clear task of establishing institutions and standards by which to subject private bureaucratic power to the values of democracy, the Rule of Law, and fairness. The law should actively intervene in labour relations, not to stifle the efforts of independent trade unions which support the interests of their members, but rather to achieve what they can never achieve—a systematic scrutiny of the exercise of bureaucratic power by all corporate enterprises, public or private, in the

[59] See H. Collins, 'Capitalist Discipline and Corporatist Law' (1982) 11 *Industrial Law J.* 78 and 170.

[60] A similar proposal is discussed in Linda Dickens *et al.*, *Dismissed: A Study of Unfair Dismissal and the Industrial Tribunal System* (Oxford, 1985), ch. 9; but these proposals are criticized in H. J. Glasbeek, 'The Utility of Model Building—Collins' Capitalist Discipline and Corporatist Law' (1984) 13 *Industrial Law J.* 133.

[61] Lawrence S. Bacow, *Bargaining for Job Safety and Health* (Cambridge, Mass., 1980).

primary or secondary labour market, unionized or not. The attractiveness of this conception of the role labour law derives from a recognition that the subordination which infuses the employment relation stems as much from the exercise of bureaucratic power as from inequality of market power. Although for many employees collective bargaining redresses the inequality of bargaining power, it has never come to grips with the problem of taming bureaucratic power. If we are to secure greater respect for the individual's rights in the workplace, we must abandon abstentionism.

5

Are Contracts Promises?*

ANNE DE MOOR

ONE proposition on which authors with widely divergent views of the theory of contract are capable of agreeing is that contracts are promises. This appears from a comparison of the work in this area of Patrick Atiyah, in this country, with that of Charles Fried, in the USA. In *Promises, Morals, and Law*,[1] Atiyah defends the view that, contrary to what we may intuitively think, we do not have an obligation to keep all promises and even where we do, such an obligation is not only far more qualified than is generally supposed, but is not actually created by the promise. The promise is only evidence for other obligations, 'which either pre-exist the making of the promise, or which anyhow would arise before, or at the same time as, the promise becomes obligatory',[2] and most commonly arise from benefits rendered to the promisor or from acts of detrimental reliance performed by the promisee. He also claims that it is the study of the operation of the rules of contract which compels this view of promissory obligation. It is this entirely original claim, not previously articulated in his work,[3] which requires the assimilation of the practice of contracting with that of promising. Indeed, if contracting were distinct from promising, why should we follow Atiyah's counsel and allow our convictions about the moral force of promises to be guided and reshaped by the legal practice of imposing contractual liability? While Atiyah imports arguments drawn from the *practice* of contracting into the theory of promising, Fried in *Contract as Promise*[4] does the opposite. He maintains that a morally sound *theory* of promissory

[1] Oxford, 1981. Unless otherwise indicated, further references to Atiyah will be to this book.

[2] Atiyah, 193; on Atiyah's view as to the evidentiary nature of promises, see J. P. W. Cartwright, 'An Evidentiary Theory of Promises' (1984) 93 *Mind* 230.

[3] Although the claim is implied in much of his other work within the theory of contract, in particular in 'Contracts, Promises and the Law of Obligations' (1978) 94 *Law Quarterly Rev.* 193; see also *The Rise and Fall of Freedom of Contract* (Oxford, 1979).

[4] *Contract as Promise: A Theory of Contractual Obligation* (Cambridge, Mass., 1981). Unless otherwise indicated, further references to Fried will be to this work.

obligation contains all the elements necessary to provide a foundation for contemporary American contract law. Both authors share the assumption that arguments for the existence and the proper measure of contractual liability and of promissory obligation are interchangeable.

In this paper I shall argue that, if adequate attention is paid to the legal doctrines and rules of differing legal systems, the equation of the concept of a legal contract with that of a promise will prove too simplistic. Doubts on that score will centre around the bilateral character of a contract. Before embarking upon an examination of the nature of contracts, however, I will outline what seems an inherently problematic feature of the transposition of justificatory arguments from the legal discourse of contract into the moral discourse of promise and vice versa, which concerns the need to do justice to the proper nature of each. So, my challenge against the simple monist view of Contract and Promise is mounted from two different angles. First I consider a formal objection; that contractual obligation is of a different kind than the obligation which inheres in promises, and so needs to be justified in a different way. The second objection is substantive; it turns on the essentially bilateral nature of contracts. While in the first two sections of this paper I deal with each of these objections separately, the third section shows how they are, in fact, connected. The argument there will be that those who equate contract and promise may be forced, by the need to respect the proper nature of contract, to say that promises too are bilateral. But the only way they can attempt to substantiate this view of promising is by enlisting the support of legal doctrines which appear to be distinctive to particular legal traditions. If this, in turn, induces the 'monist' to acknowledge the significance of institutional structures within the discourse of promise, she will be inviting the charge that she is disregarding the proper nature of promissory obligation. In conclusion, I indicate the direction which a search for the foundation of contractual liability might take. A fresh approach would seek to ground contractual liability in the value for individuals to be able to create 'special bonds' between themselves and others, capable of grounding special obligations and corresponding rights. It would radically abandon the notion of promise: special bonds may take various institutional forms the justification of which need not necessarily be related to the moral force of promises.

1. THE FORMAL OBJECTION

Contractual liability is hedged about with many incidents and requirements. The law of contract lays down authoritatively when a contract is deemed to be made, how its content and scope are determined, and what sanctions will be visited on those who do not perform it. Because of this dependence of contractual obligation upon rules, some have renounced the search for an explanation as to why a contract is binding. They have held that, because the law can only provide us with the facility to undertake contractual obligations if its rules defining both the circumstances under which they are to be held as being undertaken and the sanctions which non-performance entails are observed, the question of why a particular contract generates an obligation can only be answered by pointing at these rules.[5] Even if this conventional or 'positivist' explanation of contractual obligation may sound too extreme, its merit is to highlight a feature of contracting which, at first sight, does seem apt to distinguish the ensuing obligation from that which inheres in a promise. This is that the making of a contract is an 'institutional' act. Promising, on the other hand, is often intuitively apprehended as a natural act: while, for instance, a complex set of legal rules determine the time and place of the formation of a contract, a promise simply appears to be made when and where it was made.[6]

This 'naïve' perception of promising has been challenged, bringing into contention the claim that the dependence of contractual obligation on rules might serve to distinguish it from promissory obligation. David Hume's writings on the moral force of promises[7] marked the emergence of a now dominant philosophical account of promising which emphasizes its dependence on rules, that is the rules of the practice or institution of promising. Moral philosophers, postulating the need for an artificial institution in order, for example, to provide the motivation for people to keep their promises which human nature lacks, have been joined by linguistic philosophers, asserting that promising can only intelligibly be analysed as a speech-act within the context of an

[5] A brief statement of this position can be found in D. N. MacCormick's essay on 'Voluntary Obligations', as it appears in his *Legal Right and Social Democracy* (Oxford, 1982), 190–3.

[6] A. W. B. Simpson, 'Innovation in Nineteenth-Century Contract Law' (1975) 91 *Law Quarterly Rev.* 247, 258 ff.

[7] A brief statement of David Hume's views on promising in *A Treatise of Human Nature* (Oxford, 1896) can be found in R. S. Downie, 'Three accounts of Promising' (1985) 35 *Philosophical Quarterly* 259.

institution defining what acts 'count as' promises. Some of the most extreme of these views about the basis of promissory obligation parallel the 'conventionalist' explanation of legal obligation as being entirely dependent on, and only justifiable by reference to, the rules of the convention of promising. But even more qualified assertions of the artificial nature of promises suggest an analogy between contractual and promissory obligation.

If it is accepted, this analogy seems to warrant the view, shared by Fried and Atiyah, that arguments for the justification of contractual liability and of promissory obligation are interchangeable. If, indeed, promissory obligation is conventional and institutional, it would not be wrong to have regard to contractual practice as a source of illumination of its true nature. As, indeed, Atiyah does not fail to notice,[8] this may now have to become the primary source for understanding the binding force of promises. Conversely, an institutional account of promising is more likely to generate arguments suitable to justify contractual liability than one which stresses its 'natural' character.

While this view of the nature of promising may seem to disarm those who object to the 'substitutability thesis' on theoretical grounds, problems nevertheless reappear when that thesis is put to the test of practice. Those commenting upon Atiyah's work,[9] for instance, have regretted his failure to produce a (critical) theory of promissory obligation. The criticism seems entirely plausible. Atiyah's only evidence of contractual practice comes from English (and American) law reports and books. However, comparative law reveals a diversity of legal provisions, particularly as to what is required for a contract to come into existence; and these rules are usually anchored deep in the various legal systems' legal institutional history. If an account of the practice of promising is shaped entirely by the rules of a single legal tradition, it may well prove too insular to generate an adequate moral theory. There is, for example, something distinctly unsatisfactory about Atiyah's statement that the English law doctrine that 'an innocent party to a breach of contract cannot recover damages for a loss which he has, or even could have avoided by taking reasonable steps following the breach',[10] in some way qualifies the binding force of promises, when under French law no such

[8] Atiyah recurrently reproaches those who hold a 'social practice view' of promissory obligation for their failure to familiarize themselves with the practice of the law of contract: see, in particular, at 138.

[9] Amongst others, see J. Raz, 'Promises in Morality and Law' (1982) 95 *Harvard Law Rev.* 916, 919–20.

[10] Atiyah, 6.

'duty to mitigate (damages)' exists.[11] One might, of course, accept, with Atiyah,[12] that as the obligation to keep one's promises is, like any other moral obligation, shaped and sanctioned by the collective judgment of a particular community, a universally valid theory need not and cannot be sought.[13] But if one adheres to the more familiar view that moral principles provide rational and therefore universally valid standards for the evaluation of conduct, the objection against Atiyah's methodology seems well taken.

In contrast to Atiyah, Fried resolutely starts out by developing a critical theory about the binding force of promises, evolving from the notion of autonomy, which he goes on to claim as the basis of the contemporary American law of contract. He is aware of the difficulty of explaining contract doctrine in all its detail and complexity by reference to the simple principle that promises ought to be kept.[14] Opinions are divided amongst lawyers as to whether Fried has succeeded on the latter score (at least, since the application of his promise principle to the laws of other legal systems remains largely unexplored, as far as Anglo-American contract law is concerned).[15] What should in any case be observed is the ambuguity in Fried's philosophical defence of the promise principle. He does not make it clear whether or not his principle of individual autonomy[16] would be capable of grounding an obligation to

[11] In French law, the general position is that it is the court, not the parties themselves, which is in charge of the proceedings after a breach of contract and decides on the appropriate remedies. The consequence is that conduct aimed at mitigating her damages by the party in breach (e.g. the acquisition of substitute goods in case of failure to deliver), which may be required under English law, may, as such, amount to a breach under French law. This does not mean, of course, that the French courts never sanction a posteriori any unreasonable behaviour by 'the innocent party'.

[12] See, in particular, ch. 5.

[13] Even so one might feel uneasy about a theory of promissory obligation which, by giving their due to all incidents and qualifications of our law of contract, becomes so technical and detailed as to escape recognition by a representative member of the community whose adherence to the values it embodies is supposed to account for the theory's normative force. It is no wonder that Atiyah has been reproached for working with an oversimplified picture of the law of contract, see *inter alia* A. S. Burrows, 'Contract, Tort and Restitution—A Satisfactory Division, or Not?' (1983) 99 *Law Quarterly Rev.* 217, 264 ff.; H. Collins (1982) 45 *Modern Law Rev.* 225.

[14] Fried, chs. 1, and, in particular, 2, 6.

[15] Fried's disposal of the entirety of the body of rules relating to the doctrine of consideration on the ground that it is internally inconsistent is controversial. His repeated transferral of doctrines, such as the one defining under which conditions terms can be implied in a contract (traditionally conceived of as forming part of the law of contract) to the tort branch of the law of obligations, has also attracted criticism.

[16] Which, in any case, he leaves rather vague and indeterminate, sometimes equating it with individual will and, at other times, associating it with 'trust' and mutual confidence: see, in particular, ch. 2.

keep a promise in the absence of an 'institution' or 'convention' of promising. He plainly assigns a role to the latter, but remains obscure as to what it is. The 'institution of promising' does not create the obligation, which springs from the same source as the moral force of the institution itself, namely, the value of autonomy. At times Fried seems to restrict its role to '*defining* the practice of promising and its entailments.[17] If he believes that it is, in fact, the law of contract which thus defines and clarifies promissory obligation, his attempt to deal with the complexity of the relationship between promissory and contractual obligation is similar to that of MacCormick.[18]

MacCormick can be seen to seek a compromise. He expressly rejects the view that it is necessary in explaining promising and the obligation to keep promises, to invoke rules enshrined in a prior social practice. Yet, at the same time, he recognizes that contractual obligation is surrounded by institutional incidents. Special additional requirements and qualifications obtain for the enforceability of promises as contracts. He does not ignore the fact that these are not universal but may be elaborated by a particular legal system and distinctive to it.[19] But he does not allow this to shake his belief that a universally valid justification of contractual liability can be found in the inherently binding nature of promises stemming, in his view, from the fact that they do (and are calculated to) induce their addressees to rely upon future performance by the promisor.[20] So the discourse of promise provides a 'pure' justification for contractual obligation. The relevant legal practices only determine, in a normatively neutral way, the incidents of its application. In this way MacCormick seems to do justice both to the law of contract and to the moral discourse of promise. Institutional legal detail is kept out of the latter, leaving the possibility of a general theory unaffected. Yet none of the law's detail, complexity, and indeed insularity is reduced. However, MacCormick's description of the nature of the law's intervention is easily exposed as too minimal, once adequate attention is given to the specific nature of contract. This I now propose to do by examining the substantive objection against the assimilation of contract with promise.

[17] Fried, 17 (my emphasis).

[18] References are to *Legal Right and Social Democracy*, above, n. 5.

[19] See the discussion at 205.

[20] Ibid., 195.

2. THE SUBSTANTIVE OBJECTION

The thrust of the substantive objection is that those who assimilate contracts to promises move from an essentially two-sided, bilateral notion to one which is unilateral. How strong is this objection?

A comparative study of the contract laws of different legal systems does, indeed, reveal the central model of a contract to be a relationship, a bond between two individuals. In consequence, a contractual obligation is one that is owed to a particular individual who, even before any breach occurs, is already identifiable on the basis of his special bond with the person under the obligation. Other legal requirements carry corresponding entitlements only for specified or specifiable individuals. However, legal systems typically endow contractual obligation with at least two further distinguishing characteristics. The relationship giving rise to it is one which has been intentionally created, or at least so acknowledged, by both parties to it. Furthermore, the person to whom a contractual obligation is owed has the power and the right not only to enforce it, but also to release the obligated person: it has been said[21] that she 'holds him on a string'. I shall not here attempt to defend this picture of contract as a *vinculum iuris* between the parties. Objections have been formulated against the characterization of contract as bilateral in the sense described. Yet, as was the case with the formal objection, it is the second limb of the substantive objection, stating the unilateral nature of promise, which, in recent years, has become the more beleaguered proposition.

Indeed, in virtually all the current philosophical literature,[22] an essential feature of a promise has been seen to be the creation of an obligation to a promisee, on whom a right to the future performance of the promised action is conferred and who, consequently, has the power to release the promisor from the obligation. A seemingly useful contrast has consequently been drawn between promises and purely solitary acts, such as vows or pledges which would not confer any rights upon another determinate person. Yet the tenability of this distinction must surely depend on whether it provides an explanation of how the mere act of promising can give rise to a relationship of obligation and corresponding entitlement between promisor and promisee. What must be clarified is exactly how the person who has the right and the power over the promisor's commitment is determined. In other words: who is the

21 See M. H. Robins, *Promising, Intending and Moral Autonomy* (Cambridge, 1984), 99.

22 But see Downie, loc cit. n. 7 above, for a dissenting position.

'promisee'? To this question of 'privity', philosophers give uncertain or, in the least, widely divergent answers.

Privity of promise

(i) *Being the addressee of a promise* Could it be sufficient, in order to have the right to enforce a promise, to be the person to whom the promise is addressed? Or the one to whom it is communicated? It suffices to think of pledges made by politicians in speeches to the electorate, or of an hypothetical example of an undertaking, sealed and mailed to an arbitrarily selected telephone subscriber,[23] to dismiss that suggestion. To say that promises necessarily are addressed, or indeed communicated, to another person would not distinguish them from solitary acts like vows: the latter too can be communicated.

Could the fact of acting in reliance on a promise by a person to whom it is communicated or of the expectations created in such a person account for the distinctive character of a promise? This depends on whether these elements are apt to single out the individual with the right to enforce it. If we accept that the obligation arising from a promise is owed to the person who acts in reliance on it, we are committed to the view that promising does not give rise to obligations unless and until relied upon. Yet it is commonly felt that promises give rise to obligations as soon as they are made.[24] The assertion that it is the expectation created by the promise which determines the normative entitlement appears to escape this objection, as most promises create expectations immediately upon being made. However, it is not always the case that those to whom a promise is addressed expect the promisor to do as he promised. To avoid these difficulties, one might be tempted to say that the obligation is owed from the moment the promise is made, to the person or persons 'likely' to rely upon it. This would not be a solution either. The fact that she is likely to rely upon the promisor doing as she said she would does not sufficiently distinguish a person from the group of those who come to know of the promise to make her stand in a special relationship to the promisor.[25] The point of the objection could be put in another way: as formulated, the duty would be an unreasonably wide one.[26] MacCormick's view on the source of the binding force of

[23] I have borrowed this example from Fried, who uses it at 41.

[24] See also Raz, above, n. 9, 923.

[25] Robins's distinction (op. cit. n. 21 above, 8) between epistemic expectations/entitlements and moral expectations/entitlements seems helpful in this respect.

[26] Atiyah, 65.

promises illustrates—or, at least, could illustrate[27]—one attempt to rescue 'expectations' and 'reliance' as grounds for 'special' obligations. The person to whom such an obligation is owed would be her in whom the promisor *intended* to induce reliance (or would know, or indeed ought to know, that reliance would follow). However, it is doubtful whether the act of intentionally inducing reliance successfully distinguishes promises from solitary undertakings such as vows. Can the latter not be communicated with the intention that they be relied upon?[28]

(ii) *Assenting to a promise* Fried locates the distinction between a promise and a vow in the requirement that, in a promise, the person to whom it is made and communicated, must be 'in some sense willing to be its beneficiary.[29] He makes it plain that it is not sufficient that the promise benefits its addressee. The beneficiary must actually desire it to be made. The promise needs to be *accepted*.

The suggestion that it is its being accepted by another which makes for the relational character of a promise is intuitively attractive. Yet the difficulty is to clarify what exactly this act of accepting amounts to. By describing it as an expression by the addressee of a promise of her want or desire for it, Fried seems to invite numerous, rather obvious, counter-examples involving people seemingly successfully promising what is unwanted by the addressee.[30] If he nevertheless seems to adhere to this description, it may well be because, understood in this way, the notion of accepting fits a particular interpretation of a promise which, in turn, suggests a very popular explanation of how a promise can give rise to a relationship between promisor and promisee. This interpretation of promise is a legacy of the nineteenth-century liberal economic and political theories which insisted that the central case of legitimate obligation was one which was willed by the person obligated. Since promissory obligation was consequently held justified because, and to the extent that, the promisor willed it, a promise came to be seen as signifying the will of the promisor to be obligated on terms which are actually willed, in the sense of wanted or desired, by her. In other words the issue of the formation of the commitment (inherent in a promise)

27 In the version of his essay, to which reference is made here, MacCormick disowns his earlier view that 'the intention to create reliance' is a necessary condition of promising: loc cit., 204.

28 See also Robins, 8.

29 At 42.

30 See, for instance, W. R. Carter, 'On Promising the Unwanted' (1973) 33 *Analysis* 88.

and its content were conflated. As an act of intentionally undertaking an obligation, promising was held to require that the content of the promise should actually be wanted by the promisor. Yet surely one may just as sensibly claim to promise what one does not want as one may claim to promise what the promise's addressee does not want. The liberal interpretation of promise, requiring the content of the obligation to be willed by the promisor, is, as Raz has stressed,[31] not in any sense required by that concept. But, as suggested, it does allow a way of understanding how a promise can forge a relationship. If a promise is seen to express the desire of the promisor for a particular thing, it is easy to see how it can be matched by the corresponding desire of another, expressed by 'accepting' the promise, and how promisor and promisee are joined by the resulting agreement of will between them. If, on the other hand, a promise is seen as an undertaking of an obligation the terms of which are not necessarily wanted by the promisor, it is difficult to provide an account of how precisely the 'promise' takes up the promise and so forges a relationship between herself and the promisor.[32]

(iii) *Conditional promising* Raz, in fact, seems to offer an explanation of how this may happen;[33] it evolves from the idea of conditional promising. He specifies:

Two kinds of conditional promises are of interest here: First a promise made conditional on an action by the promisee (e.g., 'I will give you ten pounds if you

[31] Loc. cit., at 931–2.

[32] Fried touches upon, but does not elaborate, a way of understanding the acceptance of the 'promisee', not as an expression of her want for the content of the promise as such, but for it 'as a promise' (43). Indeed, one might attempt to define the promisee as a person who positively does not want the thing promised, but nevertheless signals assent to the promisor making the promise, for instance in order to please her. It is difficult, however, to see how this unilateral act of assenting would forge a bond with the promisor.

[33] Raz's discussion may actually suggest two alternative explanations. He holds that the promisee acquires a right based on the interest that promises made to him will be kept. This is the same interest (to be able to enter special bonds with people voluntarily) which is reflected in the promisor's (and his own) right to promise, including the right to make conditional promises of the kind described. Apart from the reference to the fact that the promise is made to him, which begs the question, there is no express explanation of how the right of the promisee becomes enmeshed with the duty of the promisor. It is possible that he considers that the identity of the interest which underlies both rights accounts for that. Raz also urges the reader to remember the fact that the promisee is not entirely passive; it is always up to him to waive his right under the promise. Perhaps the suggestion is that by not doing this, he assents to the promise? But we could not, of course, say that the way a right to enforce a promise is acquired is by foregoing to waive it; see Raz, 'On the Nature of Rights', (1984) 93 *Mind* 194, 202–3.

give me the books'). Second (which is in fact a special case of the above), a promise made conditional on a promise to be given by the promisee (e.g., 'I will give you 10 pounds if you promise to give me the book'). Whenever such a promise is made and the condition is fulfilled, there is an agreement between the promisor and the promisee.[34]

There are reasons for doubting whether conditional promising can give rise to the required special relationship. In the philosophical literature a distinction has been insisted upon between a conditional vow, even if the condition is an action or an undertaking to be performed by the person to whom the vow is communicated, and a promise. Only the promisee has a waivable right to enforce the other's undertaking.[35] In any case, the specificity of Raz's formulation (his choice of the sorts of conditional promises taken to be of interest) shows that his notion of conditional promising is directly derived from and modelled upon a central doctrine of the English law of contract, the doctrine of consideration. The function of this doctrine is, as I shall argue, to supply a legal contract's essential bilateral element.

Privity of contract

(i) *Being the addressee of a promise* Under English law, a mere addressee of a promise does not have a contractual right to enforce it, nor to claim damages for its breach.

It is not, of course, the case that one can always refuse to keep one's word with legal impunity. Promises contained in a sealed instrument have been held enforceable (in the action of 'covenant') since the very early common law. Moreover, the notion that an informal promise is in some sense binding has been present ever since, in the early sixteenth century, the breach of an informal undertaking was made actionable in 'assumpsit',[36] an action which evolved from a writ (that of 'trespass') which was to be the source of much of our present law of tort. Yet it is difficult to ascribe to either of these actions the aim of conferring upon the addressee of a promise a waivable right over it. The breach of an assumpsit was not initially actionable as such; specific material damage[37]

34 Raz, loc. cit. n. 33 above, 202–3.

35 Robins, 86.

36 The Latin word did not mean promise, though both words had a certain affinity in evoking the general idea of a voluntary assumption of liability; see A. W. B. Simpson, *A History of the Common Law of Contract* (Oxford, 1975), 216–17.

37 Despite the great diversity and complexity of historical explanations as to the rise of the action of 'assumpsit' from within the action of trespass, there seems to be some measure of agreement on the bridging role, played by the assumption of loss following the

caused by the breach of the undertaking to those who had relied upon it appeared to be a requirement until, by the end of the sixteenth century, success in this action was made firmly dependent upon the finding of consideration. On the other hand, until this day an undertaking contained in a deed (a document which is signed, sealed, and delivered) can be, and often is, enforced by a person (commonly, its beneficiary) who has not 'provided consideration' for it.[38] Yet this person is not necessarily an addressee of the promise. A deed may create a legal duty in favour of a beneficiary who is unaware of its existence.[39] Whatever the role of the formalities was initially, they cannot now be conceived as serving to forge a special relationship.[40]

It is sometimes suggested that in recent law,[41] due to the development of the legal doctrine referred to as promissory estoppel, informal promises have become contractually actionable by those to whom they were made, even if they have not provided consideration for them. It has to be pointed out, however, that it is not clear from the cases that one even has to be an addressee of the promise in order to invoke an estoppel. What is more significant, however, is that there is no good reason to perceive an action based on promissory estoppel as a distinctly

actual misfeasance of an obligation, 'self-disablement' from performance, or 'deceit' by the party in breach, between the tort action of trespass and the purely contractual action for mere 'nonfeasance' of an undertaking: see S. F. C. Milsom, *Historical Foundations of The Common Law* (London, 2nd edn., 1981), ch. 12.

[38] Seals are often attached to documents containing promises supported by consideration, i.e. bilateral transactions or contracts. Even there, the deed can be distinguished from the contract: see *per* Lord Denning in *Vincent* v. *Primo Enterprises* (1969) 2 All ER 1941, at 944.

[39] M. P. Furmston, *Cheshire and Fifoot's Law of Contract* (London, 11th edn., 1981), 25; also G. H. Treitel, *The Law of Contract* (London, 6th edn., 1983), 120.

[40] It was the royal courts which, certainly from the end of the thirteenth century onwards, insisted upon the formality of the seal as a condition for lending their assistance to the enforcement of 'covenants', which previously appear to have been enforced exclusively in the local courts. It has been argued that initially the requirement of 'delivery', which now is complied with simply by evidencing an intention to be bound, ensured that there had been act of communication to the 'covenantee': see D. E. C. Yale, 'The Delivery of a Deed' (1970) 28 *Camb. Law J.* 52. The shift in its function would, in that case, be similar to that undergone by the Roman *stipulatio*; for a comparison of 'covenant' with the latter, see F. H. Lawson, 'Analogues of the *Stupulatio* in English Law', in K. H. Nadelmann, A. T. von Medrea, and J. H. Hazard (eds.), *XXth Century Comparative and Conflicts Law, Legal Essays in Honor of Hessel E. Yntema* (Leyden, 1961), 117.

[41] There is, moreover, the long-standing suggestion that the case law warrants the view that a 'joint promisee' (presumably one of the promise's addressees) can enforce a promise for which another 'promisee' has made the requested response to the promise despite the fact that no 'consideration' moves from himself. But see B. Coote, 'Consideration and the Joint Promisee' (1978) 37 *Camb. Law J.* 301.

contractual action. The case law offers very little justification for assuming that the normal function of estoppel (which is to prevent the exercise of a pre-existing right rather than to create a new one) has been displaced. In any case, many of the decisions cited as authority for such an assumption insist that there should be conduct in reliance on the promise by its addressee, possibly even conduct resulting in a detriment or injury to him.[42] If this requires the addressee to show that she has suffered actual material damage by relying on the promise, the justification for allowing her to sue must be sought, not in her relationship with the promisor, but in the justice of compensating her for her loss. It is significant to note that assumpsit was not visualized as a separate action from trespass until the requirement to show damage was replaced by the requirement of consideration.

(ii) *Agreeing* The literature of English and American law is replete with references to the need for 'agreement'. To a certain extent the popularity of this term can be explained by the ambiguity of its meaning. In common linguistic usage, it is used to indicate both that between two people there is *an agreement*, and that two people are *in agreement.* In the former case the use of the term adds little to the meaning invoked by 'a deal' or indeed 'a contract'. Attention is simply drawn to the existence of a bond between two people capable of giving rise to special obligations. No suggestion is made as to the way this special relationship was forged. In the latter case the term evokes a unity of mind and/or of will.[43]

Although they do use the term in the former way, contract theorists regularly associate 'agreement' specifically with consensus or meeting of wills. Indeed, judicial interventions have been justified by the judges themselves—on numerous occasions in the nineteenth century and at least in one illustrious instance quite recently[44]—in terms of a need for

[42] On 'promissory estoppel', see, amongst others, M. P. Thompson, 'From Representation to Expectation, Estoppel as a Cause of Action' (1983) 42 *Camb. Law J.* 257, and Burrows, op. cit. n. 13, 239–44.

[43] Legal philosophers have not failed to notice this ambiguity: see R. Samek, 'Performative Utterances and the Concept of Contract' (1965) 43 *Australasian J. of Phil.* 196, 205–6, and R. Bronaugh, 'On Contracting: An Essay in Legal Philosophy', unpublished Oxford B.Litt. thesis, 35 ff.

[44] English courts have recently justified developing a defence of 'economic duress' against an action for breach of contract upon the ground that 'duress, whatever forms it takes, is a coercion of the will so as to vitiate consent' (*per* Lord Scarman in *Pao On* v. *Lau Yiu Long* (1980) AC 614, 635); the theoretical basis for the new doctrine has been criticized, most notably by Atiyah (1982) 98 *Law Quarterly Rev.* 197.

integrity of the will. This may, of course, simply indicate that the liberal interpretation of promise, as signifying the will of the promisor to be obligated on terms willed by her, remains powerful today. The perception of the relationship of promisor and promisee as one of consensus or unity of will has, however, also been firmly anchored in the theoretical framework of contract. Contract lawyers know[45] that the writers of the first English legal textbooks, which were produced in the nineteenth century during the heyday of liberalism, turned to the existing continental treatises for much badly needed theoretical support for the judicial decisions, particularly concerning the formation of a contract. Specifically, at least in that area, they seem to have borrowed from French works. As I have attempted to show elsewhere, the analysis by the French treatise writers of the process of the formation of a contract into offer and acceptance is intimately related to an account of its bilateral nature precisely in terms of a meeting of the contractual parties' wills (*accord de volontés*).[46] By this account, the meeting of an offer, expressing the willingness of one person to contract on a certain set of terms, and of the acceptance, signifying the other party's assent to those terms, is what constitutes the contract. The adoption, within English contract theory, of the notions of offer and acceptance, which came to represent the promise and counter-promise (or act upon which the promise is conditional) respectively, must have promoted a consensual account of the bilateral nature of contract, already attractive on ideological grounds.

However, as a comparison with French contract law would emphasize, such an account ill suits the bulk of Anglo-American contract jurisprudence. First of all, the cases make it plain that one cannot, at least not in English law, acquire a right to enforce a promise merely by attempting to assent to it. This has been felt to cause injustice particularly when, in return for her promise, the promisor makes the promise conditional upon the performance of an act other than a counter-promise: even if both parties are *in agreement* (in the sense that they are agreed on the content of the projected contract) the promisee cannot securely commence performing the requested act. As it is not the assent, but the performance of the requested act, which is taken to be the 'acceptance' of the offer, the promisor can normally revoke her promise at any time before the performance has been completed. Doctrinal attempts to remedy this by equating acceptance with assent

[45] Simpson, loc. cit. n. 6, has been very influential in this respect.

[46] See A. de Moor, 'Contract and Agreement in English and French Law' (1986) 6 *Oxford J. of Legal Studies* 275.

have, at least in England, had to retreat in favour of more traditional techniques.[47]

Secondly, compared to the French courts, English judges have shown themselves remarkably unreceptive to defences against actions for breach of contract which are based on the need for a concurrence of the contractual partners' wills. Under the French doctrine of Mistake (*Erreur*), the French courts are, for instance, prepared to entertain an argument that, because the parties were not in agreement on the content or scope of the purported contract, as one of them did not intend to make the precise undertaking which he in fact did make, no contract has come into existence. But even where they consider that the parties have agreed sufficiently completely about what the contract is to be about, they may, under the same doctrine, accept that it is flawed because a mistaken belief about the subject-matter of the contract has misdirected the will of one or both of them. Neither argument stands much chance of success in the common-law courts, which are quite prepared to hold a promisor to terms which he could be said to have promised but did not want or intend and on which, consequently, the parties were not in agreement. Mistaken beliefs or, for that matter, other factors[48] capable of misdirecting the will of the contracting partners are of little relevance. The fact that courts are prepared to hold parties to a contract even if there remains outstanding disagreement on its terms, is often said to be a consequence of their adoption of an *objective* test of agreement. In this way it is claimed that the courts indeed are looking for a consensus between the parties but that they use an objective method to ascertain it. This suggestion is emphasized by the characterization of the objective approach as a particular kind of estoppel, a move which presupposes the validity of the consensual model.[49] The Court of Appeal, however, has recently rejected the need to justify its objective determination of the content of a contract by means of estoppel. The 'well-established' principles of offer and acceptance were held adequate for that purpose. The court made it clear, however, that, in English law, 'offer' stands, not

[47] Techniques which artificially imply an undertaking in the promise requesting an act in return that the promisor will not impede the performance of the requested act, and those which construe the actual acts of reliance as the very acts requested, bear witness to the courts' loyalty to the orthodox view of the nexus between contracting parties based on consideration.

[48] As, until recently, commercial pressure; I have outlined the differences between the English and French laws of Contract more fully in de Moor, loc. cit. n. 46.

[49] The defendant would be estopped from denying that the plaintiff and himself were in agreement: see Samek, above, n. 43, 201.

for the expression of the proposer's will to commit herself on particular terms, but for a promise with a request for a counter-promise or some other act, and that 'acceptance' denotes the performance of the requested response.[50] In other words, the objective approach is not incongruous with the notions of offer and acceptance as long as these are tailored to the requirement of consideration.

(iii) *Providing the consideration for a promise* It is the doctrine of consideration which, within Anglo-American contract law, ensures that there exists a relationship between the plaintiff and the defendant specific enough to give rise to special obligations. It does this by requiring those claiming a right to enforce another's undertaking to show that they have done what the promisor *requested* (or, at least, specified should be done) in return for her promise.

The function of consideration is more aptly captured by the terminology of request than by that of condition. The latter suggests that the emergence of the bond between the contractual partners, indeed perhaps of the very commitment of the promisor, is entirely dependent upon a rather fortuitous event, the fulfilment of the condition.[51] 'Request', on the other hand, emphasizes that, at the moment of the initial undertaking, one of them is committing herself and, at the same time, by inviting a particular response, projects the creation of a bond capable of grounding another's entitlement over this commitment. The promisor intends to undertake an obligation towards a determinate individual, presently specifiable by means of the description of the act or counter-promise requested. But the language of request should not be taken to suggest that the courts interpret such description exclusively by reference to the desires or intentions of the maker. The doctrine of consideration can and does operate to provide a means for identifying the party who is to be at the other end of the contractual relationship even if the content of the requested act is determined objectively; just as

[50] *Centrovincial Estates* v. *Merchant Investors Assurance Co. Ltd.* (1983) Com.LR. 158

[51] Many lawyers—amongst whom Fried (28)—do construe a contractual 'offer' as a promise conditional upon a promise or an act. There are difficulties with this characterization. The formulation of the conditional promise-offer is 'to promise to promise if someone else promises or performs'. This would lead to infinite regress and may lead to difficulties of the kind mentioned by Atiyah, 205–6; see also Fried, 46–7 and footnote. The suggestion in the philosophical literature, that an undertaking made conditional upon an undertaking of another still does not amount to a bilateral act in the sense here described, derives support from the historical development of the action of assumpsit in which the notion of condition gradually gave way to that of consideration to deal with bilateral undertakings in contract.

it is perfectly compatible with an objective determination of the content of the initial promise. So we can perfectly well view the requirement of consideration as serving to forge a contractual relationship (an agreement) between the person making this kind of offer, and another who takes it up by giving the invited response, without seeing it as a way to ensure that they are in agreement. We should not be misled by nineteenth-century presentations of the doctrine which, in all likelihood, were unduly influenced by the liberal interpretation of promise and the matching continental consensual model of contract. The so-called 'bargain-theory' of consideration is neither required by the concept of promise (which need not be understood as an expression of the promisor's will to be obligated) nor necessary to account for the bilateral nature of contract (which can be accounted for in terms of the undertaking of an obligation towards the person who responds in a specified way).

3. CONTRACT AS PROMISE RE-EVALUATED

By contracting, two people can intentionally create or acknowledge a special bond between them, which is capable of conferring upon each of them a waivable right to the performance of the contract. The view that promising is a similar sort of act has proved hard to substantiate. One type of account which, in its strongest version, turns on the reliance which is engendered by a promise, fails to demonstrate how promising gives rise to special rights; another enlists what are, in effect, specific contractual doctrines in support.

The problem with the first type of explanation is not in seeing that the making of a promise may, in some circumstances, be accompanied by the emergence of rights. An addressee of a promise may incur loss by relying on the promise in circumstances where such reliance was reasonable and/or intended by the promisor. Even accepting that this actually *entitles* her to demand compensation from the promisor, however, her right is not a special right over the promise. Atiyah may well be correct in saying that the basis of this right is the judgment of the community or the group as to 'when one person is sufficiently entitled to entertain expectations, and to act upon them, so as to hold another responsible if those expectations, or conduct in reliance, are subsequently disappointed.[52] But it would be a mistake to hold that this

[52] Op. cit., 68–9.

judgment as to entitlement was the basis for an obligation created (or acknowledged) by promising.[53]

At first sight, it seems that a promise can give rise to the required special bond if it is 'taken up' by its addressee. However, there seems to be no natural way in which a promsie can be taken up (or, in other words, to describe who actually is the promisee). The descriptions offered in the philosophical literature are, as we have seen, sometimes quite openly modelled upon doctrines of the law of contract, more specifically the Anglo-American doctrine of consideration and the civilian requirement of consensus. These are distinctive to particular legal traditions. Despite the references to consensus in contract theorizing, it does not in practice seem necessary that the parties agree on the terms of the projected contract for a contractual relationship to arise in English law. Neither is it, for that matter, sufficient.[54] The requirement that, in order to enforce another's undertaking, one must have done what the promisor requested in return for her promise is alien to the civilian systems of contract law. Hence it can be seen that, by insisting that contracts are no more than promises, we may well be unwittingly paving the way for an 'institutional' theory of promissory obligation. Fried's work can conveniently be taken to illustrate how the substantive and formal objections against the simple monist view of contract and promise may, in this way, be related. His refusal to see a contract as distinct from a promise is accompanied by an express affirmation both of the bilateral character of a promise (which, as was noted earlier, he ascribes principally to the promisee's assent to the promise[55]) and of the relevance of the institution of promising to the obligation arising from promises.

Earlier I suggested that Fried's reluctance to elaborate on the precise function of that institution within his theory of promissory obligation may betray an attempt at least to contain the influx of 'institutional structures' in such a theory, whilst not denying their significance altogether. MacCormick quite openly shares this concern. His strategy seems to consist in admitting that a legal contract is an institutionally *defined* form of promising but at the same time insisting that a *justification*

[53] Atiyah admits as much when he characterizes promises as admissions of the existence of an obligation; op. cit. n. 2 above.

[54] Atiyah remarks upon this at 204–5.

[55] Despite his dismissal of the doctrine of consideration as incoherent, Fried does, in fact, admit that as consideration provides us 'with a truly necessary element to a correct view of contractual obligation', it has seemed natural to insist on it (at 42). For him, however, consideration established that 'the promise was made to me and that I desired the promise to be made' (ibid.).

for contractual obligation which is drawn from the promissory well can nevertheless remain aloof from institutional legal detail. It is important to see why such an attempt at separating the issue of the definition and of the justification of contractual liability fails. In the case of MacCormick at least, the belief that it might be successful seems to rest on a restrictive view of the purpose of the law of contract's requirements and qualifications. Those he specifically mentions are respectively acceptance in the civilian systems and the objective determination of the content of the contract in English law:

> The function which they essentially fulfill is to secure, as far as may be, that promises are not enforced unless it is clear that the 'promisor' really intended to be taken seriously, and had grounds to suppose that the promisee really took him seriously. They are rules laying down procedural prerequisites for the enforceability of voluntary obligations. Unless these prerequisites are satisfied, undertakings and promises are not to be enforced at law.[56]

As I argued earlier, MacCormick does not really attend, at least not adequately, to the bilateral character of contract. Had he done so, he may have allowed the difference in the legal prerequisites for the emergence of contractual liability (and in some of the rules qualifying such liability) from one jurisdiction to another to reveal a close connection between them and each jurisdiction's distinctive conception of what is the very nature of contract. The requirement of acceptance and 'the objective principle' are cases in point. The first, at least if seen as assent to the terms proposed by the offeror, does not fit the English perception of a contractual relationship; the second would be incongruous within the French. The aim of requirements of this kind is thus not merely to define the incidents and conditions for the legal enforcement of an obligation, which exists and can be justified independently from it. The kind of obligation which the law of contract enforces (that is a special obligation over which a determinate individual has a waivable right) is not intelligible independently of its manifestation in differing legal traditions. Legal systems actually provide the means of creating it by forging special bonds in the particular way they specify.

So even the English law of contract, under which arguably the contractual nexus ultimately does arise from a promise, cannot be justified solely by reference to that notion and without regard to the strictures inherent in its institutional development. Rather than merely being a procedural prerequisite for the legal enforcement of an obliga-

[56] Op. cit. n. 5 above, at 209.

tion which arises from the promise, compliance with the requirement of consideration actually creates an independent obligation in its own right. This occurs as a result of imbuing the commitment which inheres in the promise with a corresponding special right. Moreover, it is not clear that the liability arising from a contract under French law can at all be regarded as a transformed promissory obligation. In the absence of a doctrine of consideration, only if a promise is seen as an expression of the will of the promisor to be obligated on certain terms is it apt to give rise to a contractual relationship. But this is not the only, nor necessarily the best, way to understand a promise; and the terminology of the French law does not include the term promise, but rather that of offer and acceptance, denoting a proposition, rather than a promise, made by one and another's assent to it.

A foundation for the law of contract must radically abandon the notion of promise and draw directly upon the value of allowing individuals the possibility of creating or acknowledging between them special bonds capable of giving rise to obligations in each which are claimable by the other. Both MacCormick and Fried, in fact, acknowledge the signifance of some such value in the justification of contractual liability, as is evident from their references to 'trust' and the bond which exists between 'trusting' parties, as an alternative or additional ground of promissory liability.[57] Raz, too, has stressed the 'intrinsic desirability of forms of life in which people create or acknowledge special bonds between them and certain other individuals'.[58] Like MacCormick and Fried, he sees this as the main source for the obligatory character of promises.[59] Yet the connection with the notion of promise not only threatens the breadth of a theory of contract which evolves from this value; it also compels us to see the obligation arising from promises as an institutional obligation. I believe that by repatriating the moral force behind the concept of contract firmly within the legal discourse and

[57] The following passage of MacCormick's essay is particularly striking: 'Quite apart from particular detriments arising from particular acts of reliance, any breach of such a relationship of trust is in some degree injurious to the trusting party. It is injurious to the extent to which people set value on such relationships; and I for one am attracted by John Finnis's argument that such relationships are of fundamental and non-derivative value to human beings' (at 206). See also Fried's references to trust at 16–17, and to the bonds of trust in the footnote at 46.

[58] Raz, 'Promises and Obligations', in P. M. S. Hacker and J. Raz (eds.), *Law, Morality and Society* (Oxford, 1977), at 228.

[59] It is important to observe, however, that Raz's conception of what this bond entails differs from mine in so far as it does not seem to include the notion that the obligations created by it for one party are waivable by the other.

harnessing it to explain the specific character of legal obligation, we can as lawyers advance, if not the (moral) theory of promise, at least the (legal) theory of contract.

I cannot here even attempt to corroborate my suggestion that it would indeed be constructive to explain promising without reference to the distinctive contractual traditions of particular legal systems within which the value of creating special bonds between individuals is realized, and so to present promissory obligation as a non-institutional requirement.[60] But I hope to have canvassed some support for the claim that a theory of contract, which seeks the foundation for contractual obligation in this value, would contribute to a better understanding of the specific nature of contractual, and hence of legal obligation. Two ways could be isolated in which the development of this approach to the theory of contract might prove revealing. First, it would be made clear that, for a justificatory account of a branch of the law to be plausible, it ultimately needs to address itself to a very broad concept of the legal area in question, which captures the sense given to it by various legal traditions. Thus, in seeking a justification for the law of contract, we view contracts not as promises but as 'special bonds'. In this sense, justifying law is always a 'conceptual' enterprise. Yet the proposed approach to contract theory would also expose as futile any attempt to derive a 'pure' justification, capable of rendering the entirety of our law of contract coherent, from the moral power of the concept of contract so described. The doctrine of consideration, for instance, whose function makes it part of the very fabric of contract, cannot be accounted for without regard to its institutional development. It entered the law of assumpsit, neither suddenly nor tailor-made for its role, but with all sorts of strings already attached to it, as an amalgam of ideas which had, in one form or the other, been floating around, in particular in connection with the older action of Debt. Naturally enough, the way consideration caters for the two-sidedness of contract reflects its particular origin. This makes for a rather restrictive conception of what constitutes a contractual relationship with the result, for example, that unlike in French law, two people cannot under English law forge a contractual relationship simply by agreeing on a set of terms. So, while an undertaking by one person to offer another particular terms with which the latter concurs without, however, committing himself is a contract in the former legal system, it

[60] Robins's aim (op. cit. n. 21 above), is to develop an explanation of promissory obligation from a more primitive notion of (normative) 'commitment', and without any reference to 'conventions' or other 'social relations': see Introduction, 1 ff.

has to be dealt with in a different way, by means of different legal institutions (such as covenant, estoppel, tort, and trust) in the latter. But the fact that different legal traditions trace the boundaries between contract and these other legal institutions in various ways, whilst undoubtedly affecting the precise shape of contractual obligation, should not lead us to view the notion of contract as totally dependent upon institutional arrangements and a conventionalist account of that obligation as the only correct one. In doing this, we would be overlooking the fact that the distinctive notions of contract, which structure and unify the laws of contract of different legal systems, do represent particular ways in which special relationships can be forged. They are different conceptions of the same concept of contract.[61] Or so they should be: the particular obligation imposed by the law of contract is ultimately only justifiable to the extent that they are.

[61] I have borrowed the terminology from R.M. Dworkin, *Law's Empire* (London, 1986), 90 ff.

6

Family Law and Social Control*

JOHN EEKELAAR

I. A TYPOLOGY OF LEGAL FORMS

THE relationship between the family and society has long intrigued sociologists and historians. The family plays a pivotal role in the construction of a complete characterization of a society. Its organization determines, or reflects, the division of labour between the sexes within the society, adapts itself to the society's modes of production of economic wealth, often controls the distribution and devolution of political and economic power, and, above all, provides the foundation for the social careers of new members from their birth. Legal theory, then, may expect to profit from an examination of how a society's legal institutions are involved in that relationship. I shall argue that the changing nature of this relationship throws an important light on our appreciation of the social role of law.

Social theorists of law have commonly considered law to be a mechanism of social control. Krygier has, however, drawn attention to the obscurity of this concept.[1] It is therefore necessary to explore it further. Control might be conceived of in a coercive sense, as where determinate individuals impose a system of order on others. The traditional Marxist analysis of law as an instrument of class oppression follows this view (notwithstanding that the individuals might be impelled by impersonal forces), but it also underlies the classic positivist accounts of law in terms of 'command' theory. Law in this guise assumes a repressive character, the cutting edge of a conflict model of society. It operates to subjugate and alienate its subjects if they challenge the established order. We may, however, perceive the exercise of control in another way. Law (among other social institutions) may seek to incorporate the dissident into the dominant ideology. Just as Foucault claimed that, with the demise of the *ancien régime*, punishment no longer

[1] M. Krygier, 'The Concept of Law and Social Theory' (1982) 2 *Oxford J. of Legal Studies* 155, 162.

symbolized the victory of the sovereign power over an adversary conceived of as representing subversion, and moved away from the response of destruction (through torture) or annihilation (by execution or transportation) of the criminal's body to the scrutiny of his mind,[2] so law may seek to establish, or re-establish, behaviour patterns in conformity with a desired image of society. When it acts in this manner I describe law as 'normative' to indicate its role in spreading norms throughout a society viewed as actually or potentially an integrated whole.[3]

A third type of legal function relates yet more subtly to the idea of social control. There is, I maintain, a class of laws which seeks neither to repress nor remodel behaviour but which merely provides the means by which existing social relations are carried out. This is the aspect of law to which Hart referred when he responded to the view that law was directed at the 'bad' man:

> Why should not law be equally if not more concerned with the 'puzzled man', or 'ignorant man' who is willing to do what is required, if only he can be told what it is? Or with the 'man who wishes to arrange his affairs' if only he can be told how to do it? . . . The principal functions of the law as a means of social control are not to be seen in private litigation or prosecutions, which represent vital but still ancillary provisions for the failure of the system. It is to be seen in the diverse ways in which the law is used to control, to guide, and plan life out of court.[4]

Although Pound and Llewellyn, unlike Hart, saw the resolution of conflict as a central function of law, they nevertheless considered that law had a significant role in distributing resources and minimizing waste. But the allocation of resources and the resolution of conflicts presupposes the application of criteria for decision. These are likely to be drawn from the prevailing social order under a societal model presupposing a high degree of consensus.[5] The role of law in this sense, as where it acts as a guide for Hart's law-abiding citizen, lies in the

[2] M. Foucault, *Discipline and Punish: The Birth of the Prison* (London, 1979).

[3] A characteristic example of the view of law as an integrative mechanism is found in H. C. Bredemeier, 'Law as an Integrative Mechanism', in W. M. Evan (ed.), *Law and Sociology* (New York, 1962), 73–88. I use the expression 'normative' in a different sense from that of Joseph Raz. For Raz, all law is necessarily normative inasmuch as legal statements are statements about norms. But this must be distinguished from the social functions of law, which may (but not necessarily) include 'preventing undesirable behaviour and securing desirable behaviour': J. Raz, 'On the Functions of Law', in A. W. B. Simpson (ed.), *Oxford Essays in Jurisprudence: Second Series* (Oxford, 1973), ch. 11. I use 'normative' to refer to a social function.

[4] H. L. A. Hart, *The Concept of Law* (Oxford, 1961), 39.

[5] See A. Hunt, *The Sociological Movement in Law* (London, 1978).

provision of a mechanism for the better achievement of predetermined social goals. The law of contract and of wills serves the economic and social communities to which it relates by underwriting, and so making more effective, the organizational assumptions on which they are founded. For this reason I call this function of law 'instrumental'.[6] I do not argue that this tripartite typology exhausts the whole range of possibilities of legal functioning, but it must comprise the most significant part of it. Nor do I claim that any of the functions are exclusive to particular laws or to particular legal systems. They are likely to fluctuate between systems and across time. The same set of laws which were initiated coercively might later serve only in an instrumental fashion (an example will be given later). 'Repressive' and 'instrumental' law is essentially conservative (though both may sometimes be used to achieve radical social ends); 'normative' law is more radical, inasmuch as it directly seeks change, although such change may be sought to protect an established order. The typification will be helpful in understanding the changing character of the law as it related to family living, especially over the past two centuries.

2. DEVELOPMENTS PRIOR TO THE TWENTIETH CENTURY

It has been argued that, until recent times 'family law' in western societies had little relevance for the bulk of the population. With respect to the United States, Rheinstein wrote: 'the law of marital property, succession on death, support, divorce, parental power and guardianship took elaborate care of the needs of owners of property but paid scarce attention to those of the propertyless'.[7] This seems to be confirmed by an appreciation of the development of the law as expounded by the common-law judges. The law of guardianship originally evolved in order to protect a parent's interest in the marriage of his heir apparent;[8] legal protection of the parental relationship was confined to a father's proprietary interest in his heir's marriage, although it later extended to

[6] I have earlier used the expression 'regulatory' to describe this type of legal function. This may, however, be confused with that body of law and administration frequently referred to as 'regulation', which performs a function closer to that described here as 'normative': John Eekelaar, 'The Democratization of Family Law', Paper presented to the British Society of Population Studies, Bath, September 1983; 'Legal Systems and Families, Paper presented to the ISA–CFR Conference, Melbourne, August 1984.

[7] M. Rheinstein and R. Konig, in A. G. Chloros (ed.), *The International Encyclopedia of Comparative Law*, vol. iv, 'The Family', ch. 1; Introduction (J. C. B. Mohr, P. Siebeck, Tubingen, n.d.), 12.

[8] F. Pollock and F. W. Maitland, *The History of English Law* (Cambridge, 1968), ii. 444.

any pecuniary interest in the child.[9] Marriage was a major vehicle by which the intergenerational transmission of property was regulated. The legitimate status thereby acquired by the offspring ensured the orderly devolution of family wealth, although, when the fruits of commerce began to compete with land as a source of wealth, property lawyers developed the device of settling such property on the wife 'for her separate use', not so much to protect the wife's interests against those of her husband, but to safeguard her family's fortune should the marriage break down.[10]

We should not, however, suppose that legal institutions had no effect on the lives of the population at large. Family structure is determined by rules and these rules as they applied in pre-Christian Europe were drastically changed under the pressure of the early Church. No longer was marriage permitted with first cousins; the levirate and sororate were forbidden, the practice of adoption disappeared, and concubinage was condemned. The effect of this, it has been argued by Goody,[11] was to weaken the long-term hold family systems had over family property by restricting opportunities for the creation of heirs. When added to the prohibition on divorce and remarriage (even where no heirs had been produced), the discouragement of intestacy, and the rule of ecclesiastical celibacy, we have a powerful explanation for the massive movement of property away from families to the Church in the period AD 600–1100. If these arguments are accepted, much of the family law which in later times touched the propertyless only in an instrumental way, pointing out to them how they might construct a legally recognized family and how it might be dissolved, originally assumed a strongly coercive character.

For people with property, we find that the law was primarily concerned with family relationships *over time*. This type of law, too, was primarily instrumental. Family systems were used to deploy wealth and status intergenerationally within a regime of patriarchy.[12] Neither marriage, death, nor divorce normally interrupted the process of devolution of the patrimony. The husband's freedom of testation allowed him to disinherit his wife utterly, whatever the state of their relationship. On intestacy, his widow had no right at all to succeed to his

9 *Hall* v. *Hollaender* (1825) 4 B and C 660.

10 O. Kahn-Freund, in W. Friedman (ed.), *Matrimonial Property Law* (London, 1955).

11 J. Goody, *The Development of the Family and Marriage in Europe* (Cambridge, 1983).

12 See C. Smart, 'Regulating Families or Legitimating Patriarchy? Family Law in Britain' (1982) 10 *International J. of the Sociology of Law* 129.

land, although a right of dower to a life interest in one-third of his freehold land remained, unless barred by her husband. As to other property, much of which might have orginated from her, the widow received one-third if there were children and one-half if not. If the marriage ended in fact by divorce *a mensa et thoro*, or legally by parliamentary divorce *a vinculo*, this was not an occasion for redirecting the destination the husband's property would take by will or the laws of intestate succession. At most, the courts (and Parliament) would use their power to make alimentary provision as a means of restoring to an innocent wife some (not usually all) of the wealth she (or her family) had contributed to the marriage.[13] So important was the principle of legitimate succession through the male line that fathers were given an almost absolute right to the possession of their legitimate children, quite irrespective of the children's relationships with their mother. So it was that courts would refuse to deprive a father of the custody of a child even if it was still at the breast.[14] Nor would the moral delinquency of the father normally displace the operation of the legal mechanism giving effect to established male supremacy.[15] But in the event of serious infractions coercive law stood on the boundaries. A father, like the poet Shelley, whose actions or beliefs were considered likely to corrupt the child and thereby threaten both the perceived well-being of the child and that of society, might lose custody.[16] Exceptionally, then, the protection of the father's position offered by instrumental law was displaced by repression (exclusion from the normal incidents of fatherhood) and the transmission of norms (promotion of the desired precepts of bringing up children). Similarly, a wife whose adultery challenged male dominance and legitimate succession could be effectively cast from the married state, and her disobedience to ecclesiastical decree sanctioned by the ultimate alienation from the moral community,

[13] See further, J. Eekelaar and M. Maclean, *Maintenance after Divorce* (Oxford, 1986).

[14] *R.* v. *de Manneville* (1802) 5 East 221; *de Manneville* v. *de Manneville* (1804) 10 Ves. 52; see also *R.* v. *Greenhill* (1836) 4 A & E 624 (three girls of five, four, and two removed from mother to father). A concession towards the child's interest was made by the Custody of Infants Act 1839 which allowed courts to permit children *under seven* to stay with their mother and to order husbands to permit innocent mothers to visit children over that age in their possession.

[15] *Ball* v. *Ball* (1827) 2 Sim 35.

[16] *Shelley* v. *Westbrooke* (1821) Jac 266; *Thomas* v. *Roberts* (1850) 3 De G & Sm 758 ('I apprehend that, in England, a man who holds the opinion, that prayer . . . is no part of duty, but is superfluous; who considers, moreover, that there is not any day of the week which ought to be observed as a Sabbath . . . must be deemed to entertain opinions noxious to society, adverse to civilization . . . such opinions must disqualify him for the guardianship of an English child, whether his own son or any other'); in *re Besant* (1879) 11 Ch D 568.

excommunication.[17] In some countries, though not England, the illegitimate child suffered deprivation of legal rights, in effect, civil death.[18] Towards the end of the nineteenth century, the law of divorce began to be used normatively. The doctrine of the matrimonial offence and the basis for awarding, or declining, orders for financial support were directed at influencing moral behaviour and inculcating proper respect for the marital vows.[19]

But for most of the better-off section of the population, coercion must have been of little real significance. It was different so far as the general population was concerned. From Tudor times the law sought to compel the lineal blood relatives of any poor person who was unable to work to support that person.[20] It is there, however, where we first see legal concern with the family as a contemporaneous economic entity, for in 1718 justices were empowered to seize chattels and enter into occupation of the property of a husband who had left his family chargeable to the parish, and to provide for his family from the sale of the chattels and the rents of the land.[21] It was not, however, until 1834 that a wife was put in a similar position to that of lineal blood relatives by the provision that relief given to her should be treated as a loan to the husband, recoverable against him by the poor-law authorities. At the same time a husband was placed under an obligation with respect to 'the children of any woman he marries', who became chargeable to poor relief.[22] The law now enshrined the expectation that members of a contemporaneous social group must look for its economic support to a specific individual who had access to resources, usually through his labour.

It is important to see what the law was doing when it took this step. On the one hand we see the policy of forcing men and often children into the labour market. This was thought necessary not only on economic grounds, but also for reasons of social stability. But the law was doing more than that. It was attempting to impose, or reimpose, an ethic of family responsibility. The lengths to which this policy could go is illustrated by the repeal, in the Poor Relief Act of 1834, of any obligation on the part of the father to support his illegitimate child. In this way, by placing the 'burden, cost and obloquy' of illegitimate pregnancy on

[17] Before the Ecclesiastical Courts Act 1813, this was the major sanction available to the ecclesiastical courts.

[18] H. D. Krause, *Illegitimacy: Law and Social Policy* (Bobs Merrill, 1971), 3.

[19] Eekelaar and Maclean, op. cit. n. 13.

[20] These developments were consolidated in the Poor Relief Act 1601.

[21] Poor Relief (Deserted Wives and Children) Act 1718.

[22] Poor Relief Act 1834, ss. 56, 57.

the woman, it was hoped to promote conception within marriage.[23] That policy failed, and was abandoned ten years later. But although the mother and (later) the poor-law authorities themselves were given the right to claim against the father, discrimination against mothers of illegitimate children remained part of poor-law policy for many years.

We need to ask why the law took on this coercive, normative character, and why it did so only with respect to the poor. The answer lies in a profound disturbance in the economic basis of family living which occurred as early as the sixteenth century through the break-up of an agrarian society, although its roots may extend to the weakening of wider family structures detected by Goody in an earlier age. Within an agrarian society all family members work the land and distribute its fruits among themselves. Resources are distributed to individuals by virtue of their relationship to a family unit. Modern economic and social policy is still premissed on the assumption that resource inputs into the family will normally be distributed, in an acceptable fashion, among those of its members who share a common residence. But where resources are acquired by selling the labour of individual family members to other people, whether as agricultural or industrial workers, the basis of this assumption is weakened, particularly in times of social disruption and economic reverse. This is aggravated by scarcity of employment and the mobility caused by the need to search for it (especially in a society with primitive communications). The failure of the family support system leads in turn to poverty (especially of women and children) and the consequential threat of social unrest. The choice is a stark one. Family-based child care must either be abandoned (or severely modified) or family responsibility restored. The poor law reflects the latter choice. This was the legal and institutional response in nineteenth-century England to the perennial concern of the social reformers of that period with the link between social conditions and social unrest;[24] it was paralleled by the administrative measures taken in France at about the same time to 'restore marriage to the working classes'.[25] Despite the claim that the nineteenth century nurtured legal

[23] See O. R. McGregor and M. Finer, 'The History of the Obligation to Maintain', in the *Report of the Committee on One-Parent Families* (1947) Cmnd. 5629, ii. 114–21.

[24] A. P. Donajgrodzki, '"Social Police" and the Bureaucratic Élite: A Vision of Order in the Age of Reform', in A. P. Donajgrodzki (ed.), *Social Control in Nineteenth-Century Britain* (London, 1977).

[25] J. Donzelot, *The Policing of Families* (London, 1980).

individualism,[26] it also, as MacDonagh has shown,[27] provided notable instances of the imposition of standards of behaviour by legal regulation. The family law of the poor was one of them.

We may conclude that, while the strengthening of coercive law in the eighteenth and nineteenth centuries as far as it applied to the poor indicated concern over the operation among the working class of the assumption that the family should be the mechanism for resource distribution, especially to children, the middle- and upper-class family was not seen to be under a similar threat. Judicial divorce was not introduced until 1858, but there is no indication that the issue of post-divorce support, either for wives or for children, was seen to pose any serious problem. Indeed, when in 1839 statute first permitted the Lord Chancellor to award the legal custody of a child under seven to its mother, he was not given any power to order the father to pay for its support.[28] Nor did the common law recognize any enforceable legal duty on a father to support his child. The first occasion (outside the poor law) when a legal means for enforcing that well-perceived moral obligation appeared was in the 1857 divorce legislation itself, alongside the provisions for ordering support for a former wife. This was a sign that the picture was beginning to change. The power to order a man to support his former wife after divorce began to be used as a deterrent to reduce the threat to family responsibility posed by divorce.[29] Courts were even prepared to order men to support their *guilty* divorced wives (which the law would not have required if the parties had remained married) in order to keep the woman off public funds or the streets.[30] Policy might not yet need to 'restore' marriage to the wealthier classes, but by the turn of this century, normative law began increasingly to be applied to them.

3. MODERN DEVELOPMENTS

As the twentieth century progressed, the bulk of what is traditionally thought of as family law lost the primarily instrumental character it had assumed by the nineteenth century and became a significant channel for

[26] See A. V. Dicey, *Law and Public Opinion in England during the Nineteenth Century* (Macmillan, 1963), Lecture VI; Henry Maine, *Ancient Law* (Oxford, 1861).

[27] O. MacDonagh, '"Pre-transformations": Victorian Britain', in E. Kamenka and A. Erh-Soon Tay, *Law and Social Control* (London, 1980).

[28] Custody of Children Act 1839.

[29] *Sidney* v. *Sidney* (1865) 4 Sw & Tr 178.

[30] *Ashcroft* v. *Ashcroft* [1902] P 270; *Squires* v. *Squires* [1905] P 4.

the transmission and spread of norms of social behaviour. On the other hand, the province of instrumental law shifted from the laws governing the property and power relations of the rich to social security and tax law. The repressive, alienatory aspects of law as it touched family relations retreated and came to play a very residual and uncertain role. The power of the divorce courts to shut out petitioners whose moral lives did not meet judicial approval,[31] which had dwindled in practice, was removed in 1971.[32] With the eclipse of the doctrine of the matrimonial offence, the attempt of divorce law itself to spread normative standards was abandoned in favour of the simple instrumentality of no-fault divorce. The extent to which practices such as imprisonment for failure to pay maintenance or deprivation of parental status by removal of a child can be regarded as repressive rather than normative is open to debate.

(a) *The growth of normative law*

One of the most striking features of the development of modern family law is the way in which the law has become less concerned with the regulation of dealings between family members over time and more with the nature and quality of contemporaneous family relationships. Apart from the special considerations applicable to the poor, the first major indication that the law was beginning to apply to family life in a different way can be found in the gradual preference given to a surviving spouse over a deceased's kin or beneficiaries. The right of a surviving spouse to upset a will was first introduced in the modern common law by the New Zealand Testator's Family Maintenance Act of 1900. The principle was adopted in Victoria in 1906 and soon spread to the other Australian states. British Columbia adopted the principle in 1920.[33] In 1939 New Zealand extended this right to the case of intestate succession. Always more cautious, England conferred a similar right on the surviving spouse in 1938 in the case of testacy and in 1952 in that of intestate succession.[34] Glendon has noted an equivalent evolution in the United States,[35] which is seen as reflecting a preference for the surviving spouse

[31] The last important examples of the exercise of this discretionary power in England are reported in *King* v. *King* [1953] AC 125; *Godfrey* v. *Godfrey* [1965] AC 444; *Williams* v. *Williams* [1966] 2 All ER 614.

[32] Divorce Reform Act 1969.

[33] See J. Laufer, 'Flexible Restraints on Testamentary Freedom: A Report on Dependants' Family Maintenance Legislation' (1955) 69 *Harvard Law Rev.* 277.

[34] Inheritance (Family Provision) Act 1938; Intestates' Estates Act 1952. See now Inheritance (Provision for Family and Dependants) Act 1975.

[35] M. A. Glendon, *The New Family and the New Property* (Toronto, 1981), 23–8.

over the children. But this is to put the matter too simply. The movement represents a more profound change in ideology and economic ordering. Under the older dispensation, the children took as heirs, the legally defined channel through which political and economic status was maintained. Now the accumulation of family wealth is seen as potentially available for the enjoyment or security of all present family members who accordingly have a moral claim to it. The surviving spouse might have the dominant claim, but if dependent children remain in the family, the survivor will be expected to use the assets for their benefit. If the children are no longer dependent, the surviving spouse can expect to look to the asset build-up during marriage for his or her security in old age. The children must now fend for themselves. This represents a new ideology of family life, which may, it is true, derive from popular sentiment.[36] But in giving effect to these values, and so diverting wealth from the course it would have taken even if a married testator willed otherwise, the law has spread them throughout the population.

It took longer for the law to impose this ideology on spouses during their lifetimes. As long ago as 1895, New Zealand introduced a system of protecting the family home by registering it as a 'joint family home'. Thereafter, neither could dispose of it without the consent of the other. The home was also protected up to a certain value against the creditors of either spouse, though a court could order sale of the house and its protected value would then usually revert to the husband. Only in 1974 would this protected value be shared equally. Nineteenth-century 'homestead' legislation in the western provinces of Canada and some of the United States gave some protection against creditors. The reason was more the wish to stabilize the immigrant population by providing them with home-ownership which was safe from the claims of creditors (so that they could make a contribution to the growing economies) than to protect wives and promote values of family living. Only later was this homestead legislation linked to the policy of safeguarding the wife's occupation of the home. In England, a wife was not protected against *inter vivos* dealing by her husband with the matrimonial home until 1967, and this protection was achieved only by the clumsy device of registration.[37] But the argument is frequently made that the alienation of certain kinds of matrimonial property should be effective only if

[36] See Glendon's account of the surveys showing evidence of popular support for the claims of the surviving spouse: Glendon, 25–7.

[37] Matrimonial Homes Act 1967. This Act has generally been regarded as giving unsatisfactory protection, and the decision of the House of Lords in *Williams and Glyns Bank* v. *Boland* [1981] AC 487 extends the protection to some degree.

preceded by the agreement of both spouses.[38] These developments show how the law has been enlisted to stabilize the assumption that the property-owning spouse will, during his lifetime, use his property for the benefit of his contemporaneous family. But it is on divorce that we can best observe the strength of modern normative family law. For it is now increasingly usual for legal systems not merely to permit courts to reallocate the family assets between the partners on divorce, but to direct them to do so according to a norm of equality.[39]

How can we account for the spread of this ideology? One factor is undoubtedly the growing economic activity of married women, which may explain its early development in the Scandinavian countries. Nevertheless, the principle applies whether or not each spouse has been earning and in that sense made an economic contribution to the family's life. We must return to the assumption, to which reference was made earlier, that resources acquired by either or each of the adults will be available for the enjoyment of all family members. The payment of many welfare benefits, insurance entitlements, and the 'family wage' are all premissed on this assumption. But just as in previous centuries the expectation that membership of a family ensured participation in resources came to be undermined in the case of the poor, so now the growth of divorce among the better off has challenged these assumptions. It is surely the fact that so many divorced adults would otherwise be deprived of the long-term benefits of jointly accumulated family wealth that has led to the imposition of asset-sharing on divorce. It may not be possible to reintegrate a broken family, but the law will attempt to persuade (or compel) its members so far as possible to act in accordance with this assumption. There is another consideration to which we shall return. The democratic values of the twentieth century require (in principle) an equal share in society's resources for all citizens, a goal not to be frustrated by the failure of the citizen's family. The problems raised by these strategies will be considered in the concluding section of this essay.

Dramatic and significant as are these examples of normative law, they

[38] Law Commission, *Property Law: The Implications of Williams and Glyns Bank* v. *Boland*, Law Com. No. 115 (1982) 40–2.

[39] A full examination of different systems was made by the Ontario Law Reform Commission, *Study Prepared by the Family Law Project, Property Subjects*, ii (Toronto, 1967). See also the English Law Commission, Published Working Paper No. 42, *Family Property Law* (1975), Part 5. England and Australia are the only two major common-law jurisdictions which have not incorporated a norm of equality. Most Canadian provinces did this during the 1970s and New Zealand adopted it in 1980. See J. Eekelaar, *Family Law and Social Policy* (London, 1984), 105.

are exceeded by the development of legal and other institutional measures which affect the personal dynamics of family life. In the nineteenth century, it is true, a well-off woman who had suffered cruelty might obtain legal dispensation from her obligation to cohabit through divorce *a mensa et thoro* in the ecclesiastical courts and, latterly, full divorce, but only if the cruelty was coupled with adultery. Even for her, the social and economic consequences of seeking such relief must have been a significant deterrent. But the poor woman had to endure her lot. It was not until 1878 that a beaten wife could obtain from a court an order absolving her of her obligation to live with her husband (so that she could withdraw from him without losing her right, however flimsy, of support),[40] but even then she had to remain 'faithful' to him. Things have now greatly changed. In England, for example, the Domestic Violence and Matrimonial Proceedings Act of 1976 permits courts to expel the other spouse (or cohabitee) even if he owns the property. But legal regulation of the quality of life between adults is necessarily limited: for adults can, and to a large extent do, set their own limits of tolerance to domestic turmoil. The law responds (with a greater or lesser degree of efficiency) to cries for help. But children, especially very young children, cannot call in the law. If the law is to intervene here at all, it must be on the basis of externally imposed standards of behaviour. How does it do this?

The law has long been in one way or another concerned with children. We observed how, in earlier times, children were of significant actual or potential economic value to their parents, either as collaborators in family production or as agents for the transmission of family wealth. The concern of the law was to protect parents against possible diminution of their value by third parties. But children also attracted legal attention when they became a threat to economic or social stability. The children of the poor, or orphans, might swell the ranks of paupers; they might spread social dislocation. Thus Tudor poor laws, culminating in the Elizabethan Act of 1601, empowered justices to remove such children from destitute or vagrant parents, or to assume jurisdiction over poor orphans and apprentice them or otherwise 'set them to work'.[41] The urgency felt in the early nineteenth century about the growth of urban juvenile delinquency resulted in the creation of legal

[40] Matrimonial Causes Act 1878.

[41] I. Pinchbeck and M. Hewitt, *Children in English Society*, i (London, 1969); R. W. J. Dingwall, J. Eekelaar, and T. Murray, 'Childhood as a Social Problem: A Survey of the History of Legal Regulation' (1984) 11 *J. of Law and Society* 207.

powers to direct child beggars and vagrants to industrial schools and the eventual assimilation of these schools with reformatory schools under the dominant imperative that society should be protected from the threats posed by rootless children, *whether they had committed criminal offences or not.* Family and social factors may well have been perceived as contributing to these ills, but the legislation was not primarily directed towards improving the children's experience of their homes and wider environment. Rather, it was concerned with attempting to devise means whereby society might best protect itself from their consequences.

In 1889, however, a very significant step was taken. Under section 1 of the Prevention of Cruelty to and Protection of Children Act of that year it became an offence if anyone over sixteen who had custody, control, or charge of a boy under fourteen or a girl under sixteen wilfully ill treated, neglected, or abandoned the child in a manner likely to cause unnecessary suffering or injury to health. On conviction of the caregiver (usually the parent) the court could commit the child to the charge of a relative or anyone else willing to have the care of the child, and such a person would have 'like control over the child as if he were its parent . . . and the child shall continue to be under the control of such person, notwithstanding that it is claimed by its parents'. Concern was now decisively directed to the quality of the child's family life. The method of intervention, however, was by punishment. Conviction of the caregiver was a condition precedent to intervention. But too rigorous a pursuit of repressive law is unstable and only imperfectly achieves the growing normative ideal of this area of law. For how can we properly treat inadequate people as criminals? How are the children helped by the incarceration of their parents? Is the law to abandon its normative role unless extreme moral turpitude is present? In fact, the moral authoritarian basis for such intervention declined with the waning of Victorian Christian evangelicalism and began to give way to an overtly welfarist concern for the quality of the nation's stock. If the quality of life of the community is adversely affected by bad parenting, intervention is justified without reference to moral turpitude. In 1952, in England, the requirement that the caregivers be prosecuted was removed as a condition precedent for intervening on behalf of children believed to be in need of care or protection.[42]

[42] See J. Eekelaar, R. W. J. Dingwall, and T. Murray, 'Victims or Threats? Children in Care Proceedings' (1982) *J. of Social Welfare Law* 68.

In fact, as Donzelot has demonstrated, the liberal state had discovered a very effective means of transmitting its norms of family living to the general populace. Punishment began to be replaced by 'philanthropy', whereby the social and medical assistance provided to families became the route for the conveyance of these norms. Families became the subject of continual monitoring, a process significantly helped by state education and the development of psychoanalytically based social casework techniques. Inadequate families are 'helped', not punished, but on the state's terms. Donzelot sees its eventual outcome in a comprehensive system of state tutelage over families under which 'the family ceases to exist as an autonomous agency. The tutelary administration of families consists in reducing their horizon to supervised reproduction and in the automatic selecting-out of socializable minors.'[43] If we have reached that stage, we have surely reached the high water mark of the normative possibilities of law and administration. Family life, and therefore the foundation of social experience, is moulded to the image of the law and its agencies.

How far has this in fact happened? Many claim that sweeping child protection statutes coupled with intrusive social work intervention have seriously compromised family autonomy.[44] Without doubt, modern legal and administrative machinery has the potential to impose patterns of family behaviour upon the community and displace parental judgment about how their children should be socialized. Much legal writing has been directed to trying to devise formulas for diminishing this potential. When assessing the values at stake, it is important to discover the ideological framework within which the administrators of this system work. A recent study of English practice has suggested that it operates on the following assumptions: first, that the bringing up of children is primarily a parental, not state, responsibility; second, that parents naturally love their children and give priority to their welfare; third, that the presence of parental love will excuse a wide spectrum of behaviour which would, in the judgment of the supervising agency, otherwise adversely affect the child; fourth, that the presumption of parental love will only be defeated by strong evidence, usually of long-lasting behaviour patterns showing persistent refusal to advance the child's interests as opposed to those of the parent himself or herself; fifth, that, accordingly, parental explanations for the condition of

[43] Donzelot, op. cit. n. 25 above, 168.

[44] An outstanding plea for family autonomy is found in J. Goldstein, A. Freud, and A. H. Solnit, *Before the Best Interests of the Child* (New York, 1979).

children are prima facie accepted unless strong circumstantial evidence suggests the parent to be untrustworthy; and, finally, that the conviction that a parent does not put the child's interests first will justify coercive intervention.[45] Welfarism has thus reached a compromise with the claims of adult liberty and family autonomy. Adults may bring up their children with a wide measure of freedom. They are assumed to love them and to be committed to the principle of advancing their children's interests. Only if they act palpably contrary to these assumptions do they forfeit their ascribed role as socializers. We can conclude, therefore, that the role of child caregiving is delegated by the community to parents and is accordingly subject to potential scrutiny by the community and, ultimately, reversion to the community if the parent fails. The norm of promotion of the child's interests is entrusted to parents, subject to a right of revocation.

These modern developments surely indicate an exceptional degree of community involvement, through legal and other social institutions, in the quality of family living. How can one account for it? The answer, it is suggested, lies in the growth of democratic values and institutions. The democratic ideal embraces the whole of the community. Everyone is held entitled to participate in the community's wealth. Political and legal language talks of each citizen's 'rights'. The technological revolution of the twentieth century seemed to bring the satisfaction of those rights within potential realization. But at the same time social and economic forces undermined the ability of the family to realize these rights for its members. The growth of divorce in a society where economic power remains unequally distributed between men and women and where child-rearing remains fundamentally family-based has threatened the fair participation of women and children in economic resources. So ideology, reinforced by law, steps in and we begin to conceive of 'rights' of the homemaker and the child caregiver, which are deemed to be of equal worth (and accordingly entitled to equal economic recognition) to those of a major breadwinner. And the diminution of economic incentives to protect a family's children leaves 'natural love' as the major, but fragile, motivating force for parents to enhance the life-chances of their children. Once again, legally based ideology intervenes where this breaks down, and we speak increasingly of the 'rights' of children. The irony is that these democratic forces have led to what some have detected as antidemocratic restrictions of adult liberty, especially in

[45] R. Dingwall, J. Eekelaar, and T. Murray, *The Protection of Children: State Intervention and Family Life* (Oxford, 1983).

family living.[46] Certainly there is a conflict of values here. But this should not be presented as a conflict between good and evil but as competing conceptions of the good. If any is excluded, an important value is lost. There may be some optimal point where the values, in combination, achieve a result which best captures the aspirations of a democratic community. But the point is an elusive one. The line of compromise is likely to be controversial and subject to constant change.

(b) *Instrumental law*

The growth of democracy also accounts for the second major change of the law applicable to family living. For instrumental law no longer primarily concerns itself with the mechanisms of transmitting wealth and status among a dominant social group. Instead, it has become concerned with the allocation of resources within the community as a whole. The law of tax and social security is the twentieth-century equivalent of the instrumental laws of previous centuries—the laws of succession, strict settlements, and the ascendancy of the husband's rights. (This is not to say that such laws may not sometimes be used normatively—to instil new social values—or even repressively.) However, just as earlier instrumental law underwrote the economic and social system of former days, so present tax and social security law is premissed on economic and social assumptions about the organization of modern societies.

One such assumption is that, in receiving financial benefits, whether in the form of welfare payments or earned income, a family member normally acts as an agent for the benefit of the family as a whole. We observed earlier the extent to which normative law attempts to enforce this expectation. Instrumental law takes it for granted. Hence an adult woman, in receipt of supplementary benefit in England, will lose this entitlement on cohabiting with a man who is working full time. The practice may be criticized on the basis that it assumes and therefore perpetuates the economic dependence of women. On the other hand, if the assumption that cohabitation carries with it *de facto* distribution of the earnings of the man between the couple is usually correct, the basis for continuing supplementary benefit payments collapses. A similar problem arises in relation to the non-contributory invalid care allowance. This benefit is based on the assumption that the beneficiary has forsaken gainful employment in order to care for a severely disabled

[46] See especially C. Lasch, *A Haven in a Heartless World* (London, 1977); F. Mount, *The Subversive Family* (London, 1982).

person: yet it is not payable to married women or female cohabitees. The assumption, which is clearly ill founded, is that females within families normally stay at home anyway. Nevertheless, if it were true, the distinction could be justified on the ground that, if it were not made, most recipients would be receiving 'compensation' for a loss they did not suffer. If the payment were confined to those who actually gave up work to care for the invalid, a questionable distinction would be drawn between recipients. Perhaps such a benefit should be payable to *anyone* performing that function, irrespective of its implications for their employment, in which case the system would simply move further community resources into the family when it took over particular tasks (in this case invalid care) which would otherwise fall on the community. These points draw out the difficulties faced by instrumental law, which is simply the servant of prevalent social organization. If its assumptions are wrong, it will create severe distortion. If they are correct, the results might be unpalatable, but the cause lies in the social facts, not in the law. To ignore them could create severer anomalies. Instrumental law may well underwrite current social organization, but if society is to be changed, this should be through other agencies, other processes.

4. THE LIMITS OF SOCIAL CONTROL

It has been our argument that the most significant and most problematic developments in modern family law have been directed towards saving the family as a unit of resource distribution and primary child-rearing in the face of a progressive weakening in its structure. Family-based child care is today unstable child care. Paradoxically, the forces which impel the intervention of normative (and sometimes instrumental) law into family living are precisely those that have undermined its strength. For democratic principles have at the same time promoted adult interests, making almost universally available the option for either of the parents to leave the family and, by divorce, to create a new, legally recognized unit, and also generated awareness of the inherent rights of all children to an adequate upbringing. The attempt to reconcile this conflict has spectacularly failed. The evidence is overwhelming that the families of children broken by divorce suffer severe economic hardship which is likely to be significantly relieved only if the lone parent remarries. The reason is that the lone parent is normally the mother, and women's earnings are significantly lower than those of men. Thus that segment of the former family unit (mother and children) which had the highest calls on the family's income will now have available to it (if at all) the income of only one partner, and that the one with the weaker earning capacity. The consequences of this deprivation on the long-term welfare of the children are little understood and cannot in any case be fully known until the present generation of children affected by divorce reaches adulthood. But it is plausible to suppose that in a competitive world, childhood deprivations such as these may have adverse consequences for prospects in adult life. As for the mother, when her child-caring days are over, if she has not remarried, she pays the penalty of divorce by having to live in considerably reduced circumstances.[47] The attempt through private maintenance law or the modern forms of the poor law to alleviate the position by reasserting family responsibility counts for little, if indeed anything at all.

One possible strategy for providing for the casualties of the family-based child-care system is for the community, through instrumental law, to bear the whole cost of supporting both the one-parent family while children are being reared and the mother when this is finished. After all, it can be argued, the community saves by casting the primary burden of child care on families. While some western societies have been relatively generous in this respect, others have not. None has succeeded in redressing in full the economic loss caused by family breakdown. The cost in economic and political terms of high levels of public expenditure is regarded as too high, as was seen when the United Kingdom rejected the proposals of the Committee on One-Parent Families (the Finer Committee) (1974) for a 'guaranteed maintenance allowance' which would have brought all one-parent families up to the level of average male earnings. Nevertheless, policy-makers would do well to remember that the extent to which a family suffers by reason of loss of the major earner is mitigated to the extent that the community resources are in any event available to families, whether broken or not. In so far as housing, education, and medical care, for example, is provided by the community, the profundity of the loss is accordingly lessened.

What are the remaining options? One is to have recourse to the resources of the former partner. We have seen this approach in the principle of equal asset sharing on divorce. His earning capacity, if redirected to his former family, could provide a significant improvement of their living standards. Here normative law, like the old poor law,

[47] Eekelaar and Maclean, op. cit. n. 13.

attempts to reassert the demands of 'family responsibility'. This policy is at the heart of contemporary American moves to increase the effectiveness of the child support enforcement programmes. But a policy of this kind encounters two main obstacles. First, the process conflicts with the apparent assertion of individual freedom embodied in the rights to divorce and to enjoy one's property. Divorced men and their new partners are often said to resent this diversion of their earned income. Even the partnership ideology is open to challenge, especially if it is sought to share equally a wide range of property, particularly of a business nature, of wealthy individuals. The second obstacle is that, when these men do form new families, there are rarely sufficient resources from which they can support both sets of children. The problem of child support inevitably becomes enmeshed with the general poverty programme of the state.

A further option is to fall back on the earning capacity of the caregiving adult. This relieves the state and the other former partner. This appeal to self-sufficiency has been vigorously pursued in the United States and is taking hold in Canada and the United Kingdom. It was introduced, but with significant qualifications, in Australia in 1975 and was the fundamental orientation of New Zealand reforms in 1980 and English legislation in 1984. In these movements, we can again observe normative law at work. Support for a former spouse is not now to be ordered, under this principle, unless she (usually it will be the woman) has done all that is reasonable to become self-sufficient. The effect of such provisions will be felt not only on divorce but during marriage. For a prudent wife will try to take care that she does not allow her household or child-caregiving activities to inhibit too drastically her ability to earn. She may have to fall back on this resource should the marriage fail. Women are not to use marriage and homemaking as an escape from economic activity. Child caregiving should not exclude labour-force participation.

Will either of these two strategies solve the problem of the instability of contemporary family-based child care? It is unlikely. Resort to the resources of the former breadwinner is likely to be effective only, if at all, in the short term. Its effectiveness virtually disappears on his remarriage. The expectation that the former wife should mobilize her own earning power runs up against the rock of economic and social reality. Many women with children will be unable to reconcile child caregiving with full-time employment, even when the children are of school age. Part-time work has been shown to be a totally inadequate means of lifting these families much above poverty levels. The expectation collapses utterly in times of high unemployment.

In the case of family living, then, social control through law is hardly a success story. We may be tempted to adopt extreme positions; to abandon social control or to reassess the value of family life. But we should not reject a state of affairs on the ground that the whole comprises conflicts and contradictions. Just as every individual must confront conflicts of value and choose between them, so we can also expect contradictions within society. Indeed, their exposure is a sign of health, not weakness, for it makes us aware of the choices that are being made. *Perhaps* it would not be wise to trespass further on individual freedom in the pursuit of equity for children or mothers. There must surely be limits to intrusions into family autonomy for the protection of children. What would be the implications for economic policy either of substantially improving community services available to all families or of devoting more community resources to the casualties of broken families? Might not normative law be more appropriately applied to employment practice than to family living? Indeed, normative employment law has a long and largely successful history, which ranges from the regulation of the quality of employment to supervision over the terms of employment itself. Collins (chapter 4 above) goes further and argues for a movement from mere instrumental application of law to collective bargaining to the imposition of normative standards over employers and managers. Could not employment law transmit the expectation that both parents should be equally committed to the responsibilities of child care? Could not employment practice be required to permit their exercise? We might then be able to move more quickly than we can through equal pay or antidiscrimination legislation towards making the economic value of both sexes in employment more equal. Is our social organization prepared to undergo the compromises this would entail? Could normative law achieve such a result?

7

On 'The Critical Legal Studies Movement'*

J. M. FINNIS

I

THE Critical Legal Studies Movement is perhaps no more than a passing fashion. But one ought not to assess arguments by guessing whether they portend the wave of the future or a mere footnote for historians. And attention to the arguments of the movement can help us reflect on two of the permanent questions of legal theory: (i) Why is it illuminating to treat law as a social form which warrants a place in social theory's explanatory typology of social forms? (ii) What is the relation between the positivity of law, its ability to make obligatory now what was optional only a moment ago, and the principles or critically grounded requirements of plain practical reasonableness ('background principles')?

A preliminary remark about names. 'Critical Legal Studies Movement', like terms such as 'liberalism', 'conservatism', 'socialism', 'fascism', has no place in the language of critical social theory of legal study. It is a label chosen as an instrument of persuasion in political action within the academy. To point to the rationale of this label-choosing is not to make an adverse judgment; the choice concerned both the content and the method of legal education and thus bore directly on public life; and marshalling support for political action does need labels identifying proposals with sufficient brevity for collective deliberation (whether debate or conspiracy). Still, no one will simply take for granted that those who identify themselves by this label are really critical in method or have a clear conception of legal studies or belong to a movement fit to accomplish coherent goals by persuasion or other action. These are matters I shall not try to assess.

Rather, this essay pursues the two standing questions already mentioned, by critically reflecting upon a recent work of the most influential, philosphically adept, and historically and sociologically learned exponent of the Movement. Roberto Mangabeira Unger's 'The Critical Legal Studies Movement',[1] like his earlier books *Knowledge and Politics* (New York, 1975) and *Law in Modern Society* (New York, 1976), is rich in insight into the predicament of social theory and of those (including himself) whose intellectual stance and principle of self-interpretation includes the concern not merely to be intelligible to their contemporaries but actually to *be* modern men.

II

Unger introduces the Critical Legal Studies Movement as a movement critical of objectivism and formalism in legal thought, that is in the thinking of those who have to interpret the law and to remake it by the judicial techniques familiar in American and other common-law constitutional orders. By 'objectivism' he means 'the belief that the authoritative legal materials—the system of statutes, cases and accepted legal ideas—embody and sustain a defensible scheme of human association' (556). The critique of objectivism is said to be 'essentially the critique of the idea of types of social organisation with a built-in legal structure and of the more subtle but still powerful successors of this idea in current conceptions of substantive law and doctrine' (568). He identifies an 'insight required to launch the attack against objectivism—the discovery of the indeterminate content of abstract institutional categories like ... the market' (570).

One of the reasons for attending to Unger's work is to find ready material for a reflection on the contemporary incomprehension of the master thesis of classical legal theory, the thesis that in positive law we can find a mode of derivation of specific norms of action (that is of practical reasonableness) by an intellectual process which is not deductive and does involve free choice (human will) and yet is intelligent and directed by reason. This process Aquinas labelled *determinatio*. We might translate this by 'specification', 'concretization', or 'implementation'. His point is not securely made by any one word, but I shall hereafter use 'specification' to mean what he meant by *determinatio*. A simple example, to indicate his point, would be the process by which

[1] (1983) 96 *Harvard Law Rev.* 561–675. All otherwise unidentified parenthetical numbers, below, are page references to this article. Among the many themes of Unger's engaging article not touched on in my discussion are the organization of government and economy and the theory of 'equal protection of the law'.

architects give specificity or determinateness to building plans, in accordance with their commissions, such as the commission to build a maternity hospital for Oxford. Much can be understood by reflection on such an example.[2] But the process of specification in law has additional complexities which need to be identified, complexities derived from the fact that law works not in the order of making things (though it, of course, affects that order) but in the order of the *self*-constitution of human persons by *choosing* and doing in community with other *persons*.[3] Law shapes lives, not as a builder shapes a window-frame, but by rules which, even at their most precise, are only relatively specific guides to choice.

And even at their broadest, legal rules and principles are only *relatively* unspecific. In the passage just quoted from Unger, we see a first example of an ambiguity which is going to recur. He says that certain abstract institutional categories, such as 'the market', have an 'indeterminate content'. But what does he mean by 'indeterminate'? Formless, empty, and useless as a guide to practical reasoning and decision? Or are the notions to which he refers in fact notions which orientate and guide by calling for and suggesting further specifications—specifications whose content, however, is neither required by 'logic' nor rationally unconnected with the (partially) indeterminate notion with which we began? Not noticing this ambiguity and possibility, Unger fails to see that one might reasonably defend a set of rules and doctrines authoritatively established in the 'legal materials' (say, the current rules and doctrines of an Anglo-American law of contract), and defend them as 'embodying' and 'sustaining' a 'defensible' conception (say, of fair 'market' relationships), without claiming that, in all or even most respects, they are the uniquely reasonable rules and doctrines available for such embodiment and sustenance, or that such a conception is the only 'defensible' conception of a fair market.

To see, in principle, how this might be so (before seeing how it is so in a fragment of contract), consider the other target of the movement's critique: 'formalism'. Formalism is said to be the belief that there is 'a method of legal justification that can be clearly contrasted to open-ended disputes about the basic terms of social life ... The formalism I have in mind characteristically involves impersonal purposes, policies,

[2] See Aquinas, *Summa Theologiae* I–II, q. 95, a. 2; J. Finnis, *Natural Law and Natural Rights* (Oxford, 1980), 284–6, 294–5, 380.

[3] On the four 'orders' in which human life is lived, see Finnis, op. cit., 136–8; on the significance of choice as self-constitutive, see Finnis, *Fundamentals of Ethics* (Oxford, 1983), 139–42.

and principles as an indispensable component of legal reasoning.' (564.) 'An indispensable component': the other indispensable component(s) of legal reasoning, and the only component that could begin to 'contrast' legal with any other form of practical reasoning about social life, is carefully omitted by Unger here and virtually throughout: authority, the *fiat* of legislation, precedent, or custom, binding (though not absolutely) and determinative for legal reasoning (though not absolutely determinative) precisely because (though not only because) it has been *made* by relevant persons in relevant circumstances and because we need such exercises of authority to terminate disputes and resolve co-ordination problems both now and for the future consistently and fairly.[4] As has been seen, Unger does observe the existence of 'authoritative legal materials' (564, 577) or 'the constraints of institutional content' (572). But he never stops to ask what the authority of these 'materials' is, and what could explain it.

This failure to offer an explanation of the source of the authority of the posited rules and institutions of a political community is a weakness shared with the jurisprudence of Ronald Dworkin, a jurisprudence scornfully and not too scrupulously attacked by Unger as the 'hocus pocus' of the 'rights and principles school' (575). Dworkin's failure, to use his own terms, is a failure to do the relevant parts of political philosophy, in which, as he rightly says, jurisprudence is embedded. Unger's failure, in *his* own terms, is a failure to pursue thoroughly the typological analysis of social forms which he thinks is the legitimate successor to the largely discredited methods of classical political philosophy.[5]

Back to 'formalism'. Its vice, Unger says, is to regard the purposes, policies, and principles of 'the law' as 'indispensable' to resolve 'what would otherwise be incorrigible indeterminacy in the law' (579). Note 'indeterminacy' again, and observe in passing that, being resolvable, it cannot be *sheer* indeterminacy. Observe also: the formalist is supposed to think that the indeterminacy is 'corrigible' by reasoning; but Unger does not stay to explore how formalists suppose (as, by the definition of formalism, they must) that legal reasoning differs from 'open-ended' reasoning about 'the basic terms of social life'. (Whatever Unger may think, we may suspect that the difference has something to do with the

[4] See Finnis, 'The Authority of Law in the Predicament of Contemporary Social Theory' (1984) 1 *N.D.J. Law Eth. Pub. Pol.* 115–37.

[5] Unger, *Law in Modern Society* (New York, 1976), 43–5. On some relations between the problem of authority and the problem of the typology of social forms, see J. Finnis, 'On "Positivism" and "Legal Rational Authority"' (1985) 5 *Oxford J. of Legal Studies* 74–90.

authoritativeness, for *legal* reasoning, of the ways in which legislation and predecent specify modes of social co-operation.)

The link between objectivism and formalism, in Unger's account, is this. Formalist legal doctrines 'often included' a third level beyond the levels of (i) authoritative rules and precedents and (ii) ideal purposes, policies, and principles (579). This third level is the one with which objectivists, by definition, are concerned, the level of 'conceptions of possible and desirable human association to be enacted in different areas of social practice' (579). For 'just as the ambiguities of rules and precedents require recourse to imputed purposes or underlying policies and principles, so the ambiguities of these policies and principles can be avoided only by appealing to some background scheme of association . . .' (579). Thus, such third-level conceptions 'help make the entire body of law look intelligible and even justifiable' (578–9) by 'offer[ing] guidance about the relative reach and the specific content of the opposing principles and counter-principles which, as we shall see, are supposed to settle provisionally what would otherwise be pervasive ambiguities in the more concrete legal materials' (619).

Notice the claim: third-level ideals 'make the law look intelligible and justifiable'. But 'justifiable', in Unger's usage, hovers between 'not unjustified, not unreasonable, not wrongful' and 'required by reason, rationally necessary'. By overlooking the ambiguity, Unger insinuates what he never clearly affirms, that dominant (that is, pre-'critical', 'objectivist', and 'formalist') legal doctrine proceeds on the unwarranted belief that the third-level conceptions of possible and desirable association both (i) necessitate or require the pursuit of *this* rather than *that* particular second-level purpose, policy, or principle and *these* particular first-level rules, and (ii) are themselves necessary, that is, are conceptions of what forms of association are uniquely desirable (see, for example, 579, 633).

Unger's own conception of 'critical' legal doctrine retains the three levels. In plainly affirming this, he also affirms that the revised third level will still 'assign distinct models of human association to different sectors of social practice', on the basis that different 'kinds of human association . . . can and should prevail in different areas of social life' (619, 649). It remains simply unclear how the methodological relationships between the levels of 'critical' legal doctrine will differ from those between the supposed three levels of existing doctrines. Unger says little more than that in the 'critical' view, 'no one scheme of association has conclusive authority' and there is a process of 'mutual correction of abstract ideals and their institutional embodiments' (580). Pre-critical scholars will discern no novelty here. Unger, however, believes that they (wrongly) suppose the set of models of human association to be 'given' and 'rigidly defined' and 'natural' (633). It is time to see how he tries to show this by an examination of contract doctrine.

III

Unger's showpiece of critical legal doctrine is, in fact, his lengthy study of certain rules and principles of current Anglo-American law of contract. It aims to show two things. First, that current legal doctrine hides the relationship between its second-level principles and the controlling third-level conceptions of desirable forms of human association, and that those third-level conceptions remain uncriticized, uncorrected, and falsely supposed to be 'given' and 'rigidly defined' (prior to their embodiment in legal principles, rules, and institutions). Second, that in current doctrine, the second level consists of principles and counter-principles, the latter being only grudgingly admitted and marginalized by the principles which tend to extend 'imperialistically' to all social life (619).

So: 'The structure of reigning ideas about contract . . . can be stated with the greatest possible simplicity, in the form of two pairs of principles and counter-principles' (619). The first principle is 'that of the freedom to enter or to refuse to enter into contracts. More specifically, it is the faculty of choosing your contract partners' (619). And its counter-principle is: 'the freedom to choose the contract partner will not be allowed to work in ways that subvert the communal aspects of social life' (620). One should be uneasy about these formulations. The counter-principle is stated in a predictive or descriptive, not a normative form. Worse, the principle is never stated by Unger in other than a broken-backed form: 'the principle of freedom to enter . . .; the faculty of choosing your partner . . .'. And though Unger seems to lose sight of the freedom not to contract at all, what his formulations intend, I suppose, is something like: 'each person is to be free of obligations purportedly imposed upon him by the agreements of other persons between themselves; correspondingly, no one has the power to impose, by agreement with another, obligations on one who does not agree to them'. Unger's carelessness about the formulation of a principle is a small sign of his deep misunderstanding of the role of principle in practical thinking.

You would also be right to suspect that a principle as negative in form and content as the principle of freedom to contract is rather unlikely to extend imperialistically to all of social life. And, in the event, Unger takes the principle, its proper formulation and its intended range of application entirely for granted, and focuses instead on 'manifestations' (620) of the *counter*-principle that freedom to choose the contract partner will not be allowed to work in ways that subvert the communal aspects of social life.

The first manifestation is said to be the rules of law which, he says, 'operate to prevent the principle of freedom to contract from tracing the limits of liability so rigidly and narrowly that the fine texture of reciprocities is left entirely unprotected' (620–1). These rules include rules imposing liability 'whether contractual or delictual' (620) based on occupancy of a status or exercise of a profession, rules or supposed rules of promissory estoppel, and the rules of quasi-contract for restitution on unjust enrichment. Now, to treat these rules as manifestations of a counter-principle at work within the law of contract makes sense only on the extraordinary assumption that the 'principle' of freedom to contract is taken as asserting that one has no legal liabilities at all other than contractual (that is, those one has freely agreed to)—an assertion very remote from the legal systems Unger is discussing, even if not altogether remote from some nineteenth- and twentieth-century theories of contract.[6]

Still, Unger's treatment of those rules was intended to be no more than fleeting, and he passes on to 'the most instructive application of the counter-principle . . . the rules of contract law that discourage contract-making in non-commercial settings' (621). His example of such rules is 'the norms that govern the interpretation of the intent to contract' (621). These norms he presents as three levels of rules (analogous in structure to, but not to be confused with, the three levels of legal doctrine).

On the first level is the rule that a declaration of intent to be legally bound may be unnecessary (and is unnecessary where the parties are 'devoting themselves to self-interest in the harsh business world' (621)), and that a declaration of intent not to be bound at law may be

[6] Of course, at various times, theoretical writers have claimed that delict and contract are the only sources of obligation in common law: see, e.g., West's *Symboleographie* ((1590) 1647), pt. I, s. 3. But this (to speak only of recent centuries) never accommodated either obligations arising from status or those arising from the seventeenth- and eighteenth-century extensions of *indebitatus assumpsit*—to say nothing of Equity's supplementations of the common law.

effective. On the second level is a rule which 'guides and qualifies the interpretation of the first-level one': that 'whenever possible', intention is to be construed 'in a manner that protects justified reliance and reads the parties out of a situation in which they stand at each other's mercy' (621): the exclusion of liability will in such situations be interpreted as narrowly as possible. And on the third level is a rule which 'limits the scope of both the first-level and second-level ones' (621). It qualifies the second-level rule by determining that 'in non-commercial contexts', an intent to exclude liability is *not* to be construed as narrowly as possible. And it qualifies the first-level rule by determining that 'in family life or friendship the presumption of intent to be legally bound [is reversed]' (621).

This grand structure of three levels of rules is illusory. The so-called third-level qualification of the first-level rule is no more than a component of that complex rule, a component required to state it fully, by some such formula as: 'Business deals are presumed to be intended to have legal effect; family or friendship arrangements are presumed not to be intended to have legal effect.' The separation of this fairly straightforward rule into two different levels has a rhetorical function: to draw attention to the alleged manifestation of the counter-principle, so that 'the principle' is depicted as the principle of a business or commercial realm of contract, while the counter-principle is depicted as 'defend[ing] private community against the disruptive intervention of the law', that is the law that flows (on Unger's loose assumptions) from the principle of freedom to contract. As he says, 'classical contract theory claims to describe and seeks to define [a form of life]—an existence separated into a sphere of trade supervised by the state and an area of private family and friendship largely though not wholly beyond the reach of contract' (623). Now this important thesis about a distinction between spheres of social life, such that one sphere (family and friendship) is treated as largely beyond the reach of legal contract, is hardly reconcilable with Unger's general thesis that in current, pre-critical doctrine the principles are 'dominant' over the counter-principles, which are 'pressed to the corner' and treated as 'mere ad hoc qualifications to the dominant principles' (569). Nor is the spheres-of-social-life thesis easily reconcilable with the most striking fact about nineteenth- and twentieth-century contract theory: that its rules and principles are expressed with great generality, no distinction being made between types of party (such as trader, consumer, friend, relative) or of transaction (in corresponding terms); and that many of its leading cases[7] concern agreements between relatives, friends, or acquaintances in relationships of a sort that can only extravagantly be described as 'trade', let alone 'the pitiless world of deals' (635).

Still, we should look more closely at the working-out of the thesis that the law distinguishes sharply between spheres of social life. For the central claim of the Critical Legal Studies Movement, on Unger's account of it, is that conceptions of desirable human association can retain their controlling 'third-level' status in legal thinking without being conceived, as at present they supposedly are, as 'given', 'natural', or 'rigidly defined'. So: classical theory, according to Unger, involves a 'polemical opposition of contract to community' (625), 'stark opposition of community as selfless devotion and contract as unsentimental money-making' (641), between 'a conception of community as an idyllic haven of harmony, and contract, as a realm of unadulterated self-interest and pure calculation' (644), with 'the practical result ... [of leaving] inadequately supported the subtle interdependencies of social life that flourish outside the narrow zone of recognized community' (625).

Thus, what is wrong with pre-critical doctrine, according to Unger, is its rigid, polemical opposition, at the third level, between two forms of human association, the world of commerce conceived as devoid (in fact, in conception, and thus in law) of mutual responsibility, and the world of private community, whose 'prime instance' is 'the nineteenth century bourgeois family or its diluted successor' (623).

To make his contrast plausible, Unger must introduce the family as 'subordinat[ing] the jealous defence of individualistic prerogative to the promotion of shared purpose and the reinforcement of mutual involvement' (624) in a 'flexible give-and-take that contract law ... would disrupt' (623). But the family unbalances Unger's type-casting. Within a page his depiction of this social type has taken a contradictory form: 'the whole view of family beyond contract depends upon the interaction between an impoverished conception of community and a narrow view of law in general and contract in particular. The conception of community defines communal life largely negatively, as the absence of

[7] Consider e.g., *Chichester* v. *Cobb* (1866) 14 LT 433; *Clarke* v. *Dunraven* [1897] AC 59; *De La Bere* v. *Pearson* [1908] 1 KB 280 (the relation between a newspaper reader and the editor who offers advice is scarcely commercial); *Felthouse* v. *Bindley* (1862) 11 CBNS 869; *England* v. *Davidson* (1840) 11 Ad & El 856 (offer of reward); *Lampleigh* v. *Brathwait* (1615) Hob 105; *Roberts* v. *Gray* [1913] 1 KB 520 (contract for education); *Shadwell* v. *Shadwell* (1860) 9 CBNS 159; *Thomas* v. *Thomas* (1842) 2 QB 851; *Williams* v. *Cawardine* (1833) 5 C & P 566; *Wilson* v. *Wilson* (1848) 1 HL Cas 538.

conflict.' (625.) 'Absence of conflict'? Or 'promotion of shared purpose ... mutual involvement ... and flexible give-and-take'?[8]

And what about the other social form, the market, a 'devolution of practical life to the harshest self-interest' (622), excluding even a 'partial reconciliation between the competing claims of self-interest and attachment to other people' (623), a realm of 'equality of distrust', and so forth? This depiction overlooks vast tracts of law. We have already observed Unger's neglect of the bodies of law outside contract, such as tort and restitution, which, though not treated as contractual, are treated by the law as applicable and even primarily applicable to the world of commerce. It is now time to take into account the rules of law considered by Unger as subsumed under the second pair of principle/counter-principle.

IV

The second of the two principles governing the law of contract is freedom *of* contract, stated by Unger in, at last, a proper form: 'the parties must be free to choose the terms of their agreement. Save in special cases, they will not be second-guessed by a court, not at least as long as they stay within the ground rules that define a regime of free contract' (625). And the second counter-principle, supposedly marginalized in pre-critical law and doctrine, is 'that unfair bargains should not be enforced'. As Unger says, 'Fairness means not treating the parties, and not allowing them to treat each other, as pure gamblers unless they really see themselves this way and have the measure of equality that enables each to look out for himself.' (632.) Thus, for example, a contract made by one party under the economic duress of a party possessing significantly superior bargaining power can be treated as voidable by the weaker party. Or again, where a contract is frustrated by unforeseen circumstances, the modern law provides for a mutual adjustment of losses which Unger somewhat grandly describes as each party insuring the other against mistakes and misfortunes falling outside

[8] Of course, Unger has earlier claimed (op. cit. n. 5 above, 144) that, in 'liberal society', 'familial relationships are abandoned to the exploitation of power advantages within the family under the guise of respect for the integrity of the family group', so that 'the impersonality of the public realm and the communal character of the private one are always changing positions'. That has some plausibility as an observation on the *effect* of liberal legal doctrines. What has no plausibility is that those legal doctrines are flagrantly self-contradictory, as they would be if they were what Unger claims in 'The Critical Legal Studies Movement'.

the limited and discriminate risks defined by the contract (including its unspoken presuppositions) (632). Such a 'mutual insurance' amounts, as Unger says, to treating the contracting parties as if they were in a kind of partnership or joint enterprise—a kind of community. To this extent, as Unger rightly says, the second counter-principle, requiring fairness, intersects with (that is, reinforces) the first counter-principle.

Unger's point, now, is that in pre-critical law and doctrine, operating in a society where gross inequalities of bargaining power exist, what restrains the counter-principle of fairness from 'running wild' and correcting almost every contract (629) is the drawing of 'unstable, unjustified and unjustifiable lines ...' (629). But do we not find here the perennial sophistic complaint that wherever any line is drawn by law, 'for every situation corrected, there seems to exist another similar to it that is left untouched' (633), so that the line itself is arbitrary and thus unjustifiable and thus unjustified, that is, ripe for subversion? Those who accept this refuse to acknowledge the rationality of what I have called 'specification' (illustrated in section II, above). They cannot fix a speed limit or a scale of taxation, or divide examinees into first, second, and third class ...

And the further question, in relation to Unger's own enterprise, is whether he shows that in drawing its lines, the law is guided by some ideal of the market, an ideal stateable at a third level, that is, prior to and independent of the (counter-) principles of fairness and equality which work at the second level. To answer this question, we can look at Unger's claim that the Critical Legal Studies Movement has a counter-vision of contract based on a counter-vision of the market, yielding not a competing concern within a shared conceptual framework of contract law, but rather a new conceptual framework. Unger offers to illustrate his notion of a 'struggle between conceptual frameworks' by examining the progress of such struggle in areas of 'exemplary difficulty' in existing legal doctrine. His chosen examples are some problems concerned with mistakes made in the process of forming a contract.

Suppose that a contract is being negotiated not face to face or by telex but by correspondence, and one party changes his mind about the offer or counter-offer he has made, or about the acceptance he has sent off to the offeror, and so tries to revoke his offer or counter-offer or acceptance. A contract, once formed, cannot of course be simply revoked by one party. So the question is: precisely when is the contract irrevocably formed? And precisely when does the purported revocation take effect if it can take effect? Unger notes that the classic and current

Anglo-American contract doctrine refuses to distinguish, for these purposes, between innocent and wrongful (purported) revocations. The explanation for this, he says, is that such problems arise in a 'fully commercial context', in which the parties are engaging in 'pure gambles beyond the reach of the counter-principles of community and fairness' (643). Alternatively, he acknowledges that the current doctrine considers the relevant distinctions in the moral quality of the conduct of the revoking party to be 'too fine and fragile to serve as useful bases' (634) for rules about formation and revocation.

His 'critical' legal doctrine proposes, on the other hand, to reverse the relations between principle and counter-principle, under the guidance of a counter-vision of human association. It therefore proposes to distinguish between wrongful revocations, which will be treated as ineffective, and innocent revocations, which may be effective even after the contract itself has come into existence. And what is the proposed distinction? Wrongful revocations are those attempted 'because of afterthoughts about the profitability of the deal or changes in market conditions supervening upon the dispatch of the acceptance'. Innocent revocations are those made 'to correct a mistake that does not concern business judgment', for example 'faulty calculations or . . . a misapprehension of what [one] has agreed to do' *including* 'negligent' miscalculations and misapprehensions, and an 'ordinary' measure of imprudence (634–5, 638). And then, where the revocation is in that sense 'innocent', 'the losses ought to be divided between the offeror and the offeree according to the degree of the [revoking party's] negligence and even the comparative ability of the parties to bear the loss' (636). Comparative ability when? And which losses? Objections to Unger's proposal will spring to mind.

Unger's proposal asks A to 'insure' B in relation to the very matter over which B has exclusive control, that is over B's own conduct in making his calculations about the content of the obligations, costs, and benefits he is proposing to contract for. But as to external market conditions, affecting price, profit, feasibility of performance, and so on, each 'party' is treated as a self-insurer, a high-risk gambler, simply because these are, according to Unger, 'business judgments'. Here is a distinction which *does* seem arbitrary, not because it draws a line between 'similar situations', but because it is groundless or wrong in principle.

And if one makes this objection, one is surely not participating in the advertised 'struggle between conceptual frameworks'. Rather one is pointing out that Unger is just using, ineptly, an existing conceptual framework—a framework which does, in various contexts, take account of negligent and wrongful conduct, and which in other contexts takes account of that sort of autonomous responsibility for one's own affairs which Unger calls high-risk gambling; and that he is doing so without regard to the costs of unpredictability and of the extensive litigation required to settle, *ad hoc*, the relation between such incommensurables as 'degrees of negligence' and 'ability to bear the loss'.

Contract law has to grapple, in any case, with complex situations. Consider, for example, another of Unger's 'exemplary instances', a variant on the preceding case. A careless tenderer for a sub-contract discovers his carelessness, and seeks to revoke his bid before it has been accepted but after the general contractor has become bound to the client on terms which presupposed the tendering sub-contractor's original bid. No need to go into the details of Unger's discussion and proposal, which share the weaknesses of his earlier discussions. Notice only the fact, which he records but glides past: pre-critical contract doctrine makes the legal solution turn on the question whether the general contractor knew or had reason to know or suspect that the sub-contractor's bid was predicated on a miscalculation; for if he did have this knowledge, suspicion, or ground for suspicion, he cannot hold the sub-contractor to the bid, despite his own costly reliance on that bid (637). Unger is bound to glide past this, for it illustrates the principle of fairness already embodied in a body of law which he wrongly treated as sponsoring 'harshest self-interest', 'high-risk gambling', and so on.

Should we not rather say that existing contract law and doctrine is rich in concern for moral principles of fairness and can expand or contract its specification of those principles without engaging in any struggle between conceptual frameworks? The competition, which no one thinks can be resolved by deduction, is between such considerations as excluding the unfairness of taking advantage of another's mistake; the unfairness of defeating actual reliance; the unfairness of submitting the relations between parties with many diverse interests to the indefinite delay and unpredictability and incidental waste of litigation necessitated by rules which are indefinite because formulated in *terms* of 'fairness'; and so on.

Unger is aware of the latter problem. He confronts the objection that there is a 'need to choose between a ready but crude generality [in the legal rules] and a subtle but painstaking and uncertain particularism, with its potentially invasive probing of the springs of conduct and the nuances of moral discrimination' (642). This formulation of the objection to his counter-vision rather overdoes the concern about invasiveness and underplays the concern about certainty, predictability, consistency, and finality. Anyway, he parries it in two ways.

First, he says it is 'often' advanced as a cover for an 'ideological' attempt to 'confine to a narrow range of situations the idea of contract as a common enterprise animated by mutual loyalty' (642–3). Maybe. But the problems of early certainty about the rights and liabilities of the 'parties' remain real problems, quite apart from ideology. And it also remains that the question in issue was precisely whether there is yet a contract to which the parties ought to be loyal, or only an uncompleted negotiation.

His second parry points out that his own counter-vision itself accommodates some 'brightline' rules of contract of 'the classical form' in 'special cases'. He does not stay to consider whether, and how, there can be a (in his sense) non-arbitrary and 'justifiable' 'bright line' between 'special cases' of this sort and other situations where the critical legal doctrine is going to authorize courts to impose obligations and create entitlements in ill-defined ways unrecognized by pre-critical contract law.

V

The key move in Unger's 'critical' strategy is a fallacy. For it is a fallacy to assert that 'bright lines', that is definite rules—such as those in contract which are so formulated as to refer only to events, times, states of mind, and so on, and not at all to reasonableness or fairness or *ex post facto* ability to pay—could be justified only if there were a bright line, a 'stark contrast' (644), between ideals of human association, say between community and commerce, between family (or friendship) and the market.

On the contrary, the case for bright lines at the first level of rules is best made on the basis that the ideals of human association are related one to another in the way indicated by Aristotle's analogy of *philia*, friendship, which extends, in differing but related forms, from the central case of friendship to the friendship of fellow players, communal good neighbourliness (*philia politike*), and friendly accommodations and demarcations in business and competition.[9] And what is the substance of these lines of analogy or relationship between forms of association as

[9] See Aristotle, *Nicomachean Ethics* VIII, 2, 1155^b 17–20; 3–4: 1156^a 6–1157^b 6; Finnis, op. cit. n. 2 above, 139–44, 157–8.

different as 'real' friendship and business friendship? It consists surely in the fact that each of these forms of association exemplifies the basic human good of community and that each is structured, though in differing ways, by common principles of fairness, honesty, and responsibility.

Indeed, the realm of commerce as envisaged in the law of contract is a realm in which the mutual obligations are not only controlled by the side-constraints of fairness but are actually grounded on fairness and on the common benefits made available by respect for undertakings; and these principles of fairness and common good are not different from the principles of fairness and common good which structure forms of interdependence and loyalty *not* involving the deliberate undertaking of mutual obligations by mutual promises.[10] They are principles which have a claim and a bite more or less independently of any descriptive or ideal typology of forms of human association.

Unger does not understand the moral underpinnings of existing, pre-critical contract law and theory. According to him, it is only his counter-vision that 'treats the counter-principles of community and fairness as possible generative sources of the entire body of law and doctrine, [and] finds the standard source of obligations in the only partly deliberate ties of mutual dependence...' (569). According to him, pre-critical doctrine sees the counter-principles of community and fairness 'as mere ad hoc qualifications to the dominant principles, [and] identifies the fully articulated act of will and the unilateral imposition of a duty by the state as the two exhaustive sources of obligation' (569; compare 597, 639). In other words, before the Critical Legal Studies Movement, everyone was a voluntarist or a positivist.

A glance at the pre-critical discussions of the obligation of promises in Charles Fried's work[11] or mine[12] will correct that impression. And a fair assessment of the existing law will show what I have already indicated; first, that pre-critical doctrine treats contract as only a fraction of the legal universe, a universe abounding in duties of compensation, of restitution, of trust and fiduciary obligation...; and second, that the law of contract itself is shot through with conceptions of honesty and fair dealing and with public policies supported but not merely invented by the state.

10 Finnis, op. cit. n. 2 above, 298–307.

11 C. Fried, *Contract as Promise: A Theory of Contractual Obligation* (Cambridge, Mass., 1981), 13–17.

12 Finnis, op. cit. n. 2 above, 299, 303–8, 320–5, 344–6.

The case for having a brightline rule, such as that preventing revocation of a contract once formed but allowing free revocation of offer, counter-offer, or acceptance until the moment of formation, is a case which does not at all rest on the superstition that an act of will has some normative significance on its own or when linked with another, contemporaneous act of will. Nor does the case rest on the absurd thesis that contract, being commerce, is part of a distinct form of human association in which harshest self-interest must be allowed to flourish without the restrains of community or fairness. It is a case which points partly to the advantages to all of a 'business efficacy' enhanced by clarity and stability of expectations at each stage of conceiving and conducting a business venture; partly to the unfairness typically occasioned to third parties whenever a contract is revoked or invalidated; partly to the risks of unfairness occasioned by rules which encourage perjury; and partly to the waste, misery, and unfairness of having to leave disputes to the hazards of litigation and palm-tree justice, instead of solving them with brisk efficiency, months or years earlier, by pointing to the relevant brightline rule in the 'rule-book'.

To say this is not to say that this case is so overwhelming that reform of the law in the directions suggested by Unger and others would be irrational or unreasonable. The existing brightline rules, even where reasonable, are not *deductions* from the principles of fairness and community of which they are specifications. It is Unger who is the absolutist, that is to say the disappointed methodological absolutist, who, not finding deduction, proclaims that the movement of legal thought from his two higher levels (which I have been arguing are really but one complex, higher level) to the first-level rules is a movement 'flawed' (580, 615, 647), 'confused' (570), 'arbitrary' (577, 633), 'unjustifiable', and even 'unjustified' in (he hints) the strongly negative sense of demonstrably wrong. Most of the time—and when criticizing others, always[13]—he overlooks the distinctive reasonableness of specification. Architects, musicians, legislators, and jurists specify and particularize general ideals, commitments, and principles, by steps none of which is itself necessary and all of which could reasonably have been in some respect different—so that there is, in these myriads of instances, no uniquely correct solution. Yet all these steps are reasonable (when

[13] Cf. op. cit. n. 1 above, 615, where, in relation to his own proposed doctrine, Unger acknowledges that 'at each crucial juncture' in the steps from higher to lower levels 'different conclusions might reasonably be drawn'; his normal assumptions, however, are displayed on p. 571: 'it would be strange if the results of a coherent, richly developed normative theory were to coincide with a major portion of any extended branch of law'.

things are being done well), and none could without risk of *error* have been taken randomly or without regard to coherence with the larger whole constituted both by the initial general idea or ideas of value, commitment, or principle and by the steps already taken.

It is this requirement of coherence—of the integrity of the system both as a set of rules and principles extending analogously over many different but comparable forms of relationship and transaction, and as a set of interrelated institutions (such as a hierarchy of courts, themselves more or less subject to legislatures)—that distinguishes legal thought from 'open-ended' practical reasoning: 'formalism', if you will; fairness, 'due process and equal protection of law', and systematic integrity, if one wants more accurate labels. This is a form of that loyalty of officials—say, judges and even legislatures—to their own previously settled and announced standards, that fidelity which Lon Fuller rightly made the feature which distinguishes law from managerial direction, i.e. from the bureaucratic rule to which Weber had more or less assimilated it.

VI

Specification is a matter of practical reasoning, whose premisses are *normative* principles: the understood basic forms of human goods and the normative requirements of one of those goods, practical reasonableness. Like Anthony Kronman's positivist,[14] though with a different animus, Unger's Critical Legal Studies Movement uncritically supposes that norms and obligations can be justified simply by pointing to *facts* about the present or the past. Obligations, he says in his set-piece account of the 'premisses' of his counter-vision, 'arise primarily from relationships of mutual dependence that have been only incompletely shaped by state-imposed duties or explicit and perfected bargains' (639). The context makes clear that the vague phrase 'arise primarily from' is meant to do the work of 'are justified primarily by reason of...'.

But when is interdependence a good to be maintained, and when had it better be moderated or superseded by relative autonomy or by other forms of interrelationship? When is interdependence no more than parasitism, and what distinguishes parasitism from the honourable dependence of the infant, the unborn, the insane, the infirm? Unger does not seem to ask.

Indeed, the content of the counter-vision, of the forms or ideals of

[14] A. Kronman, *Max Weber* (London, 1983), 55 and *passim*; Finnis, op. cit. n. 5 above, 80–4.

human association to be encouraged by the movement, remains almost wholly negative. (The counter-vision now in question goes far beyond the counter-vision of contract; it is the movement's vision of social life *tout court*.) The individual is to be 'freed from the tyranny of abstract social categories'.

> The search for the less conditional and confining forms of social life is the search for a social world that can better do justice to a being whose most remarkable quality is precisely the power to overcome and revise, with time, every social structure in which he moves. (584–5)

A really critical student will have two reflections on this. First, one will reflect that the truly dependent had better look fearfully to their future when they hear these proposals to overcome every abstract social category and every social structure. For what is the aspiration and reality that Aristotle named the Rule of Law,[15] and what are the legal structures of fair trial, or of the 'welfare' rights to food and water, or of the right not to be deliberately killed, but abstract social categories and structures to be 'overcome'? The world envisaged (or at least spoken of) by the movement is not a world for children.

Second, one will reflect that the fundamental programme of the movement—of introducing a society in which 'social life makes available in the course of ordinary politics and existence the instruments of its own revision' (662)—is at war with Unger's own proposed revision of contract law on the basis of the 'counter-principles' of fairness and community. For fairness and community are conceived by him precisely as extending (not revising, breaking down, remaking, or overcoming) the interdependencies and mutual obligations of persons—obligations which, indeed, he subsumes under the name of loyalty (for example, loyalty between parties to be supposedly pre-contractual negotiation). But is not *loyalty* a strange name on the lips of those dedicated to the permanent revision of all confining social structures, all schemes of division and hierarchy? For what is contract but a device for deliberately creating obligations backed by the coercively confiscatory power of the state, for creating restrictions (on the freedom of the parties thereafter), for creating divisions (between those subject and those not subject to the obligations thus created), and for creating a kind of hierarchy (between the party who—at least legally—is dominant, because he has the unsatisfied right, and the party with the unperformed obligation . . .)?

As Unger seems to admit, his movement has no 'proposal about how

[15] *Politics* III, 10, 1286ᵃ 9.

to reconcile freedom with other ends' (662). It rests uncritically content to ignore that problem of reconciliation, or at least to put off indefinitely the task of identifying and living out those 'other ends'. I say 'uncritically' because the value of freedom, which the movement affirms, is arbitrarily exempted from its denial of objective human goods. The exemption is disguised by careful choice of words:

> if the central tradition of modernism is to be believed, nothing lies on the further side of blind constraint ... but a confrontation with the real and anguishing sense of freedom itself. ... [But] freedom, to be real, must exist in lasting forms of life; it cannot merely exhaust itself in temporary acts of context smashing. (660, 661)

Here the words 'real', 'must', and 'cannot' can conceal the affirmation of a good and the proposal to avoid an evil: a life of context smashing is not a good life ... is worthless ...

Note the assumption Unger has laid bare: '... if the central tradition of modernism is to be believed ...'. A genuinely critical social theorist will ask a few questions before believing the central tradition of anything. He might begin by asking whether Unger has offered good reasons for denying that there are any objective human goods. And he will find that Unger has offered four reasons; two of them are contradicted by himself and the other two rest on the characteristic modern failure to examine the possibility that the requirements of practical reasonableness, while ruling out a few classes of action (and thus making possible an acknowledgement of a few fully specific human rights not to be treated in certain ways), for the rest have a directive quality, far short of specifying a unique set of individual or social commitments, yet far richer than emptiness. 'To affirm objective human goods is to affirm that the mind can grasp and establish moral essences .. But this has never been shown, and the conception of reason on which it rests has been discredited in nonmoral areas of thought.'[16] But this talk of 'essences' is no more than alarmist conjuring with a word half-forgotten and sure to be misunderstood. What is actually at stake is no more and no less than the question whether the mind can understand anything and hold and communicate some definite meaning to define and express what it understands; and the 'what it understands' is no more and no less an 'essence' in thought about human good than it is in thought about geometry, biology, chemistry, or particle physics. Unger's denial of

[16] R. M. Unger, *Knowledge and Politics* (New York, 1975), 77.

essence is contradicted by many of his own affirmations, not least his acknowledgement that there is a human nature.

Equally self-contradictory is Unger's claim that 'the doctrine of objective value falsely teaches us to forget the connection between what is good for us and what we are'.[17] For he had himself, in the same book, acknowledged that 'the conception of objective value [proposes that we think] of . . . norms of conduct as ends whose fulfillment would bring our worthiest capacities to their richest development . . .'.[18] As Aquinas does not tire of saying (but is often not *heard* to say), we come to know our nature (what we are) by coming to know what are our capacities, and these we come to know by understanding what we do (our actions), and these we understand by understanding their point, their ends, the goods that they realize and participate in.[19]

Unger's third charge is that a theory of objective goods 'degenerates into either meaningless abstraction or unwarranted parochialism'.[20] With this one can and should be brisk. The charge could only be established by someone who participates in specific discussions of particular goods, particular requirements of practical reasonableness, and particular specifications of those goods and requirements in the commitments of an individual life-plan or the institutional structures and practices and legal rules and principles of a given community. Unger, for the most part, omits to engage in such discussions; his discussion of the current rules and principles of contract does not encourage confidence in his claim that there is no middle ground between meaningless abstraction and unwarranted parochialism.

Finally, and I think most near to his own heart, is the contention that the 'doctrine' of objective human goods 'denies any significance to choice other than the passive acceptance or rejection of independent truths. Our experience of moral judgment, however, seems to be one of at least contributing to shape the ends we pursue. A conception that puts this fact aside disregards the significance of choice as an expression of personality.'[21] Unger, in other words, treats the claim that there are objective human goods and moral requirements as the claim that we can 'kn[o]w the moral good with certainty, and underst[an]d all its implications and requirements perfectly',[22] to the extent that we do not need

[17] Ibid., 239.
[18] Ibid., 77.
[19] See citations and commentary, in Finnis, op. cit. n. 3 above, 20–5.
[20] Unger, op. cit. n. 16 above, 77, 239.
[21] Ibid., 77.
[22] Ibid., 93.

any individual choice of obligation-creating commitments or vocations, or any social mechanism of 'impartial adjudication', of authoritative specification.

I have tried in this essay to indicate how far this distorts our human situation. That situation is better understood in the classic social theory of Aristotle and, say, Aquinas—a social theory still to be refined and elaborated, but methodologically far sounder than the criticisms which Unger and his fellows have brought against it. To the scandal, of course, of positivists, that descriptively explanatory social theory is integrated with an explicitly normative moral and political theory. So I have also been suggesting that, in the limited but important fields here discussed, the movement's criticism of substantive and procedural social institutions fails to subvert those institutions because it fails to understand their relationship to principles of practical reasoning which not only justify them but could justify their reform.

8

Legal Doctrine and Interests in Land*

J. W. HARRIS†

I. INTRODUCTION

The expectations of the parties are oriented towards the economic and utilitarian meaning of a legal proposition. However, from the point of view of legal logic, this meaning is an 'irrational' one. . . . a 'lawyers' law' has never been and never will be brought into conformity with lay expectation unless it totally renounce that formal character which is immanent in it. This is just as true of the English law which we glorify so much to-day, as it has been of the ancient Roman jurists or of the methods of modern continental legal thought.[1]

So wrote Max Weber some seventy years ago. It constitutes one of his leading conclusions about the nature of lawyers' law. It points to a contrast between formal-doctrinal (and hence circumscribed) reasoning which, he claimed, was intrinsic to professional legal thinking, and open-ended, consequentialist controversy over the interpretation of legal propositions. If there are rival views as to the meaning of a legal rule, the layman expects the choice to be made according to which version will have the best outcome, all things considered. The professional lawyer, however, will settle the issue by reference to doctrinal arguments based upon existing legal materials.

I propose to examine this alleged contrast in the context of current issues concerning interests in land in English law. I shall argue that the dichotomy exists, but not in the stark Weberian form. Consequentialist interpretation is not, from the point of view of legal logic, 'irrational'. On the contrary, it constitutes the basis of one professionally accepted style of reasoning—what I call the 'utility model of rationality'.[2] However, the 'doctrine model of rationality'—along with two other models—also

† My thanks are due to the British Academy for a grant which enabled me to conduct research in the United States in connection with some of the themes discussed in this essay.

[1] M. Weber, *Law in Economy and Society*, ed. M. Rheinstein (Cambridge, Mass., 1954), 307–8.

[2] J. W. Harris, *Law and Legal Science* (Oxford, 1979), 143–50.

plays a crucial role in the development of the law.[3] To the extent that 'policy' can never totally displace doctrine, so long as our legal institutions retain anything like their present character, Weber was correct. As I shall try to show, this aspect of his contrast thesis is borne out by the onslaught on 'formalism' mounted by the new Critical Legal Studies Movement. For the conclusion to be drawn from this critique is that, if we want to ditch doctrine, we need to invent new institutions, new lawyers, and a new conception of 'law' itself.

2. WEBER'S ANALYSIS

To understand what Weber has in mind by 'legal logic', we must attend to a distinction not made explicit in his writings: the distinction between 'law' in the sense of a momentary legal system and 'law' as a historic congeries of materials forming part of the tradition of some body of officials.[4] Weber recognizes that law is commonly conceived of as constituted of 'prescriptive, prohibitory, and permissive' propositions.[5] This is an accurate description of a momentary legal system. It is the conception of law presupposed in the introduction to any textbook which announces that the law set forth is that in force at a certain date. Granted such a conception, juristic science assumes that logical conflicts are ruled out; one cannot affirm the existence, and also the non-existence, of a legal duty covering the same act-situation on the same occasion. Two contradictory rules cannot be simultaneously valid. Legal logic of this kind merely parallels classical propositional logic. For the most part, however, Weber conceives of law as a historical accretion of principles, maxims, definitions, and classifications, forming part of a particular juristic tradition. When a proposition (constituting part of the present law) may be formulated in different ways, reasoning, in accordance with what I have called the doctrine model, indicates which formulation is correct by reference to the inherent conceptual structure revealed in the historic system. The legal logic, peculiar to the professional lawyer, is that process of conceptual sublimation which articulates this inherent structure.

Doctrinal reasoning is not all of one kind. Its unifying feature consists in this: solutions to legal problems are to be sought from within the law

[3] Ibid., ch. 5.

[4] I have discussed this distinction in op. cit. n. 2 above, esp. at 10–14, 41–3, 65–73, 97–102, 111–22.

[5] Weber, 99.

(the historic system), whether by appeal to some overarching maxim, or by analogical reasoning, or by any other justificatory process which assumes that sufficient premisses are to be found in the established legal materials. Utility model reasoning, by contrast, invokes information going beyond the historic legal materials as the basis for consequentialist justification. The data it brings to bear may be of many different types—economic, sociological, political, moral, or religious—but they are all considerations as to which lawyers have no privileged access. Such reasoning is not 'irrational' from any point of view. It is, however, antipathetic to legal (doctrinal) 'logic'.

Weber's analysis opposes two kinds of professional legal thought to what he calls 'substantive rationality'. Substantive rationality is involved whenever a legal question is answered by reference to some general, extra-legal, moral principle. It was typical, in his view, both of some kinds of religious legal institutions and of welfarist institutions in general (whether sustained by 'patrimonial sovereigns', 'enlightened despots', or 'democratic demagogues').[6] In contrast, professional legal rationality is 'formal', in one or other of two senses, depending on the class of 'legal *honoratiores*' who control it.[7] First, it may be casuistic. Casuistry ('cautelary jurisprudence') insists that the ruling in a case must be based on precedent or analogy with some earlier ruling. Casuistry may be more or less empirical or conceptual, depending on whether precedential or analogical cogency is mediated through factual similarities or through the intrinsic meaning of the concepts in which rulings are given.[8] Second, professional legal rationality may be 'logically formal'. In this case, concepts are subsumed, in accordance with their intrinsic meaning, under highly abstract propositions, forming a consistent and 'gapless' juristic system. New legal questions may then be answered, not by reference to the facts or concepts forming the *protasis* of some particular existing legal rule, but by logical derivation from the second-order abstract propositions by which the intrinsic meanings of all legal concepts within the system are tied together.[9]

Weber argued that casuistic jurisprudence was typical of jurisdictions in which the evolution of law was in the hands of practitioners, as in early Rome and in all common-law countries. Common-law casuistry was

[6] Ibid., 63, 205–9, 224–6, 264–5, 279–83, 303–15, 318–21, 349–56.

[7] For a discussion of the varied and sometimes inconsistent senses in which Weber employs the concepts of rationality and formality, see A. T. Kronman, *Max Weber* (London, 1983), ch. 4.

[8] Weber, 61–4, 73–4, 178, 198–204, 209–20, 315–18, 349–56.

[9] Ibid., 61–4, 145, 204–5, 220–3, 266–9, 274–9, 296–8, 303–15, 349–55.

more empirical, and less conceptual, than its Roman counterpart; but casuistry of all kinds was a 'lower' form of legal science, when compared with logically formal rationality.[10] The latter was peculiar to those continental jurisdictions where legal development had been controlled by university-trained bureaucrats.

The central theme of Weber's massive work on economy and society, of which his sociology of law forms a part, is the relationship between economic behaviour in particular and social behaviour in general. Yet he stresses again and again (suggesting that his historical researches had falsified what his theoretical predilections predisposed him to believe) that distinctively economic factors play only a small part in bringing about the creation of particular legal institutions and do not account for the emergence of different kinds of professional legal thought.[11] In particular, logically formal rationality was not a necessary prerequisite for modern capitalism. The English counter-example made that clear.[12] The factors influencing professional legal thought are political and internal-intellectual ones. The political history of various jurisdictions does or does not result in monopoly of legal development resting in the hands of different kinds of legal *honoratiores*. In England, following royal centralization of the administration of justice, practising lawyers were able to obtain a guild-like exclusive control, and they developed a casuistry which suited the needs of their clients and furthered their own financial interests. In most continental jurisdictions, and especially in Germany, there was no centralization of the administration of justice. There were, however, demands, both from bourgeois entrepreneurs and from the bureaucratic staffs of princes, for a coherent corpus of law; and it was this that gave the *entrée* to the professors and their pupils. The English writ system biased internal intellectual development of legal thought towards empirical casuistry. The heritage of Roman conceptual classifications and the idea of a transcendent natural law provided the intellectual stimuli for the systematic logical formalism of the continental jurists. Lawyers of all kinds, however, have a caste tendency towards 'formal' reasoning; that is, an insistence that new legal problems should be referred, not to extra-legal ('policy') considerations, but to some feature of the already given legal materials.

[10] Ibid., 316.
[11] Ibid., 61, 131, 176, 265, 274, 304, 315.
[12] Ibid., 176, 230, 315, 318, 352–3.

3. CASUISTRY

As all readers of Weber have to bear in mind, what he says about types of anything must be understood as referring to 'pure' or 'ideal' types. Any correlation between kinds of thinking and particular jurisdictions is no more than an approximation. We should not be surprised to discover within any one jurisdiction aspects of all forms of reasoning he distinguishes. It remains to be seen whether, in the context of modern English land law, reasoning is either 'substantive' or 'formal'; and, if the latter, in which of the two senses of formality Weber describes.

Casuistry, of the conceptual kind, occurs when reasoning to a conclusion includes reference to the contours of an interest in land laid down in some analogous legal context. Common-law reasoning is replete with such casuistry. Some, but not all, restrictions on the alienability of a fee simple will be void as inconsistent with the 'natural qualities' of the estate.[13] Since a mortgage, by its nature, entails the right of the mortgagor to redeem the mortgaged property, an option for the mortgagee to purchase the property must necessarily be void if it forms part of the mortgage transaction, but not if it is entered into (a day later) as a separate transaction.[14] The right to enforce a restrictive covenant against a successor to freehold land must (like an easement) be appurtenant to dominant land;[15] but its enjoyment need not be directly associated with the user of the dominant land.[16] An easement may involve intermittent exclusive enjoyment of a servient tenement,[17] but not permanent joint possession.[18]

In such instances and many others to be found in land-law books, courts invoke doctrine to settle disputed questions about the present law. Should they do so? Weber purports to offer explanations, not justifications, of different kinds of professional legal reasoning. Yet he accepts uncritically one of the common rationales for doctrine as against policy, namely, that it augments the certainty and predictability of the law:

> Juridical formalism enables the legal system to operate like a technically rational machine. Thus it guarantees to individuals and groups within the system a

13 *Re Brown, District Bank Ltd.* v. *Brown* [1954] Ch 39.
14 *Samuel* v. *Jarrah Timber and Wood Paving Corporation Ltd.* [1904] AC 323.
15 *London County Council* v. *Allen* [1914] 3 KB 642.
16 *Gilbert* v. *Spoor* [1982] 2 All ER 576.
17 *Miller* v. *Emcer Products Ltd.* [1956] Ch 304.
18 *Copeland* v. *Greenhalf* [1952] Ch 448.

relative maximum of freedom and greatly increases for them the possibility of predicting the legal consequences of their actions.[19]

Two other justifications for doctrinal reasoning (not mentioned by Weber) lie close to the surface of present-day legal culture. They concern 'separation of powers' and 'the rule of law'. If judges resolve an uncertain question about the present law by an assessment and balancing of social consequences, are they not trespassing on the functions of the legislature? Whereas it is an established feature of the judicial role that legal doctrine should be articulated and systematized. 'Separation of powers' is, arguably, a constitutional imperative of limited scope which is, in any case, specific to certain kinds of western-style polities. 'The rule of law' provides a much broader justification for the doctrine model of rationality.

The rule of law is a political quality of institutions. Writers commonly make this quality explicit in terms of the part played within institutional structures by rules; rules must be general, non-retroactive, binding on all, and so on.[20] These are necessary, but not sufficient, features of a thorough-going observance of the rule of law. Supposing the adjudicative organs of an institutional structure were to adopt the following stance when forced to choose between rival formulations of a legal proposition: 'The law is uncertain. So close the books, and let us decide (just like parliamentarians faced with rival Bills) which of the two formulations would have best consequences for the community, all things considered.' If this happened, the rule of law would be less observed by the institutional structure than is true where (as everywhere in the modern world) the books are not simply closed when a difficult case arises. It is taken for granted that pre-existing legal materials may bear on the answer. 'Law', *tout court*, consists of rules and doctrine, and the rule of law involves both. When 'the law' (in the sense of presently valid rules) is unclear, a court which appeals to doctrine is still applying 'the law' (in the sense of the historic system or systems which form part of its tradition).

In the case of such an elusive (and yet pervasive) phenomenon as 'legal thinking', there can be no sharp divorce between justification and explanation. Mediating and going beyond these three alleged rationales for doctrine there is what Weber calls the 'internal structure of legal

[19] Weber, 226–7.

[20] See, for example, L. L. Fuller, *The Morality of Law* (New Haven, rev. edn., 1969), chs. 2 and 5; J. Raz, *The Authority of Law* (Oxford, 1979), ch. 11.

thought'.[21] The legal mind craves consistency in the evolution of legal concepts. Self-interest and self-respect alike induce in those occupying the upper strata of the ranks of legal *honoratiores* a yearning for doctrinal symmetry. As Jeremy Bentham put it, and he did not like it above half: 'The goddess of harmony has exercised more influence, however latent, over the dispensations of Themis, than her most diligent historiographers, or even her most passionate panegyrists, seem to have been aware of.'[22] Nevertheless, as Bentham also recognized, in the evolution of the common law, overt consequentialism may displace doctrinal consistency. For example, in *Lace* v. *Chantler* the Court of Appeal accepted the argument that a purported grant of a lease for the duration of the war must be void, since it is of the essence of leases to have a fixed term or a term capable of being rendered certain by the parties.[23] In *Re Midland Railway Company's Agreement*, however, the court refused to accept, as a corollary, that a restriction on a landlord's right to terminate a periodic tenancy (which might lead to its indefinite duration) was also void:

> ... the subject-matter under consideration has an air of artificiality, of remoteness from practical considerations; and in such circumstances we think the court should be unwilling to be moved by some process of logic to travel further than authority compels in the direction of holding that what parties to a transaction in plain English agreed is something impossible in law and therefore void.[24]

It is not merely that obvious bad consequences may put a casuistic terminus to a process of conceptual analogy. Sometimes, in the development of interests in land, consequentialism takes centre stage. This was true of the reasoning of both the Court of Appeal and the House of Lords in the recent controversial decision in *Williams and Glyn's Bank Ltd.* v. *Boland.*[25] The most crucial issue in the case was whether the rights of an equitable co-owner under an implied trust for sale were interests 'subsisting in reference' to land within section 70(1) of the Land Registration Act 1925. Much was at stake. Such interests arise whenever a house has been conveyed into the name of one co-owner, where the other (equitable) co-owner has paid part of the purchase price

[21] Weber, 61.

[22] J. Bentham, *An Introduction to the Principles of Morals and Legislation*, ed. E. H. Burn and H. L. A. Hart (London, 1970), 24.

[23] [1944] KB 368.

[24] [1971] Ch 725, 732 *per* Russell LJ. Contrast *Centaploy Ltd.* v. *Matlodge Ltd.* [1974] Ch 1 (total restraint on landlord's right to terminate periodic tenancy held void as inconsistent with the estate).

[25] [1979] Ch 312 (CA); [1981] AC 487 (HL). Browne LJ alone eschewed consequentialism.

or agreed to be partly responsible for paying off the mortgage. If they are interests in land within the statute, then, provided they are coupled with 'actual occupation', they can rank as 'overriding interests',[26] and will in consequence be binding on those who deal with the registered proprietor of the legal estate. Some commentators had argued that this question must be answered in the negative because, by force of the equitable doctrine of conversion, all interests under trusts for sale must be regarded as interests in money not in land. Not surprisingly, the Court of Appeal and House of Lords would not allow such important social questions to be sidestepped by reference to a highly technical doctrine which had arisen, largely, in the unrelated context of succession rules.[27] They adopted the utility model of rationality. That ruling must be chosen which would have best consequences. This entailed balancing the harm to conveyancers and their clients if unregistered interests of this sort were binding on purchasers and mortgagees against the deleterious social effects for equitable co-owners, especially wives, if they could be deprived of their homes by a transaction in which they took no part. The wives won.

Criticism of this aspect of *Boland* has largely focused on the merits of balancing. The Law Society has estimated that additional enquiries made necessary by the decision have cost the house-owning public some six and three-quarter million pounds annually.[28] There has been less complaint about the propriety of judicial attempts to weigh consequences in such a context. 'Policy considerations' are, as Weber claimed, the obverse of doctrinal legal logic; but they are not, or are no longer, considered to be extrinsic to lawyers' law.

Furthermore, Weber's typology for modern legal reasoning is incomplete. I have suggested that, in developing the law, there are in principle four models of legal rationality: the will model, the natural-meaning model, the doctrine model, and the utility model.[29] The will model appeals to historical evidence as showing that some agent who participated in the creation of the provision would have wished it to be interpreted one way rather than another. The natural-meaning model is employed when the fact that some word or phrase has (in natural English usage) a certain meaning is taken as sufficient warrant for adopting an interpretation.

[26] Land Registration Act 1925 s. 70 (1) (g).

[27] See S. Anderson, 'The Proper, Narrow Scope of Equitable Conversion in Land Law' (1984) 100 *Law Quarterly Rev.* 86.

[28] *Sol. Jo.*, 26 April 1985.

[29] Harris, ch. 5.

In Weberian terms, 'substantive rationality' is employed when the crucial reasons given for defining an interest in land one way rather than another are general (moral, social, political, economic, or religious) considerations not specifically embodied in the law. If the court has regard only to the moral claims of the individual parties without subsuming them within a wider moral principle, its decision is not 'rational' at all (since for Weber rationality entails support by general principle). It is instead an instance of 'khadi justice'.[30] If the court recognizes that its award must be subsumed under a universalized ruling, but then opts between different rulings by assessing the consequences in terms of moral, social, or economic considerations 'extrinsic' to legal materials, its reasoning is substantive, not 'formal'. Weber's substantive rationality thus equates, roughly, with what I have termed the utility model of rationality. Casuistic and logically formal reasoning are two varieties within the doctrine model. Weber did not distinguish the backward-looking elements of the will model from open-ended consequentialism. He considered any procedure for settling legal questions by reference to what individual legislators had in mind to be merely one aspect of 'substantive' reasoning.[31]

As to natural-meaning reasoning, although Weber recognized it to be distinct from other kinds of reasoning, it was not for him a genuinely 'legal' model of rationality; not an aspect of 'lawyers' law'. Only the layman (he said) supposed that interpretation could be 'literalistic' and that an interpreter was a mere 'definition-monger'.[32] Lon Fuller took a similar view when he criticized a 'pointer theory of meaning' (which he attributed to Professor Hart).[33] And yet, in recent years English judges have become obsessed with the idea that difficult issues of statutory construction should, as far as possible, be settled, not by arguments about policy or doctrine or legislative history, but by asking what is the natural (layman's) meaning of the words Parliament has employed. In a recent judgment interpreting some highly abstruse provisions of the Water Act 1973 (as amended), the House of Lords rejected any suggestion that the language should be understood in any other than its ordinary (lay) sense. In the words of Lord Scarman: '... the language of the two paragraphs consists of ordinary English words which possess by

30 Weber, 63, 229, 264, 351–2.

31 See his discussion of the Prussian *Allgemeine Landrecht* of 1794, ibid., 280 ff.

32 Ibid., 316.

33 L. L. Fuller, 'Positivism and Fidelity to Law—a Reply to Professor Hart' (1958) 71 *Harv. Law Rev.* 630, 668. Hart has acknowledged the force of this criticism: see H. L. A. Hart, *Essays in Jurisprudence and Philosophy* (Oxford, 1983), 7–8.

their very imprecision the flexibility which is the hallmark of the English language, and which is one of the reasons for the survival of English as a worldwide tongue'.[34]

Symptomatic is the outcome of the second crucial issue in *Boland*'s case, namely: how are the words 'actual occupation', in paragraph (g) of section 70(1) of the Land Registration Act 1925, to be understood? Ungoed Thomas J., at first instance in *Hodgson* v. *Marks*, had presupposed the will model of rationality in answering this question. He found in the legislative history of the paragraph evidence that those who drafted it intended that 'actual occupation' must be apparent to a purchaser.[35] Templeman J., at first instance in *Boland*'s case,[36] had applied the utility model. He held that an equitable co-owner was not 'in actual occupation' where the legal owner was himself an occupier, justifying this interpretation by reference to the unacceptable conveyancing consequences of any other view.[37] However, the Court of Appeal in *Hodgson*[38] and both the Court of Appeal and the House of Lords in *Boland*[39] rejected any restricted or technical interpretation: *because* these were words of plain English, they *must* be given their ordinary meaning.

The relative importance *inter se* of the four models of legal rationality varies from jurisdiction to jurisdiction and from one branch of law to another. Natural meaning is riding high today across much of English law, but not in the particular context of the evolution of interests in land. The reason is simple. Even when a land-law rule is comprised in a statute and so has a fixed verbal formulation, if its application turns on the meaning of some such term as 'lease', 'hereditament', or 'interest in land', there is no natural, non-technical meaning to which appeal can be made. So far as the will model is concerned, sometimes the courts do indeed refer to what the draftsman of a property statute had in mind. Commonly, however, such speculations are informed, not by genuine biographical information about his aims, but by conclusions about the doctrinal import of the concepts he used or assertions of the form 'he

[34] *South West Water Authority* v. *Rumble's* [1985] 1 All ER 513, 517.

[35] [1970] 3 All ER 513.

[36] (1978) 36 P & CR 448; and also in *Bird* v. *Syme Thomson* [1978] 3 All ER 1027.

[37] In rejecting his view, the Court of Appeal and House of Lords unfairly attributed to Templeman J. reliance upon the obsolete doctrine that husband and wife are to be regarded as one for all purposes.

[38] [1971] Ch 892.

[39] [1979] Ch 312 (CA); [1981] AC 487 (HL).

cannot have envisaged social consequences *xy*, since they are obviously so undesirable'.

On the narrow topic of evolving interests in land, therefore, the usual competitors are doctrine and utility. On the first crucial issue in *Boland*, the judges could not have decided whether a co-ownership right was an interest 'subsisting in reference' to land by referring to the natural meaning in ordinary English of the expression; and they chose not to raise difficult historical questions about the phrase's meaning for its creators. There was accordingly a straight fight between conversion doctrine and consequentialism. The latter prevailed.

Yet doctrinal consistency was not ignored. If, despite the alleged conversion, the interests of these equitable co-owners subsisted in reference to land, then that must be true of all those who acquire an interest under an implied trust. It was accepted that, if the ruling was to favour the wives in the case against the mortgagee-banks, it *must* also favour any occupant who had contributed to the original purchase price of the property against any transferee from the registered proprietor.[40]

Why should this be so? A purely consequentialist approach might have warranted a much narrower ruling, for example:

> Wives, but only wives, ought to be protected against banks, but only banks. It would be wrong to prejudice first-time home-buyers; and no-one deserves to lose out to the unregistered (and undiscoverable) mistress co-owner. Let us, therefore, construe the statute to mean that only equitable co-owners who are wives (and whose husbands have mortgaged to banks) have 'interests subsisting in reference to land'. Others in whose favour implied trusts have arisen, or wives whose husbands sell to private purchasers, shall be deemed to have interests in money only.

Parliament may enact such distinctions,[41] but it is unthinkable that an English court would. Why? It is not merely the requirement that the law, the present law comprised in a momentary legal system, must be stated in non-contradictory propositions. The above (unthinkable) ruling

[40] Lord Wilberforce said: '... the appeals do not ... involve any question of matrimonial law, or of the rights of married women or of women as such. Exactly the same issue could arise if the roles of husband and wife were reversed, or if the persons interested in the house were not married to each other.... To extend (if it be an extension) the area of risk so as to include possible interests of spouses, and indeed, in theory, of other members of the family or even outside it, may add to the burdens of purchasers ...'; [1981] AC 487, 502, 508.

[41] An attempt to confine the effect of the *Boland* case by limiting the trust-interests within paragraph (g) of section 70(1) of the Land Registration Act 1925 to those of spouses was indeed made in the ill-fated Land Registration and Law of Property Bill 1985.

observes this constraint. It announces different, mutually consistent rules for different categories of occupying equitable co-owners and different categories of transferees. The unthinkability comes from doctrinal inconsistency: either equitable co-owners' rights are interests subsisting in reference to land within the statute or they are not. The ruling infringes doctrinal 'legal logic', not propositional 'legal logic'.

4. LOGICALLY FORMAL RATIONALITY

Thus far we have considered, in relation to the evolution of interests in land, one of the two types of 'formalism' which Weber opposed to 'substantive rationality'. It is clear that, in this context, conceptual casuistry is indeed inherent in 'lawyers' law'. When the concepts employed within legal rules include either particular estates or interests or the general notion of 'interests in land', legal reasoning cannot be open-endedly consequentialist. The meaning of the concept, established within the tradition of the jurisdiction, must be taken into account. At one extreme, an interpretation may be justified solely in terms of doctrine. And even when, at the other extreme, consequentialism alone dictates the choice between two interpretations, the fact that the chosen ruling has to be expressed in conceptual language fetters the distinctions which can be made. Conceptual casuistry, at the least, hobbles policy.

What of the other kind of Weberian legal formalism, the 'higher' sort? Does the common law, contrary to Weber's depiction of it, ever engage in a formal logic wherein concepts are subsumed within a 'gapless' system?

Two versions of the idea of 'gapless system' should be distinguished. First, a system may be said to be gapless by virtue of a presupposed closure rule. It is assumed that conduct is legally prescribed or prohibited only if some rule emanating from or subsumable under a determinate list of positive sources applies to it; otherwise it is (negatively) permitted. This is the sense of 'gaplessness' defended by Kelsen.[42] Alternatively, a system may be said to be gapless in that doctrine, extrapolated from its component materials, can provide sufficient reasons to solve any disputed question of law. It is this doctrinal gaplessness which is presupposed by Weberian logically formal rationality. The difference is easier to grasp if we bear in mind the distinction

[42] H. Kelsen, *General Theory of Law and State* (Cambridge, Mass., 1945), 146–9; *Pure Theory of Law* (Berkeley, 1967), 245–50.

between momentary and non-momentary systems; for the 'gapless system' of the first type represents the present law of a jurisdiction, whereas the second kind of 'gapless system' is constituted by historically accumulated doctrine.

English lawyers take the first variety of gaplessness for granted. It underpins every assertion that behaviour is not illegal because there is nothing in the books against it. Weberian gaplessness would only be presupposed by a lawyer who thought that, whenever a 'hard case' arises, scholarly distillation of the intrinsic meanings of established legal concepts will always provide the answer. Even Professor Dworkin's super-judge, Hercules, does not believe that; for he supposes that you have to go outside the legal materials and look at community morality (in the light of critical political philosophy) in order to find your answer.[43]

Common-law reasoning does not assume doctrinal gaplessness covering all legal questions. To that extent Weber was right about the common law. But neither, especially in the context of property law, does it confine itself to casuistry. In addition to definitions of individual concepts which may be invoked (and then applied or distinguished) from one context to another, it does on occasion appeal to second-order maxims channelling or restricting the abstract process of concept-manufacture. In so doing it approaches just that kind of systematization which Weber claimed to be alien to it.[44] Perhaps Weber underestimated the extent to which professional role self-justification, as well as the demands of academic scholarship, might motivate doctrinal systematization. He assumed that the medieval law of seisin and estates was no more than a casuistic jumble,[45] whereas it actually had just the sort of internal consistency to which 'logically formal' reasoning is supposed to lead, even if we cannot share the eulogism of its last apologist, A. D. Hargreaves, who described English land-law jurisprudence as 'the greatest system of property law that the world has ever known'.[46]

[43] R. M. Dworkin, *Taking Rights Seriously* (London, 1978), 105–30.

[44] This is a facet of legal reasoning which receives no separate treatment in D. N. MacCormick's otherwise comprehensive treatment of the topic in *Legal Reasoning and Legal Theory* (Oxford, 1978). MacCormick argues that consequentialist alternatives are limited by the requirement that rules must be universalized and must then constitute a coherent and non-contradictory whole, and by the requirement that any novel ruling must be licensed by principle or analogy. It is to be added that the range of possible universalizations of rules which deploy specialist concepts is curtailed by reference to doctrinal systematization within a subset of second-order principles.

[45] Weber, 202.

[46] 'Modern Real Property' (1956) 19 *Modern Law Rev.* 14.

Even modern land law exhibits aspirations towards doctrinal gaplessness, although they tend to give way before pressing demands of substantive justice. Two second-order doctrinal tenets (and their countervailing utility-model pressures) warrant special attention.

Students of land law are introduced, usually at an early stage in their studies, to a well-known dichotomy. A claim to some use or enjoyment of land avails either only against a particular proprietor, or against all comers to the land. In the former case it is a personal right; in the latter case it is an 'interest in land'. If it does fall into the latter category, some qualification needs to be introduced into 'all comers', depending on other subclassifications of interests in land. It may be legal or equitable; it may or may not be registrable as a land charge; and (where the title to the land itself is registered) it may or may not be an 'overriding interest'. If merely equitable, the interest binds all comers *except* the bona fide purchaser of a legal estate for value without notice and those claiming through him.[47] If it is registrable as a land charge but has not been registered, it binds all save the purchaser of a legal estate for money or money's worth (or sometimes, all except a purchaser of any interest in the land).[48] If it is not an overriding interest nor protected on the registered title, it binds all except, in the case of registered dispositions, a registered transferee for valuable consideration;[49] and, in the case of unregistered dispositions, all except a purchaser of a legal estate.[50] These subclassifications qualify the range of protection. They are, however, all posterior to the initial dichotomy. If the claim is an interest in land, it binds all (with, perhaps, an excepted category). If it is not an interest in land, it can only bind a single obligor.

A classic statement of the dichotomy is to be found in the judgment of Lord Jessel MR in *London and South Western Railway Company* v. *Gomm*. The case concerned the plaintiff's right to repurchase land sold by it to the defendant's predecessor in title. The defendant bought the land with notice that this right had been reserved. The plaintiff claimed that its option was binding on the defendant, but at the same time sought to deny that it created an interest in land. (If it did create such an interest, it was void both because of the effect of the rule against perpetuities and because it would be *ultra vires* the statutory powers of the company.) Kay J., at first instance, upheld this contention: the covenant was not an

[47] *Re Nisbet and Potts' Contract* [1906] 1 Ch 386 (restrictive covenant binding on one who had acquired title by adverse possession irrespective of notice).

[48] Land Charges Act 1972, s. 4.

[49] Land Registration Act 1925, ss. 20, 23, 59.

[50] *Freer* v. *Unwins Ltd.* [1976] Ch 288.

interest in land, but it was enforceable against a purchaser with notice. That, said Lord Jessel, was a contradiction in terms:

... the company must admit that it somehow binds the land. But if it binds the land it creates an equitable interest in the land.... If it were a mere contract it was not Gomm's contract, and if it did not in equity run with the land so as to give an interest in the land it could not have been enforced against him.[51]

The doctrinal dichotomy between personal rights and interests in land dictated the Court of Appeal's conclusion. It was not that, if the law recognized claims over land which bind a defined and limited class of successors, bad things would follow. It was simply—doctrinally simply—that the right in question *must* be the one thing or the other. I shall call this 'the doctrinal cleavage'.

The doctrinal cleavage is deeply embedded in our land law. It divides restrictive from positive covenants affecting freehold land and easements from easement-like concessions which are not appurtenant to dominant land. In recent developments concerning pre-emption rights, the courts have striven to protect the cleavage in the face of some refractory materials. A decision of the Court of Appeal appeared to have laid down that such rights availed only against the party who conferred them and so were not interests in land,[52] whereas the Land Charges Act, by providing that such rights could be registered as land charges, seemed to assume the contrary.[53] Decisions at first instance fluctuated about which side of the divide they should fall, while being in agreement that they must fall one side or the other. The majority of the Court of Appeal in *Pritchard* v. *Briggs* has settled the question in an ingenious manner which respects the cleavage. Pre-emption rights as such are not interests in land. However, once the condition has occurred upon which the right to buy arises, they are transmuted into options and thereafter become interests in land. Before the transformation is triggered, no successor to the grantor of the right is bound even if it has been registered. Registered protection has effect only from the moment of transformation.[54]

Given the doctrinal cleavage, how does the law decide on which side to rank any particular claim to the use or enjoyment of land? The most often cited list of criteria appears in the judgment of Lord Wilberforce in

51 (1881) 20 Ch D 562, 580, 582.
52 *Manchester Ship Canal Co.* v. *Manchester Racecourse Co.* [1901] 2 Ch 37.
53 Land Charges Act 1972, s. 2 (4).
54 [1980] Ch 338.

National Provincial Bank Ltd. v. *Ainsworth.* I shall call it 'the doctrinal prescription'.

Before a right or an interest can be admitted into the category of property, or of a right affecting property, it must be definable, identifiable by third parties, capable in its nature of assumption by third parties, and have some degree of permanence or stability.[55]

In the result the House of Lords overruled a decade of lower court decisions, in holding that there was no such thing as 'the deserted wife's equity'. Although a wife, by virtue of her status, could be protected against her husband in the occupation of the matrimonial home, she had no right to occupy capable of binding any successor of her husband. The specific ruling was overturned by Parliament. The Matrimonial Homes Act 1967 enacted that spouses' occupation rights should bind successors, provided they were registered as land charges. The *Ainsworth* ruling has thus not formed part of the present law at any time since the Act came into force.[56] The doctrinal prescription, however, continues to form part of 'English law', in the sense of that non-momentary, historic collections of maxims (encompassed with the tradition of our courts) which is available, in accordance with the doctrine model of rationality, to guide choices between different rulings. Like the doctrinal cleavage it deals directly, not with conduct, but with concepts (interests in land) employed within some conduct-related rules. Both are second-order propositions exemplifying what Weber described as 'logically formal rationality'. Unlike his ideal type of a logically formal system, however, they do not dictate solutions through some ineluctable deductive or quasi-deductive process. They guide choices about the recognition of interests in land. They have weight within legal reasoning; but they may, as we shall see, be overriden by non-doctrinal considerations.

It emerges from the doctrinal prescription that fully fledged interests in land have three characteristics. First, they involve some defined enjoyment-content relating to land—whether a right to possess or occupy (exclusively, or jointly with others); or a right to make some use of the land less than possession; or a right to control its development; or a right to resort to the realizable value of the land as security for a debt. Second, they enjoy general protection against all comers (qualified, as we have seen, depending on whether they were invented by exercise of the court's equitable jurisdiction or, more importantly today, depending

[55] [1965] AC 1175, 1247–8.

[56] See now the Matrimonial Homes Act 1983.

on their status within registration systems). Given the doctrinal cleavage, these first two characteristics are conceptually tied to the idea of an interest in land. The third characteristic is transmissibility (either *inter vivos* or on death). Common-law jurisprudence leans in favour of this characteristic, even though it is not conceptually tied to the notion of an interest in land. Any total prohibition on the right to alienate a fee simple is void. A lease may include an absolute prohibition on assignment. Such a provision will not, however, prevent the lessee effectively assigning his estate. It will merely provide grounds for the lessor to seek forfeiture or other relief for breach of covenant upon the occasion of an assignment.[57]

According to the doctrinal prescription, a right cannot have the second characteristic (general protection) unless it also has both the other two: a well-defined enjoyment-content and transmissibility. Lord Wilberforce states that the right must be 'definable', 'identifiable by third parties', and 'have some degree of permanence or stability'; and must also be 'capable in its nature of assumption by third parties'—such being necessary 'before a right or an interest *can* be admitted into the category of property, or of a right affecting property'. The force of the 'can' is doctrinal. An 'ought' asserts the existence of a reason,[58] and its employment in justificatory discourse licenses a demand that the reason be articulated. A doctrinal 'can' or 'must' buries its second-order justificatory reasons out of reach of the inquisitive, and announces a starting-point for first-order applied reasons: 'Rights can only exist as interests in land, that is, bind successors, if they are well-defined and transmissible. Now let's see whether the right here in question has these qualities.'

In the *Ainsworth* case, the principal substantive objections to admitting that a deserted wife's right could bind her husband's successors were these: first, such successors, not being acquainted with the details of intramarital relations, could not be expected to know whether the right had arisen; and, second, the right had an evanescent quality, since it could always be terminated by the court in the exercise of its discretion. If these objections had merely been fed into a consequentialist calculation, they might have been outweighed by the injustice-consequences to wives of not recognizing the right's proprietary status. In *Boland*, precisely comparable objections were so outweighed. An equitable co-owner's interest may arise through an implied trust whose

[57] *Governors of the Peabody Donation Fund* v. *Higgins* [1983] 3 All ER 122.
[58] Cf. J. Raz, *Practical Reason and Norms* (Oxford, 1975), 29–31.

existence depends on private dealings beyond the ken of purchasers and mortgagees (not to mention the uncertainty inherent in this aspect of trust law);[59] and the duration of the possessory aspect of the equitable interest is (as we shall see) also subject to the court's discretion. The two considerations acquired special force in *Ainsworth* because, in contrast with *Boland*, the doctrine model, rather than the utility model, structured the reasoning. Their Lordships asked themselves, not whether a ruling one way or the other would have best consequences, but whether the right under review had the characteristics we expect to find in an interest in land.[60] It did not. It was obviously not transmissible by the wife; and it was lacking in clarity and permanence. In Lord Hodson's words: 'Equity may not be past the age of child-bearing but an infant of the kind suggested would lack form or shape.'[61]

5. GROWING PAINS

Doctrine pinches the reformer's foot. In recent years, English land law has been experiencing growing pains, where claims to the enjoyment of land have pressed for recognition as more than merely personal rights. These developments have strained the doctrinal prescription and even, to some extent, the doctrinal cleavage.

A sovereign parliament is not bound by case-law jurisprudence, even less by a prescription which purports to elevate doctrinal consistency above consequentialist justice. Parliament passed the Matrimonial Homes Act 1967, reversing *Ainsworth.* The Act enabled spouses to register occupation rights. Once registered, they are binding on all successors.[62] That conferred characteristic 2 (general protection) upon the wife's right and so turned it into an interest in land of a sort. It is, of course, non-transmissible; and, more importantly, Parliament made no attempt to give it a precise enjoyment-content. It has only a negative

[59] This is one of the criticisms of the *Boland* ruling stressed by the Law Commission in its report on the implications of the decision: Law Com No. 115 (1982).

[60] Lord Wilberforce was the only member of the House to appear in both cases. In *Ainsworth* he prefaced his inquiry by saying: 'The ultimate question must be whether such persons can be given the protection which social considerations of humanity evidently indicate without injustice to third parties *and a radical departure from sound principles of real property law*' ([1965] AC 1175, 1242, italics supplied). Whereas in *Boland* he said: 'The solution must be derived from a consideration in the light of current social conditions of the Land Registration Act 1925 and other property statutes' ([1981] AC 487, 502). The inhibiting effect of overarching 'sound principles' appears to have fallen away.

[61] [1965] AC 1175, 1224.

[62] The rule that such rights cannot bind a trustee in bankruptcy (Matrimonial Homes Act 1983, s. 2 (7)) has been reversed by the Insolvency Act 1985, s. 171 (2).

definition. Once a spouse's occupation right is registered, no successor of the other spouse can turn her out. She is, however, not entitled to that open-ended set of use-privileges over the land which is the incident of a right to possess; and consequently cannot invite others to share the house with her.[63]

Nor in the recent judicial evolution of controversial 'interests in land' has any consistent attention been paid to the doctrinal prescription. One such has been the interest of an equitable co-owner to which reference has already been made. How does it fare in the light of the three characteristics of a fully fledged interest in land?

Boland finally established that it enjoys the second crucial characteristic, that of general protection.[64] The first characteristic (land-related enjoyment-content) is more problematic. Since the decision of the Court of Appeal in *Bull* v. *Bull*,[65] it has been accepted that an equitable co-owner in possession of land can defend his right to remain in occupation against the legal co-owner, provided one of the purposes of the trust under which his interest arises was to provide him with a home.[66] Unlike the spouse with a registered Matrimonial Homes Act charge, he has an affirmative claim to joint possession with all its attendant privileges. When the House of Lords held that Mr Boland's mortgagees took their charge subject to Mrs Boland's rights, it followed that she was not only irremovable herself, but she could keep her defaulting husband with her (as she did).

On the other hand, the co-owner's possessory rights can be terminated if the court exercises its discretion, at the instigation of any person interested in the land, to order a sale. Where the applicant is the other co-owner, the discretion is nowadays exercised having regard to the particularistic 'justice' claims of the parties and other members of the family.[67] Where, however, he is the other co-owner's trustee in bankruptcy, case law indicated that sale followed almost automatically—the

63 *Wroth* v. *Tyler* [1974] Ch 30; see now Matrimonial Homes Act 1983, s. 1.

64 In the case of unregistered land, it binds all save bona fide purchasers without notice: *Caunce* v. *Caunce* [1969] 1 All ER 722; *King's North Trust Ltd.* v. *Tizard* [1986] 2 All ER 54. Where title is registered, it is capable of being protected by entry on the register—*Elias* v. *Mitchell* [1972] Ch 652; and (as held in *Boland*) when coupled with actual occupation it constitutes an overriding interest.

65 [1955] 1 QB 234.

66 *Barclay* v. *Barclay* [1970] 2 QB 677.

67 *Browne* v. *Pritchard* [1975] 3 All ER 721. *Williams* v. *Williams* [1976] Ch 278. Where, however, the co-owners are not spouses, it is an unsettled question whether the court should be biased in favour of ordering sale in view of the statutory trust for sale upon which the property is held: *Re Evers* [1980] 3 All ER 399; *Re Holliday* [1981] Ch 405; *Bernard* v. *Josephs* [1982] Ch 391.

exchange value of the co-ownership interest displacing its use value;[68] and Parliament has intervened in the case of married co-owners, with a compromise whereby a year must elapse after the bankruptcy before the court is to assume, unless circumstances are exceptional, 'that the interests of the bankrupt's creditors outweigh all other considerations'.[69] It has yet to be settled how the discretion should be exercised where the applicant for sale is a purchaser or mortgagee from the other co-owner.[70]

As to characteristic 3 (transmissibility), an equitable interest in property is, in principle, freely assignable. Can that really be true of a typical co-owner's interest?

For sale; my right to joint occupation with my wife, coupled with and subject to rights to ask the court to order sale.

This ludicrous possibility was actually adverted to, obliquely, by Lord Denning MR when, in *Bedson* v. *Bedson*, he denied that a spouse could sever his joint tenancy of a matrimonial home so as to produce an assignable equitable tenancy in common.[71] It was not to be contemplated that a deserting husband could dispose in favour of a third party of his rights under the co-ownership trust, since they entailed an affirmative claim to joint possession and it would have to follow that the third party could move in with the wife. The conclusion as to non-severability has been rejected in subsequent cases,[72] but the premiss has never been squarely confronted. Is the right to joint possession transmissible, or may the equitable tenant in common transmit only a right to share in proceeds when the land is sold (together with a possibly worthless *locus standi* to ask the court to order sale)?

More academic controversy has surrounded the question whether interests in land can result from mere 'licences'. If X allows Y some use of X's land, does Y acquire an interest in land by force of the contract alone (if there is a contract) or, in appropriate circumstances of

[68] *Re Turner* [1975] 1 All ER 5; *Re McCarthy* [1975] 2 All ER 857; *Re Bailey* [1977] 2 All ER 26; *Re Lowrie* [1981] 3 All ER 353. *Re Holliday* [1981] Ch 405 is an exception.

[69] Insolvency Act 1985, ss. 171 (3–5); s. 172 introduces a similar compromise where the bankrupt, whether married or not, has minor children living with him at the property.

[70] Although it has been held that sale will not be ordered in favour of a purchaser who has behaved discreditably: *Chhokar* v. *Chhokar* [1984] F. L. R. 313.

[71] [1965] 2 QB 666, 678. This view was rejected in the same case by Russell LJ, at 689–90, and repeated by Lord Denning in *Jackson* v. *Jackson* [1971] 3 All ER 774, 777. It would mean that, in many instances, a spouse co-owner could not prevent the other spouse from inheriting his share by survivorship without instituting matrimonial proceedings.

[72] *Re Draper* [1969] 1 Ch 486; *Harris* v. *Goddard* [1983] 3 All ER 242.

detrimental reliance upon some representation or acquiescence by X, by virtue of the doctrine of proprietary estoppel? A 'just' outcome in particular cases may suggest that X's successor should not go free of responsibility; but how is that to be squared with the overarching doctrinal tenets?

We may unpack some of the issues by attending again to the three characteristics to be looked for in a fully fledged interest in land. It is now clear that even a wholly executory contractual licence may confer the first characteristic, that of enjoyment-content related to the land itself, since it is enforceable by specific performance and not merely in damages.[73] Whether contractual licences have the second characteristic (general protection against all comers) is a notoriously unresolved question. Conversely, 'estoppel interests' appear to have characteristic 2,[74] but it is unclear whether they enjoy characteristic 1. One who has expended money on another's land may, should a litigated dispute arise, receive anything from just his money back[75] to an award of the fee simple.[76] Pending judicial crystallization of his rights, does he own an interest in the land or merely an equitable *locus standi* to claim one?

The answer to this latter question may be associated with two other unresolved issues: whether an estoppel interest is assignable and whether it falls within the classification of interests in land implied in the Land Registration Act 1925.[77] Given the diffuse nature of this category of rights, it will be hard to achieve both doctrinal consistency and consequentialist justice. If nascent claims based on proprietary estoppel are ordinary equitable interests in land, they may, in principle, be transmissible. And where title to the land is registered, they will bind successors to the estopped party, as overriding interests 'subsisting in reference' to the land within section 70, where the claimant is in 'actual

[73] *Verrall* v. *Great Yarmouth BC* [1981] QB 202. That a contractual licensee's rights have this land-related content has been enough to enable him to claim compensation for a lost 'interest' when, one way or another, the rights have been taken from him: *Tanner* v. *Tanner* [1975] 3 All ER 776; *DHN Food Distributors Ltd.* v. *Tower Hamlets LBC* [1976] 3 All ER 462; *Pennine Raceway Ltd.* v. *Kirklees MC* [1982] 3 All ER 628.

[74] *Dillwyn* v. *Llewellyn* (1862) 4 de G F and J 517. *Inwards* v. *Baker* [1965] 2 QB 29; *Ives (ER) Investment Ltd.* v. *High* [1967] 2 QB 379; *Griffiths* v. *Williams* [1978] 248 EG 947; *Re Sharpe* (1980) 1 All ER 198.

[75] *Dodsworth* v. *Dodsworth* [1973] 228 EG 1115.

[76] *Pascoe* v. *Turner* [1979] 2 All ER 945.

[77] In *Blacklocks* v. *JB Developments (Godalming) Ltd.* [1981] 3 All ER 392, Judge Mervyn Davies QC, in the context of the equity to rectify documents for common mistake, equated the dichotomy between personal rights which do not come within the registered-land scheme and proprietary rights which do, with the question of whether or not a right is assignable.

occupation'. Where he is not, they will fall before all transferees for valuable consideration, since the latter take subject to interests protected on the register and overriding interests,[78] 'but free from all other estates and interests whatsoever' (section 20).[79] The result will be that the court may have to exercise what is in essence an *in personam* discretionary jurisdiction between ill-assorted, and arbitrarily selected, pairs of disputants. That will be the consequence of derogating from the doctrinal prescription, of recognizing as 'interests in land' inchoate claims with no defined content.

Conversely, if uncrystallized estoppel claims are not interests in land, they will not be transmissible and will not come within the registered-land classification of interests. It will then be necessary to accommodate those cases in which successors have been affected, by derogating from the doctrinal cleavage. It would have to be contended that, although estoppel interests do not bind all comers, yet they are not enforceable merely against a single obligor. Some successors of the land-owner who made the representation upon which they are based would also be obliged to make good what had been represented, including, perhaps, those claiming under the estate of the estopped party, his trustee in bankruptcy, successors who in some way reinforced the representation, and all who took with express notice of the facts giving rise to the estoppel. On this view, an estoppel interest would be neither an overriding interest 'subsisting in reference' to land within section 70 of the Land Registration Act, nor an 'interest in land' of which a transferee could take free within section 20.[80] Consequently, whether it could be

[78] If the claimant is not in actual occupation, estoppel interests cannot rank as overriding interests within s. 70 (1) (g); and they are unlikely to be considered 'other easements not being equitable easements required to be protected by notice on the register' so as to qualify as overriding interests within s. 70 (1) (a). But see *Celsteel Ltd.* v. *Alton Holdings Ltd.* [1985] 2 All ER 562, 574–6 (Scott J.).

[79] Unless, possibly, some relevant requirement of 'good faith' were read into section 20: *Peffer* v. *Rigg* [1978] 3 All ER 745. Contra, *Miles* v. *Bull (No. 2)* [1969] 3 All ER 1585; *De Lusignan* v. *Johnson* [1974] 230 EG 499.

[80] The Law Commission, in its Working Paper No. 67, part B (4) (iv), suggests that estoppel interests fall outside the terms of section 20 (changing the view which they expressed in Working Paper No. 45, para. 70). They do not consider the argument that, even if an estoppel interest is not an 'estate' or 'interest' within section 20, it might still be held to be a 'matter' or 'claim' within section 59 (6), in which case a purchaser would not be 'concerned with' it unless it was protected by an entry on the register. However, they draw a general distinction between the questions, 'by what equitable burdens is the purchaser bound by succession?'; and 'by what equitable burdens is the conscience of the new owner bound in the circumstances?' The latter question escapes the provisions of the Act; and it would be the relevant question, on the assumption that estoppel interests fall outside the doctrinal cleavage, and so are not ordinary interests in land.

enforced against a particular successor would not turn on whether the claimant was in actual occupation. In the upshot individualized justice could be meted out, but at the price of undermining that conceptual economy (so crucial to the institution of private property in land) which the doctrinal cleavage subserves. No purchaser from an estopped party could rely on the land registration scheme. And the inchoate estoppel claim being non-transmissible, no land-owner having such a claim over his neighbour's land could dispose of his own land without first going to court for crystallization.

Another incipient sapping of the doctrinal cleavage is to be found in one of the many suggested solutions to the question of whether contractual licences bind the licensor's successors. Lord Denning's favoured answer, stated in *Errington* v. *Errington*, was that they should have the same range of protection as ordinary equitable interests in land—that they should bind all save a bona fide purchaser without notice.[81] In *Binions* v. *Evans*, however, in recognition of the opposition which this view had aroused,[82] Lord Denning offered a more limited solution: even supposing contractual licences do not rank as equitable interests in land, still the court will enforce them against a successor who expressly contracted with the licensor to give effect to the contractual licence, by imposing on him a remedial constructive trust.[83] If this view does turn out to represent the law, it will constitute another example of a claim to land-use which is neither a personal right enforceable only against a single obligor nor an interest in land availing against successors generally.

It would also provide a means of escaping an apparent statutory ban on the creation of new interests in land, to which academic critics (though not the courts) have given much attention. Section 4 (1) of the Law of Property Act 1925 provides:

> . . . and equitable interest in land shall only be capable of being validly created in any case in which an equivalent equitable interest in property real or personal could have been validly created [before the commencement of the Act].[84]

[81] [1952] 1 KB 290. This view has received *sub silentio* support from the decision of the Court of Appeal in *Midland Bank Ltd.* v. *Farm Pride Hatcheries Ltd.* (1981) 260 EG 493.

[82] *NP Bank Ltd.* v. *Hastings Car Mart Ltd.* [1964] Ch 665, 669 (Russell LJ); *NP Bank Ltd.* v. *Ainsworth* [1965] AC 1175, 1239–40 (Lord Upjohn), 1251–2 (Lord Wilberforce). *Re Solomon* [1967] Ch 573 (Goff J.).

[83] [1972] Ch 359, 368. Cf. *Lyus* v. *Prowsa Developments Ltd.* [1982] 2 All ER 953.

[84] Section 14 provides: 'This part of this Act shall not prejudicially affect the interest of any person in possession or in actual occupation of land . . .'. A technical argument could, therefore, be advanced to the effect that the elevation of contractual licences to interests in

If a contractual licence is binding only on a limited class of successors, it need not be considered an 'equitable interest' within this provision. Even if it has the wider range of protection advocated in *Errington*, it might still escape the section 4 prohibition. Contractual rights are normally freely assignable. A wide range of contractual licences over land, however, will not be, because their express or implied terms make their enjoyment-content personal to the licensee. Hence, even if contractual licences were to be held to have the first two characteristics of fully fledged interests in land, they would lack the third (transmissibility), and that might be enough to place them outside the 'equitable interests' referred to in the subsection.

Such considerations illustrate a more general point about the role of legislation in the development of doctrine. A sovereign legislature can add anything to that totality of mutually consistent propositions which constitutes 'the present law'. Any specific enactment about what must or may be done in relation to land necessarily derogates from any inconsistent rule created by courts, as when Parliament conferred some degree of irremoveability upon deserted spouses by the Matrimonial Homes Act, or upon tenants whose contractual tenancies have expired by the Rent Acts. Where, however, the legislature inserts some new principle, maxim, conceptual definition, or classification, into the congeries of doctrinal pronouncements which form part of a historic official tradition, the outcome is much less clear. Doctrinal propositions, taken in the raw, have only what Weber called 'logically formal meaning'. They make immediate sense only as part of a metaphysic created by a specialist caste of lawyers.

> Their rational, systematic character, as well as their relatively small degree of concreteness of content easily result in a far-reaching emancipation of legal thinking from the every-day needs of the public.[85]

Of course, at one remove, they have a bearing upon the trespassory and other imperative and permissive rules which constitute the momentary legal system. Although the definitions contained in the opening sections of the Law of Property Act 1925 appear to be addressed only to conveyancers and their academic collaborators, if fitted together with other material they can be related to that which may or may not be

land is not prohibited by section 4 (1), provided they are occupational contractual licences. The same limitation would make it possible to distinguish two authorities commonly thought to stand in the way of this development: *King* v. *David Allen and Sons Bill Posting Ltd.* [1916] 2 AC 54; *Clore* v. *Theatrical Properties Ltd.* [1936] 3 All ER 483.

85 Weber, 205.

lawfully done with land. For example, something like the following argument is involved in any assertion that section 4 (1) is conclusive against the possibility of contractual licences ever binding successors:

> Since X (who is in possession) asserts that he is entitled to stay there as against Y (who has duly acquired the fee simple from Z), and since (granted the doctrinal cleavage) X can only resist Y's claim if X has acquired an estate or interest in the land, and since the dealings between Z and X did not confer on X either of the legal estates recognized by section 1 of the Act nor any equitable interest which would have been known to the law in 1925, and since section 4 (1) prohibits the creation of new equitable interests, X must be a trespasser and Y be entitled as of right to recovery of the land.

The argument is far from watertight. As indicated above, its force might be sidestepped by declaring that there is an *in personam* constructive-trust jurisdiction not captured by the doctrinal cleavage, or by denying that the ban contained in section 4 (1) went beyond fully fledged (and hence transmissible) equitable interests. Or, more simply, it might be held that the subsection was no more than an instruction to conveyancers, and not a freeze on judicial doctrinal creativity at all. When the legislature throws stones in the pool of pure doctrine, the ripples must be captured by juristic speculation.

6. THE CRITICAL STUDIES ALTERNATIVE

Academic commentators have advanced a wide variety of views as to how claims to land-use, arising from informal transactions, should be accommodated to doctrine. Either it is contended that, properly understood, they represent no major departure from the doctrinal prescription or the doctrinal cleavage;[86] or that, in various ways, they constitute limited and qualified exceptions.[87] Rather than discuss the merits of these proposals, I turn now to a fundamental question which goes to the nature and propriety of doctrinal reasoning in general. Why should doctrine be accommodated at all? If such accommodation fosters

[86] See, for example, R. J. Smith, 'Licences and Constructive Trusts' (1973) 32 *Camb. Law J.* 123. G. Martin, 'Constructive Trusts and Licensees' [1980] *Conv.* 207. A. Briggs, 'Licences: Back to Basics' [1981] *Conv.* 212. S. Moriarty, 'Licences and Land Law' (1984) 100 *Law Quarterly Rev.* 376.

[87] See, for example, P. N. Todd, 'Estoppel Licences and Third Party Rights' [1981] *Conv.* 347; M. P. Thompson, 'Licences: Questioning the Basics' [1983] *Conv.* 50; J. D. Davies, 'Informal Arrangements Affecting Land' (1979) 8 *Sydney Law Rev.* 578; 'Constructive Trusts, Contract and Estoppels' (1980) 7 *Adelaide Law Rev.* 200; A. R. Everton, 'Towards a Concept of "Quasi-property"?' [1982] *Conv.* 118.

predictability and underpins the separation of powers, who benefits from that? If it promotes the rule of law, who cares? Supposing that Weber was right in his descriptive generalization about legal thinking, in contending that it is of its essence to be distinctively conceptual. Need that be accepted as an unalterable prescription? Can we not envisage a radically different kind of lawyer with a quite different approach to doctrine and, indeed, a fundamentally revised conception of law?

That we can and should is one of the major contentions of that movement amongst radical, leftist writers in the United States which is self-styled 'The Critical Legal Studies Movement'. Its adherents have ranged widely over different areas of law, bringing to bear a seemingly heterogeneous array of destructive criticisms. Fortunately, however, one of its most distinguished advocates, Professor R. M. Unger, has recently advanced a coherent and cogent exposition of the underlying themes and programmatic concerns of the movement; and it is to his essay that we may turn for an alternative approach to doctrine.[88]

Unger claims that central to the movement is a rejection of 'formalism', in the broad sense of any 'commitment to, and therefore also a belief in the possibility of, a method of legal justification that can be clearly contrasted to open-ended disputes about the basic terms of social life'.[89] Orthodox legal practice assumes that, at least sometimes, answers to controversial legal questions can be sought by a method which distances the lawyer from the political hustings. It involves working out the implications of principles underlying any given body of rules. Such an approach is offensive to the radical critic, because it must assume 'objectivism', that is, 'the belief that the authoritative legal materials—the system of statutes, cases, and accepted legal ideas—embody and sustain a defensible scheme of human association'.[90]

However (and this is the dagger point of Unger's programmatic), the opponent of the established order need not limit himself to ideological arguments establishing the unworthiness of modern political and social arrangements. If he is a legal scholar, he can subvert from inside. He can begin where the conventional lawyer does, with the given legal materials. But unlike his benighted orthodox counterpart, he will not aim at consistency in his analysis of principles. The orthodox seeks to reconcile and make coherent different facets of doctrine, allowing for

88 R. M. Unger, 'The Critical Legal Studies Movement' (1983) 96 *Harv. Law Rev.* 561.

89 Ibid., 564; see Duncan Kennedy, 'Form and Substance in Private Adjudication' (1976) 89 *Harvard Law Rev.* 1685.

90 Unger, 565.

exceptions where necessary. He is to be exposed. Given his techniques, anything can be proved and so nothing can: '. . . a doctrinal practice that puts its hope in the contrast of legal reasoning to ideology, philosophy, and political prophecy ends up as a collection of makeshift apologies'.[91]

The radical legal scholar highlights and emphasizes the dissonances and inconsistencies to be found in the legal materials. Beginning with problem areas and thence moving out across a whole branch of law, he demonstrates that wherever there is a principle there is a matching counter-principle. One must descend, not only to a second level of principles in order to apply a first level of rules, but also to a third level of ideological assumptions in order to explain the principles; and at this third level there are no defensible commitments in terms of which the principles or the rules can be coherently rationalized.[92] He thus engages in what Unger calls 'expanded' or 'deviationist' doctrine. He shows that conceptualizations within legal reasoning cannot exclude any of the empirical data and conflicting ideological claims which form part of political argument in the broadest sense:

> . . . the crucial feature of deviationist doctrine is the willingness to recognise and develop the disharmonies of the law: . . . Critical doctrine does this by finding in their disharmonies the elements of broader contests among prescriptive conceptions of society.[93]

The radical scholar destroys conventional legal analysis. He substitutes for it a new vision of the part law might play in a more acceptable social setting. Social and political arrangements must be so organized that all the hierarchies and differentiations which make modern society intolerable are destroyed and cannot re-emerge. This will necessitate redistribution of wealth and an expansion of the existing branches of government. Governmental institutions of a populist kind must entrench on areas of family and social life now exempted from them, in order that hierarchical divisions can be dissipated. With the same objective, an 'empowered democracy' must not be subjected to those checks and balances which impede truly radical change. Something like conventional courts may have a role to play in upholding 'immunity rights'. These are not defined by Unger. Presumably, they would protect the individual against the empowered democracy in such matters as life and liberty—but certainly not as regards property.

[91] Ibid., 573.
[92] Ibid., 646–8.
[93] Ibid., 578.

A crucial feature of the revised social institutions would be the 'disaggregation of the consolidated property right'.[94] The dominant conception of right accords a zone of discretion to the rightholder, enabling him to 'shoot at will in his corner of town'.[95] Property rights, in particular, 'involving as they do an essentially unlimited control of the divisible portions of social capital ... create in some people, or in the more or less stable positions that these people occupy, a power to reduce other people to dependence'.[96] The new vision replaces this conception with provisional 'market rights', 'solidarity rights', and, above all, 'destabilization rights'.[97]

Destabilization rights will be invoked to disrupt social hierarchies and differentiations. Their implementation will require new institutions and a new species of lawyer. Unger gives no details of these novelties; but he makes plain that the reconstruction necessitates the abandonment of any belief in a logic of inherent institutional roles (that is, destabilization rights are to be enforced by informal governmental processes not modelled on traditional courts); and that legal expertise will survive as a loose collection of legal, social, and political skills[98] (that is, the legal technician is replaced by the fully politicized vanguard intellectual).

Unger illustrates the application of deviationist doctrine in relation to two areas of American law—'equal protection' and contract. Let us imagine an adherent of the Critical Legal Studies Movement who applies Unger's procedures to interests in land in English law. Out of deference to the crusading zeal of the movement, we shall call him 'Hero'.

Hero will begin with troublesome putative interests—such as contractual licences, estoppel interests, options, and co-ownership interests—and deny that they can in any way be accommodated, even as qualified and limited exceptions, to any generalized description of the concept 'interest in land'. He will point out that they reflect, at a third deep level below rules and principles, irreconcilable value commitments about the terms of social life; for example, on the one hand the view that citizens should receive some part of communal wealth which is theirs to deal with at discretion, and on the other, the view that vulnerable individuals disadvantaged within social hierarchies must be given indefeasible claims to dwellings. From this starting-point, Hero will proceed to total dissolution of the doctrinal prescription and the

[94] Ibid., 596.
[95] Ibid., 597.
[96] Ibid., 655.
[97] Ibid., 600.
[98] Ibid., 668.

doctrinal cleavage across the whole range of more familiar estates and interests in land. Enjoyment-content, general protection, and transmissibility should be disunited. An open-ended set of ownership privileges should no longer be the incident of the legal estate.[99] Instead, social-revisionary criteria should determine allocation of land-use. Within these limits, 'splitting the difference' should be the loadstone for title disputes.[100] Freehold and leasehold property should no longer be conceived of as freely alienable, either *inter vivos* or on death. Purported assignments must be set aside wherever their implementation would maintain social divisions between the haves and the have-nots, or bolster patrimonial family hierarchies, or sexual role divisions, or regional, class, or racial divisions. Where transmissions are permitted but it is alleged that the right of a third party binds the transferee, the issue is to be settled, not by asking whether the right is *in personam* or *in rem*, nor even by reference to some mere exception to this dichotomy based on some such principle as 'good faith' or 'constructive trust'. We should consider, instead, whether the right has the quality of a destabilization right; whether its implementation would bring a little nearer the vision of a society in which all social hierarchy and division is outlawed.

Hero will bear in mind two programmatic limitations: scorn for institutional deference and disdain of the conventional-doctrinal crutch. He will regard it as no objection to any open-ended, politicized analysis that it is the sort of argument which could not be accepted by a judge or advanced by an advocate in a conventional court. He is a legal scholar, not a lackey of professional practice. Should anyone charge him with futility, he will point out that his analysis is not supposed to conform to the conception of doctrine which is built in to our existing law ways. He has a vision of new institutions (street committees? work-place collectives? town meetings?) wherein the new vanguard lawyer will lead the untutored along the road of destabilization. As Unger says in response to the question whether deviationist doctrine can be used by judges, 'We are neither servants of the state (not at least in the conventional sense) nor their technical assistants. We have no stake in finding a pre-established harmony between moral compulsions and institutional constraints.'[101]

[99] See J.W. Harris, 'Ownership of Land in English Law', in P. Birks and N. MacCormick (eds.), *The Legal Mind: Essays in Honour of Tony Honoré* (Oxford, 1986).

[100] Unger, 636, 638, advocates loss-sharing in disputes over contract-formation.

[101] Ibid., 581.

Conversely, disdain for doctrinal crutches entails that Hero will not employ a conventional doctrinal argument even where it happens to lead in the right direction. It might be, for example, that a modest step towards the dissolution of social hierarchy and moneyed might would be achieved by the following argument:

X advanced 10 per cent of the purchase price when her cohabitee bought the house in which they now live. If he mortgages the house to a bank without telling her, she will be able to resist any claim to possession brought by the bank. This is so for the following reasons: all the cases on co-ownership interests accept that, in such circumstances, a presumed resulting trust arises giving her an interest under an implied trust for sale; and the House of Lords have laid it down in the *Boland* case that such trust interests are overriding interests.

This is an argument Hero must not use. To do so would be tacitly to concede that there is a distinction between technical-doctrinal and open-ended ideological reasoning. Hero is a legal scholar with a radical social vision, not a mere reformer. 'The appeal to a spurious conceptual necessity may prove tactically expedient. In the end, however, it always represents a defeat for our cause...'[102]

It is beyond the scope of this essay to assess the political merits of the new vision or the social-theoretical assumptions which underpin it, central to which is Unger's claim that human beings can imagine and construct a social world completely unlike any of the types of society which our history has so far produced.[103] It is enough to record agreement with Unger's opening assertion that the Critical Legal Studies Movement (as he interprets it) substitutes 'another conception of law' to that which is presently central to modern legal thought.[104] Doctrinal reasoning is intrinsic to our legal institutions, and therefore doctrine is inherent in our conception of law. Weber overstated the contrast between 'lawyers' law' and untramelled 'substantive rationality'. His thesis is, however, essentially correct. A 'law' which referred every issue of resource allocation to unrestricted ideological controversy would have renounced that 'formal character' which is 'immanent' to the conception of law that we have. As we have seen in the context of the evolution of interests in land in English law, the interplay between doctrinal reasoning and unlimited consequentialism is complex and variegated. However, even when consequentialism dominates the elucidation of some interest made dispositive by a legal rule, as in the *Boland*

102 Ibid., 616.
103 Ibid., 648–55.
104 Ibid., 563.

case, the range of possible interpretations is limited by the immanent necessity to give the concept *some* definite meaning.

Believers in the new vision can shake off all the shackles of doctrinal consistency. Its conventional justifications are nothing to them. In place of certainty and predictability, they espouse 'destabilization'. Current separation of powers notions will have no place within the multifaceted and populist institutions of the 'empowered democracy'. And the whole idea of the rule of law is tied to the doctrine-impregnated conception of law which is to be discarded. The only 'cost' will be a necessary distancing from current institutions and existing legal practice. While he engages in direct political action, Hero must disengage from all 'constructive' legal advocacy. He must steer himself and his pupils away from any form of argumentation which might be thought formally correct within our present institutional structure. The purity of the new vision demands nothing less.

What of those who cannot share the new vision; those for whom a social theory divorced from the lessons of history is chimerical, and for whom the thought of vanguard lawyers armed with real destabilization power conjures up nightmare visions of re-education camps? For such, I suppose, the erudite activity of trying to produce doctrinal order, any doctrinal order, out of refractory materials acquires a new importance. It may be difficult or even tedious, and certainly replete with what Unger calls 'makeshift apologies'. Perhaps, as Weber claimed, the 'logical systematization of the law has been the consequence of the intrinsic intellectual needs of the legal theorists and their disciples'.[105] But for such disbelievers in Hero's alternative, it turns out to be startlingly humane.

[105] Ibid., 278.

9

Towards a Jurisprudence of Consent*

SIMON LEE†

I. INTRODUCTION

THE concept of consent features throughout the law. It is an issue, for example, in the criminal law of rape,[1] in the constitutional future of Canadian Indians[2] and Northern Ireland,[3] in the tort doctrine of *volenti non fit iniuria*,[4] and the contractual doctrine of duress.[5]

Two novel cases on consent in a medical context made their way to the House of Lords in 1984 and 1985: *Sidaway*[6] and *Gillick*.[7] Since consent is such a pervasive concept in the law, these cases were bound to be significant for jurisprudence in general as well as medical law and ethics in particular. As Lord Scarman took the opportunity in both cases to articulate his own approach to judicial decision-making, *Gillick* and *Sidaway* are twice or thrice blessed with jurisprudential interest.

Sidaway concerned a patient's right to know of the risks involved in medical treatment. Mrs Sidaway claimed that she should have been warned of the very small risk that serious injury could result from her operation. The risk had materialized and she was left severely disabled. All nine judges who heard the case dismissed her claim for damages. But the importance of the case is how the law determines whether patients like Mrs Sidaway have consented to their operations. Lord

† I would like to thank the Editors for inviting me to contribute a view from the Strand and for their comments on the first draft. I am also deeply grateful to Professor Ian Kennedy for inspiring me to think about these issues.

1 e.g. *Olugbója* (1981) 73 Cr. App. Rep. 344.

2 *Manuel* v. *Attorney General* [1983] Ch 77.

3 Northern Ireland Constitution Act 1973 s. 1.

4 See e.g. *Winfield & Jolowicz on Tort* (London, 12th edn., 1984), 700–16.

5 See e.g. *Chitty on Contracts* (London, 25th edn., 1983), ch. 7.

6 *Sidaway* v. *Board of Governors of the Bethlem Royal Hospital and the Maudsley Hospital* [1985] 2 WLR 480.

7 *Gillick* v. *DHSS* [1985] 3 WLR 830.

Scarman found the American doctrine of 'informed consent'[8] to be a good model. The other judges disagreed, being more prepared to defer to medical judgment. In practice, however, even they have provided a platform from which lawyers could create some requirements of informed consent.

Gillick raised the question of consent to contraceptive treatment for girls under 16 years old. Is the patient's consent sufficient, or should the doctor additionally seek that of her parents? Here the judges seemed to be in disarray. Mrs Gillick was unsuccessful in that the Law Lords, by a 3–2 majority, reversed a unanimous Court of Appeal and restored the first instance judge's conclusions as to the law. So the patient's capacity to consent should form the focus of a doctor's attention rather than the wishes of her parents.

2. 'CONSENT' IN LAW

Given the wide range of legal contexts in which consent appears, it seems unlikely that we can discover some 'real essence' in the concept. Lawyers manipulate the notion of consent. There are undoubtedly some limits to what could plausibly count as consent but there are undoubtedly many plausible interpretations within those limits. The questions for debate are not about the abstract 'meaning' of consent but what does the law use consent to represent and what content would we prefer the law to attribute to it? Two examples from outside the medical sphere should illustrate this.

Contract lawyers will remember a controversy between Atiyah and Tiplady over economic duress.[9] Atiyah argued that a criminal case, *Lynch* v. *D.P.P. of Northern Ireland*,[10] 'totally demolishes the theory that duress operates by "overbearing the will" of the party subject to it'. Atiyah maintained that it was not true to say that somebody acting under coercion did not intend or will the consequences of his actions. He considered it more accurate to recognize that such a person still had a

[8] By 'the American doctrine of informed consent' is meant the doctrine laid down in *Canterbury* v. *Spence* (1972) 464 F. 2d 772, a decision of the US Court of Appeals, District of Columbia Circuit, although this approach is only followed in a minority of States. Based on the right to self-determination, the doctor is liable if he omits to warn of such a risk that, in the court's view, a prudent person in the patient's situation would have regarded as significant.

[9] P. Atiyah, 'Economic Duress and the "Overborne Will"' (1982) 98 *Law Quarterly Rev.* 197; D. Tiplady, 'Concepts of Duress' (1983) 99 *Law Quarterly Rev.* 188; P. Atiyah, 'Duress and the Overborne Will Again', ibid., 353.

[10] *Lynch* v. *D.P.P. of Northern Ireland* [1975] AC 653.

choice or free will. We had then to decide, as a matter of policy, what kinds of threats should be deemed improper or what kinds of choices were intolerable. The authoritative work of reference, Chitty, adopts Atiyah's view, although this is scarcely surprising since Atiyah wrote the relevant chapter.[11] But his approach is, in any event, persuasive and instructive.

Criminal lawyers will also recognize that it is a matter of policy whether or not the law tolerates certain threats which affect 'consent'. The *actus reus* of rape is 'unlawful sexual intercourse with a woman who at the time of the intercourse does not consent to it'.[12] If we pretend that dictionary definitions resolve this problem of consent, confusion will reign.[13] As Glanville Williams has observed:

> To consent to do something and to wish or want to do it, are not the same. I may consent to visit my great-uncle George, when I decidedly 'do not want to go'. I go, complainingly, because he wants to see me, because I am told I must go by someone I do not want to offend, because I feel I ought to go, because I have some faint hope of benefiting myself from the visit, and so on. And I keep on telling you, I do not want to go, but I consent to go. Everyone who goes, consents to go, unless he is shanghaied or goes at pistol point or is tricked by being told that he is going somewhere else.[14]

Does this mean that everyone who has sexual intercourse consents to it? Well, 'shanghaied' and 'pistol point' can be developed to conclude that sexual intercourse obtained by the threat of force constitutes rape. And there are specific offences which deal with sexual intercourse obtained by some other threats. But Williams's point is that the legal validity of 'consent' depends upon the effectiveness of the choices, the capacity of the decision-maker, and the demands of public policy, which refuses to recognize 'consent' to activities which are deemed socially or morally dangerous. Both Atiyah and Williams are exposing the value judgments which underlie the law. Determining the content of consent is a creative exercise. Judges interpret it according to some vision of why consent is important and of the values which the law should espouse.

So what is the function of consent in medical law and ethics? It is a technique for safeguarding patients' autonomy. The requirement of consent before the doctor treats a patient acts as a corrective to the doctor's power and professional paternalism. If we really want equality

[11] See above, n. 5.
[12] Sexual Offences (Amendment) Act 1976, s. 1 (1) (a).
[13] See above, *Olugbója*, n. 1.
[14] G. Williams, *Textbook of Criminal Law* (London, 1983), 550.

within the doctor–patient relationship we can make consent an onerous doctrine. But if we believe that doctor really does know best and if we do not place great store by self-determination, then we can make consent merely a perfunctory step on the way to medical treatment.

Two broad approaches can be discerned among those who value autonomy.[15] Some justify its importance on utilitarian grounds. Autonomy is conducive to human welfare. We will be happier if our autonomy is respected, perhaps because we will experiment and learn from our successes and mistakes. The other rationale is to rely on a right to liberty. On this view, autonomy should be respected as the ultimate, non-instrumental value.[16] If we value autonomy only in so far as it maximizes human welfare, then we might well accept that in some cases autonomy ought to be overridden. We might conclude, for example, that heroin addiction makes people unhappy and that we should therefore countermand an autonomous decision to begin taking heroin. Do we really value autonomy more highly than this, so that we would always respect autonomous decisions, however disastrous? If we do see autonomy as the paramount value, of course, we might still face dilemmas. Autonomy is a capacity which we can possess to a greater or lesser extent and one which we can enjoy through time. By restricting the autonomy of the potential heroin addict now, we might preserve his autonomy for the future. Properly understood, autonomy does not preclude paternalism. Choices still remain. We need to decide when and under what conditions a person is capable of autonomous decision-making, and when we should override exercises of autonomy. This requires consideration of at least the following issues.[17]

(1) Does the person concerned have the capacity to consent?
(2) If not, who is in the best position to act as proxy and on what criteria should the proxy decide?
(3) Is the 'consent' voluntary?
(4) Is the 'consent' based on information as to the risks of the course of conduct?
(5) Is the 'consent' based on information as to the alternative courses of action?
(6) Even if the above conditions are satisfied, is there any overriding reason to invalidate the consent?

[15] See J. Raz, *The Morality of Freedom* (Oxford, 1986), for a detailed analysis of autonomy.

[16] Most famously, Kant's moral philosophy is based on this.

[17] i.e. to develop a full doctrine. In this essay, of course, we can do no more than begin to consider a couple of these issues.

3. THE GILLICK CASE

Sidaway and *Gillick* together make a substantial contribution to filling in the detail of that structure. The judgments of Lord Scarman are of particular interest in this regard. Lord Scarman's public service has been quite outstanding on a number of fronts. He is well known to the general public as the Great Reporter, having inquired into the troubles of Northern Ireland, Red Lion Square, Grunwick, and most famously Brixton. He was the first chairman of the Law Commission. He has been a persistent advocate of constitutional reform, calling in particular for a Bill of Rights. He has been an active participant in the House of Lords' legislative capacity. And he has also been a judicial activist. In that role, he has gone out of his way to explain what he is doing and why he is doing it. In his latter years on the bench he seems to have taken Dworkin seriously, talking in terms of principle rather than policy. In *McLoughlin* v. *O'Brian*,[18] for example, Lord Scarman sought to distinguish principle from policy, much to the surprise and regret of his colleagues.[19] Unabashed by their criticism, he relied on his own speech in *McLoughlin* when repeating that emphasis on principle in *Sidaway*.[20] But his celebration of principle is best captured by his masterly judgment in *Gillick*.[21] His quest for a principle yields several different formulations.

(1) 'The principle of the law, as I shall endeavour to show, is that parental rights are derived from parental duty and exist only so long as they are needed for the protection of the person and property of the child.'[22]

(2) 'The principle is that parental right or power of control of the person and property of his child exists primarily to enable the parent to discharge his duty of maintenance, protection, and education until he reaches such an age as to be able to look after himself and make his own decision.'[23]

(3) 'The underlying principle of the law was exposed by Blackstone and can be seen to have been acknowledged in the case law. It is that parental right yields to the child's right to make his own decisions when he reaches a sufficient understanding and intelli-

18 [1982] 2 WLR 982, 987.
19 Ibid., at 995, 996, 997.
20 [1985] 2 WLR 480, 492.
21 [1985] 3 WLR 830, 852–3.
22 Ibid., 853.
23 Ibid., 855.
24 Ibid.

gence to be capable of making up his own mind on the matter requiring decision.'[24]

(4) 'The principle underlying (the age of discretion cases) was plainly that an order would be refused if the child had sufficient intelligence and understanding to make up his own mind.'[25]

(5) 'The principle is clear ... we can agree with Cockburn C.J. as to the principle of the law—the attainment by a child of an age of sufficient discretion to enable him or her to exercise a wise choice in his or her own interests.'[26]

(6) 'I would hold that as a matter of law the parental right to determine whether or not their minor child below the age of 16 will have medical treatment terminates if and when the child achieves a sufficient understanding and intelligence to enable him or her to understand fully what is proposed.'[27]

Lord Scarman presumably regards these several statements as identical or at least as representing the same principle. But others might think that some of the variations on the common theme are significantly different: (2), (3), and (4) are along the same lines, emphasizing the requirement that the child must have sufficient understanding and intelligence to be capable of making up her own mind; but (5) talks of a wise choice and (6) talks of understanding fully what is proposed; (1) seems to be on a different tack altogether, focusing on the need to protect the child.

The various formulations do not necessarily coincide to produce the same result. A girl could be capable of making up her mind (satisfying (2), (3), and (4)) in favour of what others deem an unwise choice (thus not satisfying (5)). There may be a difference between understanding ((2), (3), and (4)) and understanding fully ((6)). But most seriously there is a potential conflict between (1) and the others. Suppose a girl is capable of making up her own mind but the judges feel that she is making a mistake and that her parents' counter-wishes would actually be in the girl's best interests. A judge could argue under (1) that parental rights are still needed here to protect the child. But under (3), for example, the parental protective role is irrelevant if the child can make up her own mind.

One might distinguish (1) and perhaps (5) as being motivated by paternalism, whereas the other statements of principle reflect a con-

[25] Ibid., 856.
[26] Ibid., 857.
[27] Ibid., 858.

fidence in autonomy as the ultimate value which the law should promote. Lord Fraser's orientation seems to be based on paternalism. Although he states that 'In practice most wise parents relax their control gradually as the child develops and encourage him or her to become increasingly independent',[28] nevertheless his primary focus is on what is in the 'best interests' of the particular child. This may not be the same as what the child would decide. It is because of his view that 'in the overwhelming majority of cases the best judges of a child's welfare are his or her parents'[29] that their views should normally be sought. But where the patient's 'best interests require (the doctor) to give her contraceptive advice, treatment, or both without the parental consent',[30] then her understanding and the doctor's judgment of her welfare become decisive.

Lord Fraser is more concerned that the decision be in the girl's best interests than in who makes that decision. His unarticulated assumptions are that the provision of contraception is likely to be in the girl's interests in at least some of these cases and that parents will be reluctant to accept that. Hence Lord Fraser believes that it is safer to rely on the young person herself and particularly her doctor to safeguard her welfare. Lord Fraser's five guidelines according to which contraceptive treatment may be given without consulting parents emphasize the significance of the girl's 'best interests':

(1) that the girl (although under 16 years of age) will understand his advice;
(2) that he cannot persuade her to inform her parents or to allow him to inform the parents that she is seeking contraceptive advice;
(3) that she is very likely to begin or to continue having sexual intercourse with or without contraceptive treatment;
(4) that unless she receives contraceptive advice or treatment her physical or mental health or both are likely to suffer;
(5) that her best interests require him to give her contraceptive advice, treatment, or both without the parental consent.[31]

If read in this way, we may conclude that the *Gillick* majority places different emphases on the values of autonomy and paternalism. Lord Bridge does not exercise his casting vote. On these matters, he is content

[28] Ibid., 842.
[29] Ibid., 843.
[30] Ibid., 844.
[31] Ibid., 844.

to adopt the reasoning of both Lord Fraser and Lord Scarman.[32] This provides a clue, as does the opening of Lord Scarman's opinion, where he approves of Lord Fraser's speech and explains that he is trying to make the same points in his own language in deference to the importance of the case.[33] So perhaps the majority *is* united.

It is possible to reconcile Lord Scarman's concern for the young girl's autonomy and Lord Fraser's safeguards in her best interests. Both judges may have concluded, consciously or subconsciously, that some girls will indulge in early sexual activity with or without contraception and that this may result in pregnancy and then early motherhood or abortion. The commitment of bringing up a baby on the one hand and the emotional trauma of abortion or having a baby adopted on the other hand may be seen as autonomy-reducing. Options and lifestyles may be closed to the mature person because of decisions made or abdicated when less mature. Their Lordships might therefore have decided that the law ought to allow contraceptive advice and treatment for under-16-year-olds. Then they have to explain that decision in legal terminology. If they believe that the girls and the doctors are more likely than the parents to allow contraception, then they can either stress the capacity of the girl herself or the responsibility of doctors and others to decide in the girl's 'best interests'. For this might amount to the same thing in our 'second-best' world where youthful sexual activity does occur. If the overriding aim is to protect those who will be at risk from abortion or early motherhood, then the doctrine of consent can be manipulated to achieve that in various ways. In effect, legal and medical paternalism and the young girl's own wishes are ranged against what is seen as misguided parental paternalism.

Lord Scarman's exquisite legal prose, of course, leads us to believe that the enterprise is one of searching for a principle underlying earlier cases and then applying it to contemporary reality.[34] My point is that there are many different ways of rendering the principle and they seem to stem from different motivations. This might lead us to believe that there is more than one principle available for the great judge to discover or that the great judge is perhaps discovering the principle he wants to discover. We can reconcile the variations if we accept that paternalistic intervention is not always the antithesis of respect for autonomy. But it should be clear that the judge can arrive at the same destination by

[32] Ibid., 864.
[33] Ibid., 846.
[34] Ibid., 853.

different routes. The concept of consent does not control the judges. They control it. The weight they ascribe to values such as autonomy and their hunches as to the practical consequences of imposing a strict or weak test of capacity will influence their approach to the pre-existing law.[35]

Even if we agree on one principle such as Lord Scarman's third formulation, it still provides plenty of scope for manœuvre within the concept of consent. We could lay down a strong or weak test of what is meant by capacity to understand what is involved. Indeed, there seems to be some confusion among their Lordships as to whether the question is capacity to understand or actual understanding.[35a] Apart from that problem, we could pitch the requirement of understanding at different levels. Lord Scarman seems to place a very high premium on understanding:

> When applying these conclusions to contraceptive advice and treatment it has to be borne in mind that there is much that has to be understood by a girl under the age of 16 if she is to have legal capacity to consent to such treatment. It is not enough that she should understand the nature of the advice which is being given: she must also have a sufficient maturity to understand what is involved. There are moral and family questions, especially her relationship with her parents; long-term problems associated with the emotional impact of pregnancy and its termination; and there are the risks to health of sexual intercourse at her age, risks which contraception may diminish but cannot eliminate. It follows that a doctor will have to satisfy himself that she is able to appraise these factors before he can safely proceed on the basis that she has at law capacity to consent to contraceptive treatment. And it further follows that ordinarily the proper course will be for him, as the guidance lays down, first to seek to persuade the girl to bring her parents into consultation, and, if she refuses, not to prescribe contraceptive treatment unless he is satisfied that her circumstances are such that he ought to proceed without parental knowledge and consent.[36]

It may be that very few adults could meet Lord Scarman's criteria. Again, we do not really know what he means throughout that passage by the verb 'to understand'. But Mrs Gillick could have hailed this emphasis on the difficulty of surmounting the hurdle of consent as a victory for her belief that under-16-year-olds should not be entrusted with this decision. The tenor of the rest of Lord Scarman's judgment suggests that he thought under-16-year-olds could fulfil his require-

[35] S. Lee, *Law and Morals* (Oxford 1986).

[35a] And, particularly, in the context of the essay, it is interesting to consider the relationship between Lord Scarman's approach in *Sidaway* and here.

[36] [1985] 3 WLR 830, 858.

ments as to understanding and maturity. One of the dissentients, however, more or less adopts the same test but with the opposite conclusion. Lord Templeman believes that under-16s do not possess such a degree of understanding and maturity. Lord Templeman argued that:

I accept also that a doctor may lawfully carry out some forms of treatment with the consent of an infant patient and against the opposition of a parent based on religious or any other grounds. The effect of the consent of the infant depends on the nature of the treatment and the age and understanding of the infant. For example, a doctor with the consent of an intelligent boy or girl of 15 could in my opinion safely remove tonsils or a troublesome appendix. But any decision on the part of a girl to practise sex and contraception requires not only knowledge of the facts of life and of the dangers of pregnancy and disease but also an understanding of the emotional and other consequences to her family, her male partner and to herself. I doubt whether a girl under the age of 16 is capable of a balanced judgment to embark on frequent, regular or casual sexual intercourse fortified by the illusion that medical science can protect her in mind and body and ignoring the danger of leaping from childhood to adulthood without the difficult formative transitional experiences of adolescence. There are many things which a girl under 16 needs to practise but sex is not one of them.[37]

But he thought that there were exceptions:

The position seems to me to be as follows. A doctor is not entitled to decide whether a girl under the age of 16 shall be provided with contraceptive facilities if a parent who is in charge of the girl is ready and willing to make that decision in exercise of parental rights. The doctor is entitled in exceptional circumstances and in emergencies to make provision, normally temporary provision, for contraception but in most cases would be bound to inform the parent of the treatment. The court would not hold the doctor liable for providing contraceptive facilities if the doctor had reasonable grounds for believing that the parent had abandoned or abused parental rights or that there was no parent immediately available for consultation or that there was no parent who was responsible for the girl. But exceptional circumstances and emergencies cannot be expanded into a general discretion for the doctor to provide contraceptive facilities without the knowledge of the parent because of the possibility that a girl to whom contraceptive facilities are not available may irresponsibly court the risk of pregnancy. Such a discretion would enable any girl to obtain contraception on request by threatening to sleep with a man.[38]

In the first passage, Lord Templeman comes close to accepting Lord Scarman's third formulation of common-law principle. In applying the

[37] Ibid., 869.
[38] Ibid., 873.

principle, however, he disagrees with the majority in that Lord Templeman does not believe that a 15-year-old could reach the requisite level of understanding in the complex case of contraception. In the second passage, Lord Templeman seems to come close to Lord Scarman's first formulation. Lord Templeman's priority is the protection of the child and he will focus on parental consent so long as the parents will exercise it in such a way as to protect the child. If parental involvement is likely to be counter-productive, however, then the protection of the child points towards some other proxy. So Lord Templeman then turns to the doctor.

The real motivation for Lord Templeman's dissent seems to be his opinion that girls under 16 will be best protected, in general, by the absence of contraceptive facilities: 'Some girls would come under pressure if contraceptive facilities were known to be available.'[39] But for his disagreement with the majority on the practical consequences of providing contraception for under 16s, therefore, his Lordship might have been prepared to accept a principle of capacity to consent along the lines suggested by Lord Scarman. It is difficult to be more precise on Lord Templeman's view of the common-law principle since his seven-page judgment eschews case law, only once mentioning a case, *Sidaway*, and then only in passing.[40]

Another way of manipulating the concept of consent comes into play in the second passage cited from Lord Templeman's judgment. The rigours of requiring a high level of understanding for a valid consent can be mitigated by allowing exceptions. Not only Lord Templeman but also Lord Scarman employed this technique, so even if we adopt a restrictive approach based on Lord Scarman's list of what a girl must understand, we can turn to the passage which immediately precedes that and which invokes exceptional circumstances as a ground for dispensing with the requirement of consent (or, at least, as allowing the doctor to act as proxy in giving consent):

> ... I would hold that as a matter of law the parental right to determine whether or not their minor child below the age of 16 will have medical treatment terminates if and when the child achieves a sufficient understanding and intelligence to enable him or her to understand fully what is proposed. It will be a question of fact whether a child seeking advice has sufficient understanding of what is involved to give a consent valid in law. Until the child achieves the capacity to

[39] Ibid., 871.

[40] In *Sidaway* itself he also resisted a survey of the precedents, again mentioning only one case.

consent, the parental right to make the decision continues save only in exceptional circumstances. Emergency, parental neglect, abandonment of the child or inability to find the parent are examples of exceptional situations justifying the doctor proceeding to treat the child without parental knowledge and consent; but there will arise, no doubt, other exceptional situations in which it will be reasonable for the doctor to proceed without the parent's consent.[41]

Obviously, the width of the exceptions contribute to the overall picture of the significance of consent. A judge can concoct a mixture of tests and exceptions to suit his vision of how the law should be tackling the problem of teenage contraception.

I am not doubting that there are some general guidelines in the pre-existing common law which point the judge in a particular direction. Nor do I doubt that in this case, the majority better captured the spirit of those guidelines as compared to the minority. Indeed, it is significant that the minority did not attempt to counter the majority's magisterial surveys of the common law. Lord Templeman, as I have said, eschewed case law without any explanation. Lord Brandon avoided discussion of principle by concentrating on public policy. He explained that the question whether contraceptive advice or treatment was lawful 'appears to me to be one of public policy, the answer to which is to be gathered from an examination of the statutory provisions which Parliament has enacted from time to time in relation to men having sexual intercourse with girls either under the age of thirteen or between the ages of thirteen and sixteen'.[42]

But *why* is the question one of public policy and why does any such public policy have to be gathered from those statutes rather than the National Health Service Act 1977, which places no age-limits on the Secretary of State's duty to provide contraception facilities? I have explored these issues elsewhere.[43] For present purposes, we should at least acknowledge that public policy is a cover behind which a judge may fashion his preferred vision of the law. By 'public policy' he might mean the point behind the common law *as he sees it*,[44] or the point behind some statutes *as he sees it*[45] (and he can select which statutes to examine), or the likely consequences of the law *as he sees it.*[46]

41 [1985] 3 WLR 830, 858.
42 Ibid., 864.
43 S. Lee, 'Judges and Public Policy', O'Sullivan Memorial Lecture, forthcoming in *Law & Justice.*
44 Although Lord Brandon does not seem to regard this as a common-law case.
45 [1985] 3 WLR 830, 864.
46 Ibid., 866.

Yet these may well conflict. Statutes may have been introduced precisely to counter the attitude of the common law. We should talk of public policies rather than public policy. And if we are to choose public policies in this case, we may prefer the majority's rebuttal of Lord Brandon's arguments. Lord Scarman was of the opinion that, 'It cannot be said that there is anything necessarily contrary to public policy in medical contraceptive treatment if it be medically indicated as in the interest of the patient's health; for the provision of such treatment is recognized as legitimate by Parliament: see s. 5 of the National Health Service Act 1977.'[47] And Lord Bridge concluded:

> On the issue of public policy, it seems to me that the policy consideration underlying the criminal sanction imposed by statute on men who have intercourse with girls under sixteen is the protection of young girls from the untoward consequences of intercourse. Foremost among these must surely be the risk of pregnancy leading either to abortion or the birth of a child to an immature and irresponsible mother. In circumstances where it is apparent that the criminal sanction will not, or is unlikely to, afford the necessary protection it cannot, in my opinion, be contrary to public policy to prescribe contraception as the only effective means of avoiding a wholly undesirable pregnancy.[48]

The question remains: why did Lord Brandon rely on these public policy arguments rather than challenge the majority's understanding of the common-law principles? I imagine that he was embarrassed by the central authority on which the majority relied, namely his own decision in *R.* v. *D.*[49] In that case, Lord Brandon had rejected calendar age as the test for a child's legal capacity to consent. He considered it 'a question of fact . . . whether the child concerned has sufficient understanding and intelligence to give its consent'.[50] How are we to explain Lord Brandon's change of heart? He could quite simply have observed that the context of *R.* v. *D.* was very different. The case concerned a father 'kidnapping' his own son and relying on the defence that the child 'consented' to the abduction. But perhaps Lord Brandon felt that the logic of his observations did apply to the *Gillick* controversy on consent. In which case why not just echo his earlier observations? Presumably, his Lordship had not realized how his words in *R.* v. *D.* might come to be used in regard to contraception for young people and he did not like the consequences of

47 Ibid., 860.
48 Ibid., 863.
49 [1984] AC 778.
50 [1984] AC 778, 858.

their application. So he ignored his earlier statement of common-law principle and sought statutory grounds for overriding it.

The *Gillick* case demonstrates, therefore, a variety of judicial techniques which are used to establish the law on capacity to consent. It highlights the truism that legal concepts are our tools not our masters. It should have given legal philosophers the incentive to clarify the underlying value disputes which we can sometimes glimpse at the surface of the judgments.

4. THE SIDAWAY CASE

If we now turn to the *Sidaway* case, we see that questions of capacity are only one aspect of the concept of consent. Even if we establish that a girl has the capacity to understand the treatment, what knowledge should be imparted to her before the law agrees that her consent is sufficiently informed as to be valid?

Consent must be based on some knowledge. But how much information and what kind of information should we require? But for Glanville Williams's assertion that 'The decision of the Court of Criminal Appeal in *Williams* is clearly wrong',[51] I would have assumed that *Williams*[52] was clearly right in deciding that without the most basic level of information and understanding, a 'consent' is invalid.

Law students rarely forget the salacious cases like *Williams*. It is one of several examples in the law reports of girls 'consenting' to sexual intercourse in the mistaken belief that they were consenting to something else; sometimes the something else was an operation, there it was singing instruction. Let me illustrate the point with the facts of *Williams*:

> ... the choirmaster of a Presbyterian church, by reason of that fact, became acquainted about Christmas 1921, with Vera, a girl of sixteen years of age, and it was arranged by her parents that she should take lessons in singing and voice production from him. On the occasion of the second singing lesson on January 17 the (choirmaster) said that she was not singing as she should and was not getting her notes properly and told her to lie down on a settee. He then removed a portion of her clothing and placed upon the lower part of her body an instrument—which was in the nature of an aneroid barometer and according to the evidence was not in working order and would not in any event have been affected by the breathing of the girl—and then told her to take a deep breath three times. He looked at the instrument and purported to write something in a

[51] Williams, op. cit. n. 14 above, 561.
[52] *R.* v. *Williams* [1923] 1 KB 340.

book. He then dropped on to her and proceeded to have sexual intercourse with her. She said: 'What are you going to do?' He said: 'It is quite all right; do not worry. I am going to make an air passage. This is my method of training. Your breathing is not quite right and I have to make an air passage to make it right. Your parents know all about it, it has all been arranged; before God, Vera, it is quite right. I will not do you any harm.' The girl made no resistance as she believed what he told her and did not know that what he did was wrong—nor did she know that he was having sexual intercourse with her. The choirmaster was committed of rape and his appeal was dismissed.[53]

Beyond Vera's tragic innocence, however, it might be difficult to judge how much information and understanding the law ought to require for a valid consent. The philosophers' emphasis seems to be on the existence and knowledge of alternative courses of action while the law has been more concerned with knowledge of the risks attached to the chosen option.

A truly informed consent, or a truly autonomous choice, must rest on an understanding of the alternatives. In the medical sphere, for instance, this would suggest reconsideration of everyday practice in the general practitioner's surgery. A woman who seeks contraceptive advice and treatment is not giving a meaningful consent to one method unless the range of contraceptive options is explained to her.[54] In the hospital, a woman suffering from breast cancer ought to be informed of the possibilities of chemotherapy treatment rather than led to believe that removal of the breast is the only option. Why would a doctor ever fail to reveal alternatives? Limited time, familiarity with the issue, and a paternalistic concern to direct us towards the 'right' decision could all explain such a failure. The doctor's power here is enormous. He can shape our decisions. The doctor will presumably do so in what he considers to be the patient's best interests, but is that good enough?

The legal battle on informed consent has arisen over knowledge of the risks inherent in a proposed course of action. Here again the doctor might believe that our uninformed consent to his proposal will be in our best interests. The doctor may suspect that if we know of a slight risk we may be deterred from an operation which, in the doctor's view, is in our best interests. This was the dilemma considered by the courts in *Sidaway*. Lord Scarman championed the patient's 'right to know'. The other Law Lords seemed to disagree. But in some vital respects they in

53 Ibid.

54 See S. Lee, *The Practitioner*, December 1985, 1081.

fact came close to Lord Scarman's preferred conclusion. They just reached it in a more circumspect manner.

Lord Scarman's opinion centred on 'the right of "self-determination"—the description applied by some to what is no more or no less than the right of a patient to determine for himself whether he will or will not accept the doctor's advice'.[55] At the simplest level, relevant information ought to be communicated to the patient because a doctor

must acknowledge that in very many cases factors other than the purely medical will play a significant part in his patient's decision-making process. The doctor's concern is with health and the relief of pain. These are the medical objectives. But a patient may well have in mind circumstances, objectives, and values which he may have reasonably not made known to the doctor but which may lead him to a different decision from that suggested by a purely medical opinion. The doctor's duty can be seen therefore to be one which requires him not only to advise as to medical treatment but also to provide his patient with the information needed to enable the patient to consider and balance the medical advantages and risks alongside other relevant matters, such as, for example, his family, business or social responsibilities of which the doctor may be only partially, if at all, informed. I conclude, therefore, that there is room in our law for a legal duty to warn a patient of the risks inherent in the treatment proposed.[56]

Even Lord Diplock, who gave the most restrictive judgment, acknowledged a right to informed consent for *some* patients:

But when it comes to warning about risks, the kind of training and experience that a judge will have undergone at the Bar makes it natural for him to say (correctly) it is my right to decide whether any particular thing is done to my body, and I want to be fully informed of any risks there may be involved of which I am not already aware from my general knowledge as a highly educated man of experience, so that I may form my own judgment as to whether to refuse the advised treatment or not. No doubt if the patient in fact manifested this attitude by means of questioning, the doctor would tell him whatever it was the patient wanted to know.[57]

Lord Bridge, with whom Lord Keith concurred, agreed on the questioning patient's right to informed consent: 'when questioned specifically by a patient of apparently sound mind about risks involved in a particular treatment proposed, the doctor's duty must, in my opinion, be

55 [1985] 2 WLR 480, 488.
56 Ibid., 491.
57 Ibid., 500.

to answer both truthfully and as fully as the questioner requires'.[58] Lord Templeman completes the unanimous agreement on this point when he says that 'the patient cannot complain of lack of information unless the patient asks in vain for more information'.[59]

Beyond this minimum requirement of informed consent for the questioning patient, would the Law Lords intervene on behalf of the uninformed but silent patient? Yes, in some circumstances. Lord Scarman was the most expansive:

> My conclusion as to the law is therefore this. To the extent that I have indicated I think that English law must recognize a duty of the doctor to warn his patient of risk inherent in the treatment which he is proposing: and especially so, if the treatment be surgery. The critical limitation is that the duty is confined to material risk. The test of materiality is whether in the circumstances of the particular case the court is satisfied that a reasonable person in the patient's position would be likely to attach significance to the risk. Even if the risk be material, the doctor will not be liable if upon a reasonable assessment of his patient's condition he takes the view that a warning would be detrimental to his patient's health.[60]

Lord Diplock was the least likely to interfere with the doctor's decision. He fully endorsed the *Bolam*[61] test, arguing that 'the criterion of the duty of care owed by a doctor to his patient is whether he has acted in accordance with a practice accepted as proper by a body of responsible and skilled medical opinion'.[62] But the remaining three Law Lords adopted an intermediate position. They shared Lord Diplock's starting-point of medical practice, but they shared some of Lord Scarman's willingness to override medical practice where necessary. Lord Bridge, for instance, was not prepared 'to hand over to the medical profession the entire question of the scope of the duty of disclosure, including the question whether there has been a breach of that duty'.[63] His Lordship considered that, 'the judge might in certain circumstances come to the conclusion that disclosure of a risk was so obviously necessary to an informed choice on the part of the patient that no reasonably prudent medical man would fail to make it'.[64]

58 Ibid., 503.
59 Ibid., 507.
60 Ibid., 495.
61 *Bolam* v. *Friern Hospital Management Committee* [1957] 1 WLR 582.
62 [1985] 2 WLR 480, 498.
63 The quotation is from Laskin CJC in *Reibl* v. *Hughes* (114) DLR (3d) 1, 13; cited by Lord Bridge at [1985] 2 WLR 480, 504.
64 [1985] 2 WLR 480, 505.

The demystification of medicine will gradually lead to more and more patients demanding to know more and more information before they consent to treatment. Law students tend to be incensed at the medical paternalism revealed by *Sidaway*. As patients, they will be in the vanguard of those insisting on their right to know. As future judges, of course, they are precisely the people to do so, if we are to adopt Lord Diplock's reasoning. But what if we apply the lessons of *Sidaway* to the legal profession? If, for instance, someone is contemplating a divorce and asks a solicitor for advice, the paternalism of the legal profession might emerge. The lawyer begins to take over the decision-making, perhaps limiting the revelation of alternatives and risks in the belief that the client ought to be directed towards the 'best' course of action. Does the client really 'consent'? Medical law and ethics is in vogue, but what about legal law and ethics? Informed consent requirements can be used to protect us from professional paternalism at the hands of various experts. We can expect the experts concerned to resist the device of informed consent as it applies to themselves. Nor is a paternalistic concern to gloss over alternatives and risks confined only to 'professionals'. Do we really give an informed consent to plumbers, car mechanics, and others who provide a service?

I suspect that medical law and ethics is getting ahead of the field. There is tremendous interest in the concept of consent as it applies to medicine, but the rest of our lives may not match the ideal of informed consent. This is clearly something to consider in a variety of contexts. Decisions on a range of major and minor matters (marriage, career, university, degree subject) may seem relatively uninformed. Who next once the law has pushed the powerful doctors towards informed consent? I have little doubt that *Sidaway* will come to be seen as a significant expansion of the ambit of informed consent. Medical negligence cases seem to take years to come to court but I imagine that ever since *Sidaway* plaintiffs have been tacking on to claims of negligent treatment a claim that they were not in a position to give an informed consent. Once those cases come to court, if not before, medical practice will alter to cover against such actions in the future. But there is still much work to be done on the detail of what information is necessary for informed consent.

5. CONSENT ISSUES AND THE NATURE OF JUDICIAL REASONING

For present purposes, however, what is intriguing is the methodology adopted by the different judges. None felt able to deny completely the relevance of informed consent. Some saw 'policy' dangers in embracing the doctrine too openly or readily but left grounds for hope that it could be developed. Lord Scarman preferred a clear statement of principle and preferred to leave any 'policy' problems to the legislature.[65] This seems strange since it was precisely the policy issues which troubled his brethren and Lord Scarman hinted that he could, were it appropriate, have allayed those fears.[66] Instead of developing the rejoinders he falls back on his own disapproved dictum in *McLoughlin*.[67]

What light does all this shed on judicial decision-making? And what does it suggest about the ways in which jurisprudence can help the judges to develop a well-rounded doctrine of consent in medical law?

The debate about theories of adjudication seems to have become unduly distanced from actual case law. It is also difficult to see that, in the current state of the art, there is much practical difference between the protagonists. Everybody seems to believe that in hard cases judges act as interstitial lawmakers. Even those who seem to disagree, particularly Dworkin, can only maintain that position by some strained definitional ploys. The real issue is what limits or constraints there are on judicial discretion. As Atiyah has asserted,[68] all decisions are made under limited terms of reference. The question is whether we can capture the terms of judicial reference by some bold distinction, such as Dworkin's dichotomy of principle and policy,[69] which seems to have crept into Lord Scarman's judicial thinking. I doubt whether this works. The boldness of the distinction rests on some curious stipulative definitions and retrenchments, a process which Barry encapsulates perfectly:

> Let me describe the life-cycle of the typical Dworkinian controversy. In the first stage Dworkin announces some thesis which is unorthodox and striking. The second stage is marked by attacks on the thesis by critics who bring up all kinds of difficulties. Dworkin then replies to his critics and defends the thesis. Like a prudent sea-captain in a storm, however, he usually jettisons some of the cargo to save the rest. In the process of defending the thesis, terms are subtly redefined and claims modified so that at the end it loses in power what it has gained in plausibility. This is the third stage. Subsequent stages can be generated indefinitely by the iteration of the second and third stages. The theoretical limit

65 Ibid., 492.
66 Ibid.
67 [1983] 1 AC 410.
68 (1980) 15 *Israel Law Rev.* 346.
69 See e.g. R. M. Dworkin, *Taking Rights Seriously* (London, 1978).

of the sequence is constituted by a state of entropy in which the thesis, while undeniable, is no longer worth denying because it no longer says anything distinctive.[70]

As Barry observes, the principle–policy distinction is a classic illustration of this pattern. While Lord Scarman's judgments in *Sidaway* and *Gillick* are masterpieces, I do not think their strength lies in the separation of principle from policy. Indeed, they would have been stronger if the so-called policy arguments which inevitably underlay them had been articulated. The proper counter to poor policy arguments (as illustrated by Lord Brandon in *Gillick*), lies in good policy arguments in reply (as shown by Lord Scarman's rebuttal). Since I believe that value judgments have to be made in order to shape the law on consent, the depressing aspect of judicial decision-making is that the values are hidden within legalistic argument or not even broached at all. Nor were the facts on which to base such judgments made available to their Lordships. There was no factual evidence of any kind in *Gillick*, so the judges were left to their own (conflicting) hunches as to the likely consequences of alternative interpretations of the law. It does not follow that judges should simply ignore these considerations. But we should consider how to adapt and improve procedure in our appellate courts to cope with the function they perform of choosing what to make of concepts such as consent.

So perhaps jurisprudence should return from sterile, abstract debate about judicial law-making and focus more closely on assessing its actual practice. The work of Alan Paterson, for example, is valuable in considering the process of judicial decision-making and the purpose of giving reasoned judgments.[71] Whom are the Law Lords addressing in *Gillick* and *Sidaway*? There are undoubtedly many different audiences. In so far as they are addressing each other, however, one frequently disappointing feature of appellate judgments is the reluctance to counter specifically the arguments put forward by judicial brethren with whom one disagrees. Judicial comity is obviously one inhibiting factor, as is the extra delay involved in giving judgment if each judge is to respond to his colleagues, and then perhaps to launch a counter-rebuttal. As a compromise, therefore, it is at least encouraging that Lord Scarman concluded his judicial career by taking pains to articulate his own approach. If other judges follow suit, we may soon get down to the

[70] *Times Literary Supplement*, 25 October 1985, 1195.

[71] *The Law Lords* (London, 1982).

necessary detail of considering which kind of consideration is relevant for judges in various circumstances. Dividing the proper from the improper will surely require more labels than principle and policy.

But jurisprudence involves more than descriptions of, and prescriptions for, judicial behaviour. One of the encouraging features of medical law and ethics is the interaction between lawyer, philosopher, theologian, economist, and doctor. Theory can affect praxis. There is no need to regard jurisprudence as irrelevant to the practice of the law.

If we accept that consent is a concept which lawyers and others can shape, then we need next to consider from where the shapers will derive their ideas. Lord Scarman's *Sidaway* judgment included an expansive appreciation of academic influences. The American landmark case of *Canterbury* v. *Spence*, said Lord Scarman, is

> discussed learnedly and lucidly in an article published in the Law Quarterly Review, upon which I have drawn extensively in reaching my opinion in this appeal. I wish to put on record my deep appreciation of the help I have derived from the article, the author of which is Mr. Gerald Robertson, 'Informed Consent to Medical Treatment', (1981) 97 L.Q.R. 102. The author deals so comprehensively with the American, Canadian and other countries' case law that I find it unnecessary to refer to any of the cases to which our attention has been drawn, interesting and instructive though they are, other than *Canterbury* v. *Spence* and *Reibl* v. *Hughes* (1980) 114 D.L.R. (3d) 1, in which the judgment of the Supreme Court of Canada came too late to be considered by Mr. Robertson in his article. I have also been greatly assisted by the note on the present case by Professor Ian Kennedy in the Modern Law Review (1984) 47 M.L.R. 454.[72]

This influence is not to be underrated. Nor should one ignore the imaginative move of the DHSS in *Gillick* to engage as junior counsel for the appeal to the House of Lords the leading academic in the field, the aforementioned Ian Kennedy. With this kind of interaction between legal theory and practice, one can only hope that legal philosophers will be encouraged to contribute towards the emerging jurisprudence of consent. In particular, the medical context merits serious consideration. On the way towards developing medical law and ethics, legal philosophers will also lay the ghost of H. L. A. Hart's uncharacteristically parochial dismissal of speculation about the nature of medicine. Although *The Concept of Law* is for many of us the premier source of jurisprudential wisdom, Hart began the book with the surprising claim that

72 [1985] 2 WLR 480, 492.

No vast literature is dedicated to answering the question . . . 'What is medicine?' as it is to the question 'What is law?' A few lines on the opening page of an elementary textbook is all that the student . . . is asked to consider; and the answers he is given are of a very different kind from those tendered to the student of law. No one has thought it illuminating or important to insist that medicine is 'what doctors do about illnesses' or 'a prediction of what doctors will do'.[73]

In fact, as the current controversies over 'alternative medicine' demonstrate, the heat of debate[74] over what is medicine may come as a revelation to law students who often find it difficult to summon up enthusiasm for the fundamental question 'what is law?', believing that the answers do not really matter. There are striking analogies in arguments about the concepts of law and medicine beyond the realization that the aura surrounding the terms 'law' and 'medicine' is a prize worth seeking.[75]

With judges prepared to heed academic thought as in *Sidaway*, another spectre can be challenged, namely Lord Denning's verdict on jurisprudence: 'Jurisprudence was too abstract a subject for my liking. All about ideologies, legal norms and basic norms, "ought" and "is", realism and behaviourism, and goodness knows what else. The jargon of the philosopher has always been beyond me.'[76] Many judges, lawyers, students, and law teachers no doubt share that view. But jurisprudence is also about law and law rests on jurisprudence. We cannot argue cases in the appellate courts without raising jurisprudential issues, such as the role of judges, the role of concepts, and the values which should shape those concepts. Just as Monsieur Jourdain was surprised to discover, once he understood the term 'prose', that he had been speaking prose all his life without knowing it,[77] so lawyers, law students, and judges should be pleased to know that they are already thinking jurisprudentially.

[73] H. L. A. Hart, *The Concept of Law* (Oxford, 1961), 1.

[74] See I. M. Kennedy, *The Unmasking of Medicine* (London, 1983) and the debate in *Journal of Medical Ethics*, December 1981.

[75] See e.g. Kennedy, *passim.*

[76] Lord Denning, *The Family Story* (London, 1981), 38.

[77] Molière, *Le Bourgeois Gentilhomme* (1670) II. iv.

10

Community and Discrimination*

CHRISTOPHER McCRUDDEN†

I

WHAT weight should legislators and judges give to considerations of 'community' given that it has become increasingly popular in recent legal philosophical literature to argue that greater weight should be given to such considerations?[1] My primary concerns in this article are modest and limited. They are, first, to attempt to distinguish a number of different strands of argument among those concerned with promoting 'community values';[2] second, to point to the variety of ways in which communitarianism may be put into operation; third, to examine how these distinctions may help in understanding the relationship between communitarianism and legal rights; and, fourth, as an illustration, to examine the extent to which antidiscrimination law may usefully be seen as providing a forum where some of the implications of giving greater attention to community values may be tested. I argue that one should generally be sceptical of such arguments.

II

What is a 'communitarian'? An 'ideal communitarian' is concerned to argue for the importance of ideas of 'community' as an aspect of 'the good'. 'Community in this context is a philosophical ideal; an amalga-

† I would like to thank the following for their comments on earlier drafts: John Bell, Jules Coleman, Robert Cover, Perry Dane, John Eekelaar, Leslie Green, Geoffrey Hazard, Tony Honoré, Joseph Raz, Denise Reaume, Carol Rose, Judith Jarvis Thomson, and William Twining. I presented an earlier draft at workshops at the Law Schools of Berkeley, Harvard, Osgoode Hall, and Yale. In each the discussions were helpful and penetrating.

1 An interesting question which I do not consider here is *why* this development has taken place at this time.

2 An earlier discussion is in C.J. Friedrich (ed.), *Community* (Nomos II, 1959). A particularly interesting recent discussion is R. Plant, 'Community: Concept, Conception, and Ideology' (1978) 8 *Politics and Society* 79.

mation of different virtues: friendship, altruism, trust, love, solidarity, and so on. It is important, however, to distinguish the different weights given to ideal communitarian arguments in different philosophical traditions.

In *Liberalism and the Limits of Justice*,[3] Michael Sandel develops a complex and stimulating critique of deontological liberalism using Kant and Rawls[4] as particular targets. Kantian (and Rawlsian) liberals, he argues, draw a distinction between the 'right' and the 'good', between a framework of basic rights and liberties and the conceptions of the good that people may choose to pursue within that framework. For them, the right is prior to the good in two senses: first, in the sense that rights cannot be sacrificed for the sake of the general good; second, in the sense that the principles of justice that ground these rights are not premissed on any particular vision of the good life. What justifies the rights is not that they maximize the general welfare or otherwise promote the good, but rather that they comprise a fair framework within which individuals and groups can choose their own values and ends, consistent with a similar liberty for others. This ethic is based on a conception of the person as a separate, choosing individual, independent of the desires and ends he or she may have at any moment—but who is not by nature either exclusively selfish or egoistic. A person is not defined by his aims and attachments but is capable of standing back to survey, assess, and if necesssary revise them.

The Rawlsian conception of community is to see it as an aspect of the good; important and necessary but not something which defines a person. Rawls resists the idea that placing community as subject to justice is necessarily individualistic. It does not, in other words, necessarily encourage 'ways of life that lead individuals to pursue their own way and to have no concern for the interests of others . . .'.[5] Rawls conceives the idea of community (I adopt Sandel's terms) not only in 'instrumental' terms[6] (that is, where individuals regard social arrangements as a necessary burden and co-operate only for the sake of pursuing their private ends) but also in 'sentimental' terms. The latter (Rawls's own preferred view of community) is one where participants have certain 'shared final ends' and regard the scheme of co-operation as a good in itself. Affection, benevolence, and sentiment may all play a

[3] (Cambridge, 1982) (hereafter 'Sandel').
[4] J. Rawls, *A Theory of Justice* (Oxford, 1971) (hereafter 'Rawls').
[5] J. Rawls, 'Fairness to Goodness' (1975) 84 *Philosophical Rev.* 536, 550.
[6] Sandel, 148.

part. Such actions are not, however, demanded 'as a matter of justice by the basic structure of society'.[7]

Sandel challenges each of these elements of Kantian and Rawlsian liberalism. For the purposes of this discussion, however, I concentrate on two of Sandel's arguments and begin with his alternative conception of community. His philosophical ideal (constitutive communitarianism) is where one's sense of community should be a 'mode of self-understanding partly constitutive of the [person's] identify. On this . . . view, to say that the members of a society are bound by a sense of community is not simply to say that a great many of them profess communitarian sentiments and pursue communitarian aims, but rather that they conceive their identify . . . as defined to some extent by the community of which they are a part. For them, community describes not just what they *have* as fellow citizens but what they *are*, not a relationship they choose (as in a voluntary association) but an attachment they discover, not merely an attribute but a constituent of their identity.'[8]

Sandel also challenges the priority in Rawlsian liberalism of justice over 'the good'. Where a spirit of fraternity or benevolence prevails, he argues, justice should not be brought into play. In such a situation increasing the justness of the group may actually diminish the good and in these circumstances attachment to justice is a vice. Justice should therefore not be given priority.[9]

Several aspects of Sandel's discussion arouse concern.[10] One is his argument, just mentioned, which rejects a system where justice is prior to the good on the grounds of its supposed debasement of fraternity and benevolence. As others have pointed out this result is by no means a necessary one. Baker, for example, has argued that, 'The justness of institutions says nothing about whether a person will, or should, push to the limit their rightful claims to various advantages . . . At most, Rawls' theory of justice requires that we support institutions that *permit* people to obtain what justice would make available.'[11]

A second concern involves the extent to which Sandel wants not only to have the 'constituents' of a person's identity *recognized* but also preserved and protected. When he writes that for a society to be a community in a 'strong' sense, 'community must be constitutive of the

[7] Rawls, 178.

[8] Sandel, 150.

[9] Sandel, 32–5.

[10] See A. Gutmann, 'Communitarian Critics of Liberalism' (1985) 14 *Philosophy and Public Affairs* 308.

[11] C. E. Baker, 'Sandel on Rawls' (1985) 133 *U. Penn. Law Rev.* 895, 918.

shared self-understandings of the participants and embodied in their institutional arrangements . . .',[12] what is the implication of 'must be' and 'embodied'? It is unclear whether, as Baker argues, Sandel necessarily assumes situations in which the preservation of communal sentiment and benevolence 'requires the subordination of some people',[13] and whether he considers that coercion is justified in the name of the preservation of the 'constituents' of a person's identity. It does not seem, however, to be a necessary element in constitutive communitarianism that any particular *existing* relationships are defended or forced on people, only that some are necessary and should be encouraged and fostered.

A third concern lies in uncertainty as to whether he espouses a hierarchical or a non-hierarchical vision of his ideal community. Sandel's book is arguably consistent with a hierarchical approach.[14] But a considerable number of those who urge that more concern be given now to communitarian values can be seen as rejecting a hierarchical ideal of constitutive communitarianism. Some indeed would see such a notion as the antithesis of their ideal of community. They would therefore presumably not resist developments which sought to undermine this (to them) false view of community. The constitutive communitarianism which recent advocates embrace is non-hierarchical.[15]

III

A constitutive communitarian will, of course, be concerned to put his or her ideal into operation. There are a number of ways in which this has been attempted. But first, a further distinction must be made. Ideals may be operationalized at either the *constitutional* level[16] or that of individual *acts.* Some recent 'communitarians' appear to argue that the preferred way to operationalize ideal constitutive communitarianism is to have no (or few) mediating institutions. One should attempt to apply the ideal moment by moment, person by person, act by act. I shall term

12 Sandel, 173.

13 Ibid., 920.

14 Others have been clearer in recent years in espousing such an approach, notably I. Illich, *Gender* (London, 1983).

15 See e.g. A. Hutchinson and P. Monahan, 'The "Rights" Stuff: Roberto Unger and Beyond' (1984) 62 *Texas Law Rev.* 1477.

16 I am grateful to Jules Coleman for drawing my attention to the term; see J. Coleman, 'Foundations of Constitutional Economics', in *Constitutional Economics: Containing the Economic Powers at Government*, ed. R. McKenzie (Lexington, 1984).

such writers 'act communitarians'.[17] Such an approach, if espoused as a generally preferred method, is Utopian in that it ignores many of the problems engendered by industrialization, the scale of the modern state, and the interdependence of groups within it. This approach is ultimately paralysed by, and unable to cope with, fundamental disagreements of principle within or between communities.

In contrast, those who believe that the philosophical ideal is best operationalized by the establishment of institutions, I shall call 'constitutional communitarians'. One particularly prominent 'constitutional communitarian' argument is that adopted by what I shall call 'institutional communitarians'. The latter adopts a two-stage argument. First, particular historical periods and distinct institutions, like 'the family', 'the Church', 'the employment relationship', 'the neighbourhood', 'the nation', and so on, can be usefully analysed and described along a continuum stretching from a sociological idea of society (or contract) at one end to a sociological idea of community at the other.[18] Most famously this was expressed in Tönnies's distinction between *Gemeinschaft* and *Gesellschaft*.[19] A *Gesellschaft* institution emphasizes values of achievement, efficiency, rationality, and objectivity. A *Gemeinschaft* notion attaches more importance to intuitive judgments, humanistic considerations not susceptable of empirical verification, the preservation of tradition and local autonomy, and membership in ascriptive groups. Second (and this is the crucial move), institutional communitarians argue that those particular institutions provide a necessary means by which to achieve ideal communitarianism and therefore are good in themselves, and should be protected and fostered as such;[20] that a belief in ideal communitarianism leads *necessarily* to

[17] I adopt the term 'act communitarian' in a conscious attempt to echo the term 'act utilitarian'. A recent example of act communitarianism is to be found in K. L. Karst, 'Woman's Constitution' (1984) *Duke Law J.* 447, 488. See also M. Minnow, 'Legal Treatment of Mental Incompetence: Problems of Status, Classification, and Relationships' (paper delivered to the Legal Theory Workshop, Yale Law School, 5 December 1985). Karst, however, recognizes the difficulties raised in the text, at 490.

[18] An interesting recent example is R. W. Gordon, 'The Devil and David Webster' (1984) 94 *Yale Law J.* 445, 458–9.

[19] F. Tönnies, *Community and Society* (trans. and ed. C. P. Loomis, Ann Arbor, 1957). For discussions of this tradition, see R. A. Nisbet, *The Sociological Tradition* (London, 1967), 47–106; H. M. Miner, 'Community—Society Continua', *International Encyclopedia of the Social Sciences*, ed. D. L. Sills (London and New York, 1968), 174–80.

[20] For an example of institutional communitarianism, see R. R. Garet, 'Communality and Existence: The Rights of Groups' (1982–3) 56 *S. California Law Rev.* 1001. This is also found among some recent American legal historians, see R. W. Gordon, 'Critical Legal Histories' (1984) 36 *Stanford Law Rev.* 57, 96–7 (on M. Horwitz, *The Transformation of American Law*).

particular *institutional* communitarian consequences; that without institutional communitarianism, without those institutions which may be identified as closer to *Gemeinschaft*, constitutive communitarianism is impossible.

One can, however, quite consistently be a constitutive without being an institutional communitarian because institutional communitarianism is but one way to put that ideal into operation. It is easy, however, to fall into the trap of assuming that the ideal requires either institutional or act communitarianism. Sometimes constitutive communitarians seem to do just that. The danger, of course, is that this confusion may lead communitarians to defending institutional or act communitarianism in a way, and to a degree, that I for one would regard as very risky. One should, in particular, be sceptical whether particular communitarian institutions do in practice further constitutive communitarian ideals.[21] In the absence of an existing ideal of philosophical community it may be a mistake to opt for what seems the second-best institutional form. The 'next best thing' in this case is not necessarily the institution which seems the closest reflection of the ideal. That is too often a mirage.

The upshot is that 'community values' can give rise to and be incorporated in different philosophical traditions, though in differing degrees. A second, more interesting point is that ideal communitarianism can be put into operation in different ways; no one structure is indispensable.

By this time the reader may find it useful to have a diagrammatic illustration of the structure of the different communitarian arguments outlined above and to be developed below (see Figure (i)).

IV

The question which will now be addressed is the extent to which, if one were a constitutive communitarian, that should influence one's legal decision-making. Roberto Unger[22] implies that to provide a platform of legal rights (as currently defined) will delay the advent of constitutive communitarianism because legal rights are currently exclusionary

[21] Within feminist jurisprudence there is now fortunately emerging a growing scepticism of the 'impoverished forms of "community" forced on women'; see F. Olsen, 'Statutory Rape; A Feminist Critique of Rights Analysis' (1984) 63 *Texas Law Rev.* 387, 430.

[22] R. M. Unger, 'The Critical Legal Studies Movement' (1983) 96 *Harvard Law Rev.* 561 (hereafter 'Unger').

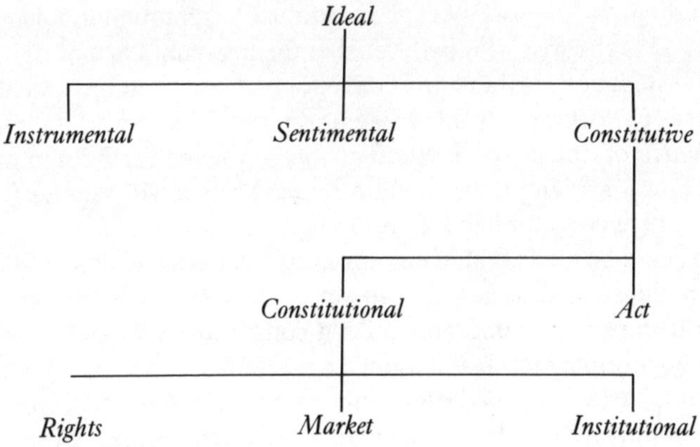

FIG. (i)

zones.[23] Carol Gilligan perhaps makes a similar point when she argues that in claiming rights women confront a dilemma.[24] An imposed idea of self-sacrifice and of the 'natural' relationship between women and caring clash with the need for self-respect and self-development, yet any challenge to an ethic of self-sacrifice will be met by others (and often by women themselves) by the rebuke of selfishness. The problem identified by Gilligan is whether women may achieve self-development and self-respect through a morality of rights 'that dissolve "natural bonds" in support of individuals' claims', without abandoning the 'old virtues' of responsibility and care.[25]

These arguments seem to me to be misguided for two main reasons. The first is that they repeat Sandel's mistake since they assume that a system of rights leaves no room for benevolence or communal sentiment. Second, there is implicit in the arguments a tendency to conflate moral and legal rights. One can, at one and the same time, consistently be a deontological liberal who believes in the pre-eminence and priority of the moral right over the good, without being a legal rights theorist who believes in the pre-eminence of rights in the legal system. So too one can be both a communitarian who believes in the pre-eminence of 'the good'

[23] Unger, 597–8. On the idea of legal rights as preserving a self-destructive and alienated form of human consciousness, see further P. Gabel, 'The Phenomenology of Rights Consciousness and the Pact of the Withdrawn Selves' (1984) 62 *Texas Law Rev.* 1563.

[24] C. Gilligan, *In a Different Voice* (Cambridge, Mass., 1982). See also K. L. Karst, 'Woman's Constitution' (1984) *Duke Law J.* 475–80.

[25] At 132.

(including the importance of constitutive communitarianism) and a legal rights theorist who believes that the pre-eminence of rights in the legal system best furthers that conception of 'the good'. A system of legal rights is not necessarily inconsistent, therefore, with a belief in the pre-eminence of 'the good', including a belief in constitutive community.

I am not arguing that a system of legal rights will *necessarily* further constitutive communitarianism, though I suspect that a coherent argument could be made that in certain circumstances it would.[26] Indeed it is not implausible to argue that to set up a system of rights might be a second[27] method of operationalizing constitutive communitarianism at the constitutional level, and indeed a rather better one than institutional communitarianism.[28] Whether this argument is true, however, can for present purposes be left undecided. The relationship between the two seems to me contingent on factors other than the form of legal right and to vary over time, place, and circumstance. In order to see whether a system of legal rights is consistent with the achievement of 'the good', we have to take each situation as it comes. There is no reason why providing a platform of legal rights should necessarily delay the advent of constitutive communitarianism. Whether it will is largely an empirical question and not one that can be answered a priori.[29] It is equally an empirical question whether giving institutional communitarian arguments a favoured legal status will advance the philosophical idea of the good. But, on *historical* grounds, one should be sceptical of the uses to which institutional communitarianism may be put in practice.[30]

Let us assume, however, what is clearly true—that some institutional

[26] See e.g. R. M. Cover, 'Foreword: Nomos and Narrative' (1983) 97 *Harvard Law Rev.* 4.

[27] A third method of operationalizing constitutive communitarianism may be the market, see J. Coleman, 'Libertarian and Rational Choice Contractarianism: Consensus and the Market' (unpublished paper).

[28] The question as to whether legal rights have the *desired* effect is equally a contingent question. My argument is directed at those who see legal rights as having the necessary effects discussed in the text. It does not assume that they will be effective in practice.

[29] See L. Green, 'Legality and Community' (1985) 5 *Oxford J. of Legal Studies* 483, 468–9.

[30] This rather pessimistic view of communitarianism may be more characteristic of Europeans than Americans. Perhaps the most dramatic and consistent use of the institutional communitarian argument is to be found in Nazi ideology, including legal ideology. See F. Neumann, *Behemoth* (Oxford, 1944) at 419 ff. and F. Neumann, *The Democratic and the Authoritarian State* (New York, 1957), ch. 6. I am grateful to Spiros Simitis for these references. American institutional communities have often been seen as less coercive, see M. Novak, 'The Communitarian Individual in America' (1982) 68 *Public Interest* 3, 5–9. But cf. A. A. Leff, 'Memorandum' (1977) 29 *Stanford Law Rev.* 879, 889.

communities are necessary and valuable, in particular because they mediate between the individual and society in a way which reduces isolation.[31] Let us also assume what is less certain—that these institutional communities will not ultimately become oppressive. Given these assumptions, should legal interpretation draw more widely on constitutive communitarianism in the interpretation and construction of legal principles? Should constitutive communitarianism be, *can* it be, promoted by legal intervention, as Unger argues it ultimately must? Here too, though for different reasons, one should be sceptical of the extent to which a constitutive community can be encouraged directly by politically (including legally) based mechanisms. Let me try now to illustrate these arguments by considering the 'antidiscrimination principle', that is the principle that one should not discriminate.

IV

In the last twenty years the antidiscrimination principle has come to take on an expanded legal meaning in certain contexts.[32] It has come to be used to challenge not only actions done with a discriminatory purpose but also those which have the *effect* of disproportionately disadvantaging a protected group in ways which are neither 'necessary' nor 'justifiable'. In the United States and Europe this development has led to the construction of two (arguably) different legal theories of discrimination: the (American) 'disparate treatment' and (European) 'direct' discrimination theory which captures the idea of intention to discriminate; and the more recent (American) 'disparate impact' and (European) 'indirect' discrimination theory which rely on the 'effects' test.

On the effects test, where an employer's practices perpetuate or aggravate the subordinate position of a protected group then they are presumptively invalid. The adverse impact is taken as evidence that the interests of the minority group or, in the case of women, the majority have not been adequately taken into account. Unless the presumption which arises from that evidence is rebutted or other considerations are allowed to override it, society requires that more account be taken of

31 This idea has, of course, a long history, see A. Kronman, 'Aristotle's Idea of Political Fraternity' (1979) 24 *American J. of Jurisprudence* 144. For a recent discussion of the need for mediating institutions, see e.g. G. E. Frug, 'The City as a Legal Concept' (1980) 93 *Harvard Law Rev.* 1057, though query whether giving them powers requires 'a basic rethinking of liberalism' (at 1154).

32 C. McCrudden, 'Institutional Discrimination' (1982) 2 *Oxford J. of Legal Studies* 303, 361.

those interests. The grounds on which the presumptive invalidity may be rebutted, the degree to which the employer is allowed to justify his practices, are, therefore, vital. If communitarian arguments are to be brought to bear on the construction or interpretation of the antidiscrimination principle, this is one of the key points.[33]

What, then, is the relationship between this antidiscrimination principle[34] and the various communitarian arguments? Most recently the antidiscrimination principle has been defended by invoking a principle of justice within the Kantian tradition. Indeed recent debates within deontological liberalism, in particular between Rawls and Nozick, have stimulated much debate as to the justification of the antidiscrimination principle in recent years.[35] Even deontological liberalism, as we have seen, requires some conception of common enterprise before a conception of justice can be relevant. In that sense it is therefore dependent on some limited notion of 'community', though this would not satisfy constitutive communitarians like Sandel.

However, the antidiscrimination principle seems consistent both with a deontological liberal and a constitutive communitarian approach.[36] It might be seen, on a liberal theory of justice, as justified in the name of human dignity and respect for persons, whether by reason of the difference principle (Rawls) or because it remedies historical injustice (Nozick[37]). But the antidiscrimination principle seems equally justified within a constitutive communitarian tradition, as Sandel himself has subsequently written, 'in the name of recognizing the full membership of fellow citizens wrongly excluded from the common life of the

[33] Ibid., 361. Another area of importance which I do not consider further here is the substantive and procedural law of antidiscrimination *remedies*. See e.g. P. Gewirtz, 'Remedies and Resistance' (1983) 92 *Yale Law J.* 585; O. M. Fiss, 'Against Settlement' (1983) 93 *Yale Law J.* 1073; A. W. McThenia and T. L. Shaffer, 'For Reconciliation' (1985) 94 *Yale Law J.* 1660; O. M. Fiss, 'Out of Eden', ibid., 1669. On the growing use of communitarian arguments by the United States Supreme Court, see R. D. Chesler, 'Imagery of Community, Ideology of Authority: The Moral Reasoning of Chief Justice Burger' (1983) 18 *Harvard Civil Rights—Civil Liberties Law Rev.* 457.

[34] I shall not attempt to defend this conception of the antidiscrimination principle here. See C. McCrudden, 'Changing Notions of Discrimination', in S. Guest and A. Milne, *Equality and Discrimination: Essays in Freedom and Justice* (Stuttgart, 1985).

[35] Contrast e.g. P. Brest, 'In Defense of the Antidiscrimination Principle' (1976) 90 *Harvard Law Rev.* 1 with Fiss, 'Groups and the Equal Protection Clause' (1975–6) 5 *Philosophy and Public Affairs* 107.

[36] If Olsen is arguing to the contrary then she is unconvincing; see F. Olsen, 'The Family and the Market: A Study of Ideology and Legal Reform' (1983) 96 *Harvard Law Rev.* 1497, 1552.

[37] R. Nozick, *Anarchy, State, and Utopia* (New York, 1974).

nation'.[38] (Though, one can point, in passing, to the ambiguity of the words 'membership' and 'common'.)

I do not underestimate the importance of the debate between those who see the principle as best justified by the Kantian or the ideal communitarian traditions but that debate is not the primary concern of this essay. My purpose is a more modest one. It is, first, to point to the relative ease with which the antidiscrimination principle can be accommodated within a communitarian tradition, and that has been the argument of the previous paragraph. I want now to go further, however, and to argue that the tensions that do arise between 'communitarian' approaches and the legal antidiscrimination principle arise from an espousal of *institutional* communitarianism.

How, then, might institutional communitarianism conflict with the antidiscrimination principle? One of the most powerful attacks on traditional forms of community is that of Karl Marx in describing the rural village communities of India in 1853:

> We must not forget that these idyllic village communities, inoffensive though they may appear, had always been the solid foundation of Oriental despotism, that they restrained the human mind within the smallest possible compass, making it the unresisting tool of superstition, enslaving it beneath traditional rules, depriving it of all grandeur and historical energies... We must not forget that these little communities were contaminated by distinction of caste and by slavery, that they subjugated man to external circumstances instead of elevating man to the sovereign of circumstances, that they transformed a self-developing social stage into never changing natural destiny....[39]

The circumstances in which the antidiscrimination principle *currently* comes into conflict with existing institutional communities of a *Gemeinschaft*-type are not hard to find. The extended family, the neighbourhood, the legal profession, the school, the place of employment, the union, the Church, and the nation have all been challenged in one form or another, in one country or another, at one time or another, as contravening the antidiscrimination principle.[40] A few examples must suffice. As I write, a black couple and their 7-year-old son have

[38] Sandel, 'Morality and the Liberal Ideal', *New Republic*, 8 May 1984, 17. See also J. Schaar, 'Equality of Opportunity, and Beyond', in Nomos IX, *Equality* (Nomos IX), ed. J. R. Pennock and J. W. Chapman (New York, Atherton, 1967), 265.

[39] K. Marx, *Selected Works*, i. 350–1.

[40] See generally on United States developments, K. L. Karst, 'Equality and Community: Lessons from the Civil Rights Era' (1980) 56 *Notre Dame Lawyer* 183. Challenges to the family raise one of the most problematic issues; see J. Fishkin, *Justice, Equal Opportunity and the Family* (New Haven, 1983).

reportedly been expelled from a white working-class neighbourhood in Philadelphia apparently to preserve the sense of community which their neighbours felt would be challenged by the family's presence.[41] A recent study of a ten-year dispute in Boston, Massachusetts, over school desegregation illustrates yet again, in the words of the author, the conflicts between 'community and equality'.[42] On the other side of the Atlantic, too, examples are numerous, perhaps most obviously in Northern Ireland. Other more specific cases involving discrimination on grounds of race and national origin in England illustrate my argument.

In *Bohon-Mitchell* v. *Council of Legal Education*,[43] for example, the body responsible for training barristers had refused to waive a requirement that those seeking to join the Bar must take a two-year course of study provided by the Council. A waiver of one year was normally given where the student had even a non-law degree from a British or Irish university. In this case the student, a non-citizen resident in Britain, had a degree in English Literature from New York City's Columbia University. The Council argued that without a home degree the student would not have the necessary knowledge of 'the English way of life'.[44] The condition was held not to be 'justifiable' and to be indirectly discriminatory on grounds of national origin. In *Mandla* v. *Lee*[45] a Sikh boy applied for admission to a private school. His faith required him to wear a turban; the school refused to admit him if he did so, stipulating that all pupils must wear the existing school uniform and that this rule was justifiable in order 'to minimize external differences between races and social classes, to discourage the "competitive" fashions which [were] said to exist in a teenage community, and to present a Christian image of the school to outsiders, including prospective parents'. The House of Lords held these grounds did not justify the rule, which was indirectly discriminatory. So too in the area of sex discrimination, examples abound. In *Ohio Civil Rights Commission* v. *Dayton Christian Schools*[46] a teacher in a private Christian school became pregnant. She wanted to continue working after her child was born. School officials told her that

[41] See *New York Times*, 27 November 1985 (editorial: 'Prejudice Triumphs in Philadelphia').

[42] The book is J. Anthony Lukas, *Common Ground* (New York, 1985). The phrase is taken from an article by the same author, 'Community and Equality in Conflict', *New York Times*, 8 September 1985).

[43] [1978] IRLR 525 (IT).

[44] At 528.

[45] [1983] IRLR 209 (HL).

[46] 106 S. Ct. 2718 (1986).

they would not renew her contract for the next year because the school's religious belief was that a mother should stay home with small children. When she consulted a lawyer, she was immediately dismissed for failure to follow the biblical chain of command.[47]

The issue of immigration control provides a final, more considered example relevant to both the United States and Europe. Successive administrations have argued that their cultural communities should be protected from certain types of immigrants. Of course it is possible to see these claims as a pretext for an unacceptable policy based on racism. Preservation of the cultural community, in this explanation, has become a code term for preservation of 'race'. There seems to me to be much truth in this explanation. But it is nevertheless important to examine such claims on their own merits. Peter Schuck, for example, develops a similar claim at some length and draws attention to the danger that a more open American immigration policy 'will encourage further social and cultural fragmentation, intergroup hostility, and political conflict, and that these developments may impair at some point the quality of American democracy. To endure and flourish, a polity as pluralistic as ours must maintain a core of common values, public symbols, and social commitments; it must develop and preserve a communal memory and vision of the future that can contain the chaotic centrifugal force exerted by new pressures and events; it must be able to guide that force into politically creative channels.'[48]

The case of *Abdulaziz, Cabales and Balkandali* v. *The United Kingdom*, which was decided by the European Court of Human Rights in May 1985, provides a limited but suggestive illustration of the wider issue in a practical context.[49] The applicants were lawfully and permanently resident in the United Kingdom. In accordance with the immigration rules in force at the material time their husbands were refused permission to remain with or join them in that country. The applicants claimed that they had been victims of a practice of discrimination on the ground of sex, race, and, in the case of Mrs Balkandali, birth. They alleged violations, *inter alia*, of Article 8 of the European Convention on Human Rights (which guarantees the right to respect for family life), taken alone

[47] Cf. St Paul's admonition to the early Christians: 'Must brother go to law with brother and before unbelievers? Indeed, you already fall below your standard in going to law with one another at all. Why not rather suffer injury? 1 Cor. 6: 6–7.

[48] P. Schuck, 'Immigration Law and the Problem of Community', in N. Glazer (ed.), *Clamour at the Gates*, 285, 302–3.

[49] *Abdulaziz, Cabales and Balkandali* v. *United Kingdom* (1985) 7 EHRR 471.

and in conjunction with Article 14 (which provides that enjoyment of the Convention rights and freedoms is to be secured without discrimination), and of Article 3 (prohibition of degrading treatment).

The authorities' decisions concerning the applicants' husbands were taken in accordance with the immigration rules in force at the relevant time. Prior to 1983, their general effect was that a foreign husband wishing to join or remain with his wife lawfully living in the United Kingdom would not be granted leave to enter or stay unless, *inter alia*, she was a citizen of the United Kingdom. On the other hand, a foreign wife wishing to join or remain with her husband lawfully living in the United Kingdom could, prior to 1983, obtain leave to enter or stay, whether or not he was a citizen of the United Kingdom and Colonies with the territorial birth link.

The European Court of Human Rights held that Article 8 had not been breached. Nor did the provisions contravene the Convention on the grounds of breach of the prohibition of racial or ethnic discrimination in Article 14 read together with Article 8. The court did, however, accept the more limited claim that the law was sexually discriminatory. The aim of protecting the domestic labour market was found to be the primary purpose of the legislation and 'without doubt legitimate'.[50] Contracting states also enjoyed 'a certain "margin of appreciation" in assessing whether and to what extent differences in otherwise similar situations justify a different treatment'.[51] Nevertheless, given that 'the advancement of the equality of the sexes is today a major goal in the member States of the Council of Europe . . . very weighty reasons would have to be advanced before a difference of treatment on the ground of sex could be regarded as compatible with the Convention'.[52] The court found that the reasons advanced by the British government did not pass this degree of scrutiny. The court also rejected the argument that men would have a markedly heavier impact on the labour market than women and was equally sceptical that the measures would advance the aim of securing public tranquillity. The government had argued that 'Immigration caused strains on society . . . firm and fair [immigration] control secured good relations between the different communities living in the United Kingdom.'[53] The European Commission on Human Rights (the body which investigates and

[50] At 501.
[51] Ibid.
[52] Ibid.
[53] At 500.

decides whether a complaint is justified before it goes to the European Court of Human Rights) had found instead that 'they might create resentment in part of the immigrant population'.[54]

The third applicant, Mrs Balkandali, it will be remembered, had also complained of discrimination *on the ground of her place of birth.* She was a United Kingdom citizen but was treated differently from other United Kingdom women citizens as neither she nor her parents were born in United Kingdom territory. The government contended that the advantage given to the foreign husbands of United Kingdom citizen women with a birth link to the United Kingdom was justified in view of the hardship that would be caused to women with 'close ties' with the United Kingdom being compelled to live in a country with which they had no personal connection. The European Commission on Human Rights considered that 'in granting a person citizenship, a State accepts that the individual has established close ties with its territory ... [A] difference based ... on the mere accident of birth, with no account being taken ... of the individual's personal circumstances or merits [was] discrimination ... on the ground of birth.'[55]

The European *Court* of Human Rights, however, disagreed and held that the law was not discriminatory on grounds of birth. While agreeing that the law established a difference of treatment on the ground of birth, the court held that it had an 'objective and reasonable justification'. 'It is true that a person who ... has been settled in a country for several years may also have formed close ties with it, even if he or she was not born there. Nevertheless there are in general persuasive social reasons for giving special treatment to those whose link with a country stems from birth within it.'[56]

What is important about these examples is not only that they illustrate the tension between particular existing institutional communities and the antidiscrimination principle, but also (and more importantly) that in each case arguments reflecting institutional communitarian thinking are made in defence of the discrimination. If constitutive communitarianism necessarily depends upon institutional communitarianism, then constitutive communitarians are on the horns of a dilemma. For the reasons discussed above, however, it does not. Thus, though the legal antidiscrimination principle *is* difficult to reconcile with institutional

54 At 501.
55 *Abdulaziz, Cabales and Balkandali* v. *United Kingdom* (1983) 6 EHRR 28, 43.
56 Court, 505–6.

communitarianism, with *Gemeinschaft* institutions, and tends toward the *Gesellschaft* end of the spectrum,[57] this does not mean that it is necessarily inconsistent with a belief in the constitutive communitarian ideal.

These examples illustrate another point mentioned previously. The extent to which constitutive community can be encouraged directly by legally based mechanisms was viewed sceptically above. This scepticism can now be justified, perhaps, by examining more closely the question of what is meant by a cultural community in the immigration context. There is, of course, a massive literature from anthropologists on the issue of culture but I will restrict myself to one of the most informative, Clifford Geertz's *The Interpretation of Cultures*.[58] He discusses and rejects a number of different approaches to the meaning of 'culture'. The most important of these, for our purposes (because it comes closest to the argument that 'immigration restrictions are justified in order to protect our culture') is the approach which treats culture 'purely as a symbolic system by isolating its elements, specifying the internal relationships among those elements, and then characterizing the whole system in some general way according to the core symbols around which it is organized, the underlying structures of which it is a surface expression, or the ideological principles upon which it is based.[59] This Geertz rejects as involving the danger 'of locking cultural analysis away from its proper object, the informal logic of actual life'.[60] The approach favoured by Geertz is to view the analysis of culture not as 'an experimental science in search of law but an interpretive one in search of meaning'. 'Believing', he writes, 'that man is an animal suspended in webs of significance he himself has spun, I take culture to be those webs.'[61]

My argument against attempts to protect 'community' is based first on a view that the institutional community sought to be protected is often a fearsomely restrictive and exclusionary entity; but second, even if it is

[57] On the *Gesellschaft* effect of antidiscrimination law, see A. Bickel, *The Supreme Court and the Idea of Progress* (New Haven, 1978) at 104 where he describes the tendency of the Warren Court 'in pursuit of the idea of equality' to 'circumscribe and displace private ordering, to legalize the society, to rationalize it in the sense in which the great industrial consolidators spoke of rationalizing the economy, to impose order on the market of norms, values, and institutions. There was evidence ... of an imperfectly bridled managerial drive.'

[58] C. Geertz, *The Interpretation of Cultures* (New York, 1973).

[59] At 17.

[60] Ibid.

[61] At 5.

not, the law is almost certain to attempt to protect an impoverished view of that culture;[62] and third, that very attempt may have deleterious effects on the 'webs of significance' which already exist. If we blunder in, trying to preserve them, there is a significant danger that they will be destroyed. It has long been recognized that the analysis of one's own culture raises a number of special problems. If the political (in which I include the legal) institutions of the society are ill equipped to view the culture of the society in which they operate in a way which is likely to be satisfying, they are even less equipped to assess the culture of another society or the impact of immigrants from that society on their own culture. The government is likely to be a poor anthropologist. Legislating culture (in the sense in which Geertz uses it) just seems silly. Its fluid, subtle, textured, changing nature seems unsuited to the 'protection' of law. A culture cannot be set in aspic. Nor should those voluntary institutions which have a valuable role in bridging the gulf between the individual and society be frozen by law. My argument is not to disparage these institutions, but rather to respect them, which involves restraint and often means not interfering.

This scepticism of the legal recognition of 'community values' is essentially contingent. In certain circumstances there may be little alternative and, ironically, this is sometimes the case when the antidiscrimination principle itself is applied. The challenge to the British birth-link immigration rules on antidiscrimination grounds was just such an occasion. There are serious arguments in favour of alternative approaches to that taken by the European court. One would have allowed a challenge to the very conception of community advanced by the British government and thus required the development and articulation of an alternative vision of community. It would then have used a communitarian argument to interpret the antidiscrimination principle. A second would have allowed a challenge to the means–ends rationality of the immigration rule based on birth. While accepting the government's conception of community, it might have refused to accept the likelihood of their immigration policy actually furthering this conception. Both approaches would involve risks: that the court might be drawn into an attempt to substitute its view of institutional community for that of the government and thus fall into the difficulties exposed by Geertz; second, that acceptable non-rational criteria might potentially be

[62] On the difficulty of artificially recreating a lost culture and the potential for creating an impoverished version of it if one tries, see e.g. G. Calabresi, *Ideals, Beliefs, Attitudes and the Law* (Syracuse, NY, 1985), 30–1.

underestimated and the in-court conversation be conducted in narrowly instrumental terms, which might spill over outside the courtroom. But neither approach is for these reasons alone unacceptable.

V

To conclude. There are a number of different types of communitarian argument. The legal antidiscrimination principle is antagonistic to institutional communitarianism. It is not, however, hostile towards (indeed it is compatible with) ideal constitutive communitarianism. Though arguments based on this ideal will be present in the legal context, putting the ideal into operation is too easily corrupted and too uncertain in its effects to be safely *encouraged* in a setting where the antidiscrimination principle is being considered.

11

Economic Theory v. Property Law: The *Numerus Clausus* Problem*

BERNARD RUDDEN†

1. INTRODUCTION

THE issue to be discussed is the apparent conflict between a modern economic theory of property rights and the law. The first tells me that things will be used efficiently only if people have property rights over them and that these rights should be protected against others, transferrable to the highest bidder, and universal, that is, permitted to inhere in all resources whose supply is limited. But, so far as I know, (1) the law of all 'non-feudal' systems lays down a restricted list of entitlements which it will permit to count as property interests, or 'real rights'. Anything else sounds only, if at all, in contract. But (2) the well-advised citizen can, at some cost, almost always obtain results denied to him by one legal device by using another. My question is, why? Answers abound and will be cited later, but they all leave me in doubt.

It may be helpful to explain the terminology used in the following discussion. By 'property interests' or 'real rights', I mean entitlements good against people with whom we have no contract, in short, strangers. My definition is deliberately vague: I do not insist that these property interests be good *erga omnes*. It will suffice that they are good against a smaller class (usually, those with notice). I use the word 'good' because I am not here concerned with exactly *how* they are protected against

† This essay has seen seen several false starts. I am grateful, above all, for the long discussions with William Bishop of the London School of Economics, with whom, at one stage, it was planned as a collaborative work. Others whose comments have been of great assistance are: Stuart Anderson of Hertford College, Oxford; Tony Honoré of All Souls College, Oxford; Gregory Alexander, Peter Martin, Al Neimeth, and Bob Summers of Cornell Law School; Richard Epstein of Chicago University Law School; Hans Baade, Michael Sturley, and Michael Tigar of the Law School of the University of Texas at Austin. Responsibility for any errors is my own.

strangers.[1] For all interests apparently excluded from the *numerus clausus* of real rights, I shall use the compendious, if contemptuous word 'fancy' taken from Lord Brougham LC's judgment in *Keppel* v. *Bailey* (1834).[2] In order to save space, I borrow from the civilians the phrase 'universal successors' to mean heir, executor, trustee-in-bankruptcy, and so on of an obligor; and 'singular successors' to mean those who take the thing in respect of which the right, real or fancy, is asserted.

I shall deal only with immovable things and, in order to isolate the problem, shall try to distinguish the content of a property interest from the rules governing its creation. English case law and doctrine, in particular, persistently treat the two together. I shall assume, however, that the system's formal requirements—deed, recording, notarized act, engraving on stone, or whatever—have been scrupulously complied with, and that the parties want to create an entitlement good against strangers. This will enable me to focus on the content of the entitlement so created in order to see whether they are permitted to do so.

The issues may, perhaps, be presented more clearly by the use of a threefold classification of the relation between a person's obligations and his things.

1. If A owes B a pure contract debt—say, to repay an unsecured loan—A and his universal successors have an obligation, for satisfaction of which all his things are liable, but only while they are his. The singular successor of any particular thing takes free of both obligation and liability.[3]

2. If A has given security—say a land mortgage—for the loan, then:

(i) as before, A and his universal successors are obliged, and all his things are liable while he has them (so if he transfers to another,

[1] G. Calabresi and D. Melamed save the word 'property' to describe the protection afforded by a rule that anyone who wishes to remove the entitlement must buy it in a voluntary transaction at a price agreed with the seller: 'Property Rules, Liability Rules, and Inalienability: One View of the Cathedral' (1972) 85 *Harvard Law Rev.* 1089. This fits their scheme of thought, but leaves me with nagging (if incoherent) doubts about a use of the word which excludes the Roman owner. Gaius (4.48) is explicit: in an action to recover his thing, the owner gets only money, assessed by the judge: *omnis condemnatio pecuniaria.*

[2] (1834) 2 My & K 517, 535. The same word is used, in the same sense, in the English Law Commission's Report (No. 147) on *Land Obligations* 6. 4) (1984). The general problem is discussed comparatively, but briefly, by V. Bolgar, 'Why no Trusts in the Civil Law?' (1953) 2 *Am. J. Comp. Law* 204, 213, and by J. Merryman, 'Policy, Autonomy, and the *Numerus Clausus* in Italian and American Property Law' (1963) 12 ibid., 224.

[3] I ignore the *actio Pauliana* and its common-law equivalent, covering alienation in fraud of creditors.

or even abandons to the lender, the thing charged, his other assets may be taken for any balance owing); but

(ii) if he alienates the one thing charged, the singular successor has no obligation to repay either interest or capital and all his other assets are free of liability; but, as to the thing acquired from the mortgagor, he is subject to a liability (correlative to the mortgagee's powers of foreclosure, sale, and so on) which is *limited* in amount, in object, and in time. It never exceeds the value of the thing; it does not extend to his other assets; and, once he abandons or transfers the thing charged, he is free of the burden. (Furthermore, with the limited liability runs the power to repay and redeem.)

3. The third class covers the case where A has undertaken a 'real' obligation by, say, giving B, his neighbour, a right of way over A's property, Whiteacre. In the previous example, A, as borrower, was bound by an obligation for which all his assets were liable (while his), and they remained so liable after alienation of the land charged; but his singular successor to that land had no obligation at all. Here, when A transfers Whiteacre, his obligation ceases, as must the liability, for breach, of his other belongings. His singular successor, however, has an obligation, for which all his other assets are liable, to respect the neighbour's right of way; both obligation and general liability will last until he too alienates Whiteacre.[4]

Thus in (1) things become liable because of their owner; in (3) owners become liable because of their thing; in (2) the borrower's things are liable because he owns them, but his singular successor is liable only on the thing he has acquired. Lessor stands to lessee, and vice versa, as in (1), but those who take their respective interests as singular successors may be subject to obligations and to general liability as in (3).

2. THE LAW

In all 'non-feudal' systems with which I am familiar (whether earlier, as at Rome, or later), the pattern is (in very general terms) similar: there are less than a dozen sorts of property entitlement. Three confer possession, either now or later, good against strangers: fee (ownership, full or

[4] According to Ulpian, Labeo used to encapsulate this by saying that 'the thing, not the man, owes the service' (D 8.5.6.2). This expresses neatly the entire liberation of the alienor of the servient land, but, in so far as it suggests that his successor's other assets are not liable, seems too wide.

bare), life estate (usufruct), and lease.[5] The non-possessory and non-security real rights will be given the name 'servitudes'. The common law fragments this class into an overlapping host of easements, profits, restrictive covenants, equitable servitudes, real covenants, land obligations.[6] The classical Roman texts mostly give a list of examples: way, water, light, and so on. Pomponius, however, divides the whole class of real servitudes into two, depending on whether the servient owner permits or merely abstains (D 8.1.15.1). The first covers rights of way and the like, the second rights of light and restrictive covenants. Affirmative duties were, in principle, not allowed to run as servitudes. Finally, there are security interests over immovables which, despite their different names, everywhere give the lender similar powers, which may (but need not) include possession. All three categories of entitlement (the possessory, the servitude, and the security) may normally be held by co-proprietors, in indivision or jointly.

There are, of course, many differences of detail. Generally speaking, however, only American states, Israel,[7] and the feudal systems burden a person with the obligation to do something and may make all his assets liable for satisfaction, just because, although he has made no contract, he acquired an immovable. The largest merchant homebuilders in the United States, Levitt & Sons Inc., impose on the singular successors of their buyers an obligation to mow and weed their lawns weekly during the summer months.[8] I am far from suggesting that this is not a good

[5] The civil-law systems (save Scotland and some Roman-Dutch areas) have added this last only since the nineteenth century. In most of continental Europe the immovables lease was for centuries merely contract, not good against strangers. For over a thousand years the source of this rule is cited as the *lex Emptorem* (C 4.65.9, Alexander Severus, AD 234) although the classification is older still: D 19.2.25.1: Gaius (AD *c.* 150 if not interpolated). The earliest statutory 'repeal' I can trace is the Prussian *Allgemeines Landrecht* I 21 358 (1794), and the fashion then spread. The Scots Leases Act 1449 achieves the same result (fifty years before the English case law protecting lessees), but this was long before the reception of Roman law in Scotland.

[6] An entire recent issue of the *Southern California Law Review* is devoted to the problem; its 270 pages give exhaustive references to US case law and doctrine: (1982) 55 *S. Cal. Law Rev.* 1179 ff. An interesting recent contribution is S. E. Serk, 'Freedom from Freedom of Contract: The Enduring Value of Servitude Restrictions' (1985) 70 *Iowa Law Rev.* 615.

[7] Israeli Land Law 1969 s. 93 (b): 'An easement for the benefit of property may also provide that the owner of the servient property shall carry out a specific act in respect thereof...'. Sections 92 and 95 permit easements in gross, as does the New Zealand Property Law Act 1905 s. 13: see now Property Law Act 1952 s. 122.

[8] e.g. Deed of Declaration of 21 Nov. 1949, Levittown, Nassau County NY, Liber 3959 cp. 428. And see R. C. Ellickson, 'Alternatives to Zoning: Covenants, Nuisance Rules and Fines as Land Use Controls' (1973) 40 *U. Chi. Law Rev.* 681, 713 n. 122.

thing; my problem is why it is often so difficult to achieve. The same is true of obligations to pay money. It seems curious that a system will allow a right of way to be given for nothing or for a lump sum, but will balk at an annual payment; yet, when the obligation is secured by lien (as in the USA *Neponsit* line of cases[9]) it may run with the land, although liability is limited to that land. The puzzle is darkened by the fact that all systems now permit positive obligations to bind the singular successors of the interest of lessor and lessee (and make all their assets liable for performance), so that leasehold conveyancing has gained an unmerited popularity in some countries.

In very general terms, then, all systems limit, or at least greatly restrict, the creation of real rights: 'fancies' are for contract, not property.

2.1 *The codified systems*

Many systems enact as a basic rule the proposition that 'no real rights can be created other than those provided for in this Code or other legislation' (Japanese CC 175; similar provisions occur in Argentine CC 2536, Ethiopian CC 1204 (2), Korean CC 185, Louisiana CC 476–8, Thai CC 1298, and perhaps by implication from Israeli Land Law 1969 sections 2–5). As far as I know, only one country then enacts the logical corollary. The Argentine CC 2536 continues:

> Any contract or testamentary disposition which constitutes or modifies real rights otherwise than as recognized by this Code is valid only, if at all, as a constitution of personal rights.

The primary sources of the Romans, French, and Germans are not so explicit, but a strong current of doctrine and case law[10] insists that the only entitlements permitted to prevail against strangers are those listed in the law and patterned as described above.[11]

[9] 278 NY 248, 15 NE (2d) 793 (1938). The numerous cases following this are conveniently cited by Uriel Reichman, 'Residential Private Governments: An Introductory Survey' (1976) 43 *U. Chi. Law Rev.* 257 n. 15. An English court has enforced a continuing payment obligation collateral to an easement on the principle *qui sentit commodum sentire debet et onus*: *Halsall* v. *Brizell* [1957] 1 All ER 371 (Ch. D.). The liability on the obligation seems to extend to all the debtor's assets, but if he surrenders the easement he, and they, are free: Upjohn J. at 377G. Doctrine suggests a device which is contractual but even more artificial: 'treating use of the roads by each successor as acceptance of an implied offer of the right to use them on payment of the contribution' (R. E. Megarry & H. W. R. Wade, *Real Property* (London, 4th edn., 1975), 750).

[10] F. Bauer, *Lehrbuch des Sachenrechts* (Munich, 12th edn., 1983), I. ii. 2; S. Ginossar, *Droit réel, propriété et créance* (Paris, 1960).

[11] An English-language version of the German categories will be found in Albert Kocourek's translation of Karl Gareis's *Introduction to the Science of Law* ss. 20, 21 (Boston, 1911).

2.2 *The uncodified systems*

Similar assertions are often to be found as the major premiss of a common-law syllogism. The best known are:

Brougham LC: 'There are certain known incidents to property and its enjoyment; among others, certain burthens . . . recognized by the law . . . But it must not therefore be supposed that interests of a novel kind can be devised . . .'[12]

Pollock CB: 'A new species of incorporeal hereditament cannot be created at the will and pleasure of an individual owner of an estate; he must be content to take the sort of estate and the right to dispose of it as he finds the law settled by decisions, or controlled by act of Parliament.'[13]

Wilde B.: 'It is a well settled principle of law that new modes of holding and enjoying real property cannot be created.'[14]

Bramwell B.: 'New rights of property cannot be created.'[15]

Holmes J.: 'The question remains whether, even if we make the further assumption that the covenant was valid as a contract between the parties, it is of a kind that the law permits to be attached to land . . .'[16]

Holmes O. W.: 'New and unusual burdens cannot be imposed on land. It strikes our ears strangely to hear a right of services from an individual called a right of property as distinguished from contract.'[17]

Olney J.: 'Such servitudes . . . are opposed to the rule that the owner of land may not create new and heretofore unknown estates.'[18]

In England, though many feudal property interests have died, only one new type, the restrictive covenant, has been admitted. Since the Romans allowed this, the feat can hardly be said to be strikingly

[12] *Keppel* v. *Bailey* (1834) 2 My & K 517, 535.

[13] *Hill* v. *Tupper* (1863) 2 Hurlst & C 121.

[14] *Stockport Wwks.* v. *Potter* (1864) 3 H & C 300, 314.

[15] Ibid., 321.

[16] *Norcross* v. *James* (1885) 140 Mass 188, 2 NE 946, 948. Most of these quotations are, in fact, from cases in which what was at issue was an attempt to use property law to secure some business advantage, such as captive clientele, or some other protection against competition. It seems to me, however, that before considering competition policy, logically one ought to know why even non-competitive fancies are excluded from the list of entitlements good against strangers. My essay is, therefore, addressed only to that issue.

[17] *The Common Law* (Cambridge, Mass., 1967), 3301, 316. The passages are, of course, descriptive not normative.

[18] *Werner* v. *Graham* 183 P 945, 947 (1919, Cal Sup Ct).

creative.[19] US common-law courts and Israeli and (since 1977) Louisiana law have gone further and permit the running of certain affirmative burdens (*servitutes in faciendo*), but as far as I know the major premiss has not been challenged. The US Restatement, Property (1944) (No. 537 com. a) says that unless such a burden has some compensating advantage 'the running of the promise by which it was created is not permitted'.

3. THE REASONS AND THEIR FLAWS

3.1 *Legal reasons*

Absence of demand The first reason given (or at least assumed) in the legal texts is that the present list of permitted property interests/real rights covers all that one could conceivably want: possession for life, for years, or for ever; certain servitudes; and security. The first objection to this is simply one of suspicion. It is possible that our perception of what people want is conditioned by the fact that they take what we let them have. More precise objections also spring to mind. The possessory interests have in common the factors of space and time. As to the first, 'exclusive possession' is necessary; but it is conceivable that someone might wish to create a shared entitlement to possession ('front-of-house rights' in a theatre, vending concessions) which does not fall easily within the present categories of co-ownership. As to the element of time, the standard interests confer entitlement to a continuous period of possession; but it is becoming increasingly common that people wish to hold a *property* interest which will confer the right to exclusive possession for short periods at repeated intervals. The Irish peasant knew this as conacre; its modern name is *time-sharing*.

It seems to be the closed category of servitudes which has seen most strain of late. The restriction that, to count as real rights, they must not impose positive obligations on the singular successor of an immovable has been avoided by case law in the common-law USA, by legislation in Israel and Louisiana, and in England by statute for local authorities,[20]

[19] D 8.4.13 (Ulpian). Singular successors are bound by clause against opening a tuna-fishery imposed on the sale of one lot for the benefit of that retained (it may have been aimed at restricting competition—*ne contra eum piscatio thynaria exerceatur*). Although English judges did not take the hint, the Real Property Commissioners of 1832, without distinguishing positive and restrictive covenants, recommended that specific enforcement be generally available: 3rd Report pp. 51, 72 (1832).

[20] Housing Act 1974 s. 126. The technique is to treat singular successors as if they were parties to the contract.

while the rest of us must continue to use the leasehold regime until rescued by the enactment of the Law Commission's 1984 bill. As to security interests, the present powers, as well as the caution, of lenders have led to little discernible demand for the fashioning of new types of mortgage of immovables (movables and corporate debt are another matter). One innovation, however, is still in the limbo of uncertainty: the *anti-lien* under which the lender takes no charge but prohibits alienation by the borrower.[21]

Absence of notice One of the main reasons given in common and civil law for the *numerus clausus* of real rights is the problem a purchaser would face in finding out about fancies. German doctrine makes much of this and in the common law of Massachussets we find Field CJ averring as axiomatic that 'interests in land, a knowledge of which cannot be obtained from a view of the land itself, or a search in the proper registry, certainly ought not to be extended'.[22]

There is clearly much to be said for this view, yet it seems open to two objections. First, one may ask why, if there is a functioning Landbook, should not a fancy be registered and enforced, with its creator paying all recording costs. Second, in no system I know is notice either necessary or sufficient for the validity of all property rights. Many countries accept the importance of notice, but contrive to tolerate large exceptions. In Germany, leases are not registrable; if the tenant is in possession, the lessor's singular successor is bound both by that possession and by the pertinent positive landlord's obligations.[23] The same is true of short leases and prescriptive claims in many other systems with recording requirements (such as France, the Australian states, and other countries with a Torrens system). Notice is not sufficient, because no system holds a fancy binding as property just because the acquirer of land knows all about it. Indeed, were this not so, common-lawyers would be spared all that dreary learning on 'touch and concern'. The assignee of a lease normally reads it and knows all about the tenant's covenants, as did the defendant in *Keppel* v. *Bailey*;[24] but he is bound only by some.

[21] See U. Reichman, 'The Anti-Lien: Another Security Interest in Land' (1974) 41 *U. Chi. Law Rev.* 685.

[22] Bauer, op. cit. n. 10 above, I. ii. 3; *Whittendon Mfrg.* v. *Staples* (1895) 164 Mass 319, 41 NE 441, 448 (in a dissent).

[23] On the whole, German and French doctrine denies that the tenant's entitlement is real, despite its protection against the landlord's singular successors. Without discussing the decades of dispute, I note only that, in 1811, the Austrian legislator, in enacting its protection, said it was to be treated as *ein dingliches Recht* (ABGB 1095).

[24] (1834) 2 My & K 517.

Absence of consent All systems require consent for contracts; so it would follow that you ought not to have certain types of obligations unless you undertook them. Of course, whether you like it or not, you may have an obligation *not* to do things, or even a positive duty to take care not to do bad things: that is what the law of tort is for. But obligations to do good, to cut your lawn or, worse still, your neighbours', ought to arise from your agreement and not from your owning a garden.[25]

The objection to this is that all systems recognize that in certain cases you may have to do good things although you never said you would. Even the Romans, though not without argument, accepted this for duties to maintain the support of your neighbour's beam and the like, and they are copied by the French and others.[26] But these systems shrink from imposing on the singular successor an obligation for which all his assets are liable. They limit liability to the servient tenement and provide, scrupulously if unrealistically, that he may escape the obligation by abandoning the land. Louisiana, for instance, announces as a general proposition that 'the owner of the servient estate is not obliged to do anything. His obligation is to abstain . . . or to permit' (CC 651). It then, however, dutifully follows the tradition of some two thousand years and provides for a servitude of support under which 'the owner of the servient estate is bound to keep the wall fit for the exercise of the servitude, but he may be relieved of this charge by abandoning the wall' (CC 700).[27] The Ethiopian Civil Code of 1960, drafted by a most learned comparativist, is still grudging: 'A servitude may only accessorily cast upon the servient owner the burden to commit any act' (CC 1360).

Some common-law US courts nowadays make positive obligations run.[28] Certainly they do this where performance is secured by lien so that only the servient thing is liable to be taken in satisfaction for breach. Professor Susan F. French emphasizes the function of the lien here, saying that 'this effectively insulates the general assets of a subsequent purchaser from liability on the servitude'.[29] Apparently, however, if an

[25] D 44.7.3.pr.

[26] D. 8.5.6.2. Ulpian describing the argument between Gallus and Labeo; Paul D 8.2.23 and 8.5.7. French CC 698–9; BGB 1021; Japanese CC 286–7.

[27] While keeping the Code as given in the text, Louisiana introduced in 1977 a category of real rights called 'building restrictions'. Despite the name they 'may impose affirmative duties that are reasonable and necessary' and 'may be enforced by mandatory and prohibitory injunctions' (CC 778–9).

[28] For the full story, see U. Reichman, 'Toward a Unified Concept of Servitudes' (1982) 55 *S. Cal. Law Rev.* 1179.

[29] S.F. French, 'Toward a Modern Law of Servitudes: Reweaving the Ancient Strands' (1982) 55 *S. Cal. Law Rev.* 1261, 1302.

obligation is called a 'real covenant' it escapes both the strict common law and this constraint. Its breach may impose liability on all the servient owner's assets, thus going further than the traditional civil law. If US courts issue an injunction to perform, backed by the contempt sanction and the threat of imprisonment, then not merely the owner's assets but his *body* is liable, and feudalism is come again. Casner says the courts do this, Krasnowiecki says they do not.[30] The Restatement is very hesitant here, emphasizing that 'covenants running with the land still furnish the unique example of the possibility of one being sued as a promisor upon a promise he had not made' (1944, V pt. III intro. note).

But the most powerful response to the 'consent' argument is surely that the singular successors of lessor and lessee, everywhere, have to do things to which they did not consent and for which all their assets are liable, provided that the obligations 'touch and concern' the land.[31]

Pyramiding An obvious objection is to point out that if one owner is permitted to bind his land to the performance of fancies, then his successors in title will expect the same power, and so the land will become encrusted with layers of obligation. This appears to recall the problems of subinfeudation or those of modern Ireland, where the provisions of Deasy's Act 1860 allowed a whole pyramid of obligations.

This objection is clearly weighty, and in reply I can make only the following points. First, the historical objection to subinfeudation was not, in practice, to the layers of services exigible from an owner in possession (tenant in fee in demesne) but to the fact that the worth to lords paramount of the feudal incidents (above all for escheat on want of heirs, whether in fact or by the ancestor's death on the gallows) was measured, not by the value of the land, but by that of the services due from mesne tenants. Second, and more realistically, if there is thought to be some value in a system which permits a wider class of property interests, then excesses could be checked either by a modern *Quia Emptores* or by permitting a tribunal to cancel them, if necessary against compensation. Third, and the question will recur again, why does the law have to solve these problems, if the market can?

30 2 ALP 9.36; J. Z. Krasnowiecki, 'Townhouses with Homes Associations: A New Perspective' (1975) 123 *U. Pa. Law Rev.* 711, 717 n. 28. It is more than likely that I have simply failed to understand the American law.

31 In the civil law, the BGB 571 (1900) enacts this, making explicit what had been added by case law in France and Austria to the provision preventing the lessor's singular successors from evicting the tenant during the term of the lease (French CC 1743 (1804), AGBG 1095 (1811)). It has since been copied in many other systems.

Doctrinaire assertions Civilian doctrine has so little doubt that a closed list of real rights is necessary that its justifications are perfunctory. The standard commentary on the Argentine CC quoted above says only:

> A multiplicity of real rights over one and the same thing is a fertile source of complications and lawsuits and can greatly injure the exploitation of the thing itself. Properties are devalued and lawsuits born...[32]

The basic Italian work avers:

> In the general interests of production, the legal system does not consider it appropriate to permit private citizens the power to burden property by limitations differing from those provided for by law [i.e. the Code], since the latter correspond to socially relevant interests: thus real interests are a *numerous clausus*. The will of a private citizen is not free to create [other] patterns.[33]

What these 'socially relevant interests' are, is not revealed.

3.2 *Philosophical reasons*

Kant and Austin The premiss is that property rights are good against all; they are, in words cited by Austin, *jura quae valent in alios generatim*. 'The right of property', he says, 'is resolvable into two elements: 1st, the power of using indefinitely the subject of the right ... 2ndly, a power of excluding others. [Both involve] equally rights to forbearance on the part of persons generally.'[34] From this premiss follow three conclusions: (1) A univeral obligation, binding all subjects of a legal system, can be imposed only by a general norm of that system, and not by the individual will. Kant argues that 'An individual, unilateral will—and the same applies to a dual or other particular will—cannot impose *on all* an obligation which is contingent in itself. This requires an omnilateral or universal will, which is not contingent but *a priori*, and which is therefore united and *legislative*.'[35] (2) A norm which binds everyone binds those not *sui juris*; hence it must be negative in content, it must command us

[32] J. N. Mustapich, *Codigo Civil* (Madrid, 1960), ann. ad 2502–3.

[33] A. Torerente, *Manuale di Diritto Privato* No. 171 (Milan, 1965).

[34] J. Austin, *Lectures on Jurisprudence* (5th edn., ed. R. Campbell, 2 vols., London, 1885), ii. 808, 938. Similar views are found in France and Germany: A. Colin, H. Capitant, and L. Julliot de la Morandière, *Cours élémentaire de droit civil français* (Paris, 1947), i. 124; M. Planiol and G. Ripert, *Traité pratique, les biens* (Paris, 2nd edn., 1952), iii. 48; Bauer, op. cit. n. 10, I. ii.

[35] *Philosophy of Law* (tr. W. Hastie, Edinburgh, 1887), i. 14. Similarly, Tony Honoré: 'the duties corresponding to claims *in rem* are created by a general title—being subject to a given legal system'. ('Rights of Exclusion and Immunities against Divesting' (1960) 34 *Tul. Law Rev.* 453, 456.)

not to do something. (3) Therefore, the correlative of a real right cannot require action; affirmative burdens do not run.

Hegelian/historical The legal system roughly described as 'feudal' imposed on landholders any number of obligations to do things to which they had not consented. It does not matter, for my purposes here, whether by the seventeenth century this structure was wicked or diseconomic. The point is that it was perceived to be so. Tenurial obligations were, in effect, abolished by the Massachussets Body of Liberties of 1641, and the English followed suit in 1660. And the word 'servitude' covers both slavery and easements.

It was Hegel, more than any other writer, whose philosophical version of this history profoundly influenced the German Pandectists and, through them, the law in the books of Latin America and the Orient. The first propositions of his section on property emphasize the interrelation between freedom of persons and of things.

> A person must translate his freedom into an external sphere in order to exist as idea. He has as his substantive end the right of putting his will into any and every thing and thereby making it his, because it has no such end in itself and derives its destiny and its soul from his will.

Hegel's insistence on the primacy of the will is translated into my area of concern in these words:

> It is about a millenium and a half since the freedom of personality began to blossom. But it was only yesterday, we might say, that the principles of the freedom of property became recognized.

Further, he depicted the standardization of property interests as

> The march of mental development [which] is the long and hard struggle to free a feudal content from its sensuous and immediate form.[36]

Thus, for Hegel, we are fully free only when our property is (relatively) free.

Hohfeldian: cloning claims The utility of a Hohfeldian analysis is that, while it does not seek to give us policy reasons, it demonstrates the true effect on strangers of creating property entitlements. To the best of my knowledge, this analysis has not been attempted before.[37]

[36] Hegel, *Philosophy of Right*, tr. T. M. Knox (Oxford, 1942), 41, 44, 62, 217. See H. Hattenhauer, *Grundbegriffe des Bürgerliches Rechts* (Munich, 1982), 7. IV.

[37] It may be latent in the stimulating, but (to me) difficult 'Comment' by Bernard E. Jacob, 55 *S. Cal. Law Rev.* 1369, 1377.

At first blush, one might assume with Gaius (D 3.5.38) that one person has the power to alter another's legal position *without his consent* only if the alteration is for the better. Thus an offer, once received, enriches the offeree's position whether he likes it or not, by conferring a power he did not have before, namely by unilateral declaration of his will to accept and thus to subject the offeror to duties. The latter's legal position is thereby 'worsened', but, of course, he consented by making the offer.

However, the effect of creating a property interest may be to alter *for the worse* the legal position of people who did not consent thereto. I take the simplest example. Black owns Blackacre and White, Whiteacre next door. The property interest under discussion is a straightforward right of way over the latter land for the benefit of the former; if created, it will prevent building on part of Whiteacre (so that the effect to be considered is the same as might be produced by a right to light or a restrictive covenant; these are not pigeon-holed in many systems; all are 'servitudes').

In the absence of such a servitude, everyone in the world has a privilege *not* to build, and no-right that anyone build, on Whiteacre. As to the privilege *to build*, White has it in relation to everyone. They have it in relation to each other, but not in relation to White. In other words, White, as owner, has a claim that no one else build. But Black has no such claim. As far as he is concerned, anyone can build next door.

If the servitude be given by White to Black, then the universal privilege *not* to build is unaltered. As to the privilege *to build*, White has it in relation to everyone except Black—his position is worse, but he has consented. Black has it in relation to everyone save White (which was his position before). Everyone else has it between themselves, but not in relation to White *and Black*. Thus their legal position is worse. The transaction creating the servitude did not transfer to Black White's claim that no one build. It *cloned* the claim, handing a replica to Black and so subjecting everyone else to a duty-not owed to two people: White as owner of the land and Black as owner of the servitude. Before the grant of the servitude, everyone had a privilege as against Black to build on Whiteacre. Now no one has. *But only White and Black consented.*[38]

Are we approaching the mysterious gap in Hohfeld's scheme? The correlative of a no-right is a no-duty. I have no right that you build a wall

[38] The problem worried the Romans: D 43.19.3.5. It is also the issue in *Hill* v. *Tupper*; the case is not, as some authors seem to think, about easements in gross: Casner, ALP No. 8.6 fn. 2; No. 9.32 fn. 3.

on your land; you have no duty to build. But the correlative of a no-right-*not* is no-duty-*not.* I have no right that you not build a wall; you have no duty not to build. In the example of the servitude given above, we saw that everyone's no-duty to build remains unaffected. What is altered is their duty-not. In relation to Black, they used to have no duty-not to build on Whiteacre. Now, by an act of White's and Black's will, they owe Black a duty-not to build.

The general refusal of the civilian and common-law systems (except the American and Israeli) to permit the running of affirmative burdens (duties-to) may now be explained by a combination of Kantian, Hegelian, and Hohfeldian terms. Save by legislation, our legal position may be altered without our consent only by adding the negative after, not by subtracting the one before, the word 'duty'. A duty-not-to may be imposed, but a no-duty-to cannot be removed. White's and Black's will alone can add another claimant (Black) to everyone's duty-not; it cannot do so in respect of a duty-to. Therefore, in a non-feudal system, it cannot do so as regards singular successors. Duties-not are frequently imposed on us without our consent, as in the example just given, or by the law of tort. Duties-to are not.

It must be admitted that this whole intriguing analysis fails to explain why the singular successors of lessors and lessees are bound by onerous duties-to, to which they certainly did not consent. One is tempted to think that the Romans were right to prevent this, by excluding leases from the law of property.

3.3 *Economic reasons*

Marketability A reason commonly given by the Restatement and by common-law doctrine is that fancies, if permitted to enure as property rights, hamper the marketability of land. The recent English Law Commission's Report (1984) on *Land Obligations* proposes that certain restricted affirmative duties be permitted to run but states:

> It would be wrong to allow an owner to use the new law to impose obligations to his fancy. The old rule that a covenant must 'touch and concern' or be for the benefit of the dominant *land* was established for good reasons.[39]

In the USA, Powell writes:

> Burdens running with the land may make the land less attractive to potential buyers. Outside Landlord and Tenant, the running of the burden of a promise

[39] Law Commission Report, No. 147, 6. 4, emphasis in original (1984).

has inherent in it risks which are difficult to avoid. The possibility of its existence necessarily has to some degree a hampering effect on the alienability of title to land.[40]

Rau agrees:

Such burdens encumber title, thereby reducing marketability.[41]

The Restatement (1944) number 537, comment *h*:

Free alienability of land is socially desirable. The running of the burden or a promise with land tends to interfere with the free alienability of the land and thus in a socially undesirable direction. [*sic*]

I find all this confusing. Hampering marketability could mean (*a*) restricting the power to alienate; (*b*) increasing the liability of the buyer's *other* assets to be taken in execution of the obligation; (*c*) increasing the costs of investigating title; (*d*) increasing the negotiation costs of the purchase. Now, (*a*) is not in issue here; (*d*) is present whether there are weird property interests or not, since the seller can seek to impose, *as a matter of contract*, whatever takes his fancy. The persistence of (*b*) and (*c*) would not reduce marketability; they would affect only the price. What the Restatement does not explain is why the courts, and not the market, should decide these difficult problems of land utilization. As Richard Epstein puts it, 'if a seller insists that a personal covenant bind the land ... [he] will have to accept a reduction in price'.[42]

Standardization Economists point out that one feature of markets is that devices develop to standardize the products on offer, so as to reduce the costs of exchange. A trader who sells a non-standard commodity imposes a cost which he and his buyer do not bear, since the mere existence of his oddity obliges all buyers to seek information on all deals. Thus there may well be reasons why, in order to favour routine trading, the law should not facilitate the coming into being of markets in non-standard packages. But my problem in the context of this paper, is twofold. First, nowhere does there exist an active wholesale market in immovables; second, every buyer may know today that, as a matter of property law, he could be bound only by certain stereotyped obligations,

40 5 *Real Property* (New York, 1981), No. 60.43.

41 'Covenants Running with the Land: Viable Doctrine or Common-Law Relic?' (1978) 7 *Hofstra Law Rev.* 139, 142.

42 'Notice and Freedom of Contract in the Law of Servitudes' (1982) 55 *S. Cal. Law Rev.* 1353, 1360.

but he does not know what fancies any particular seller will seek to exact as a matter of contract.

Market economy It is easy to see why contract develops once the market becomes an important institution. What is not so obvious is why property law becomes more restrictive. Does a market economy require a restricted list of property rights? If an owner wants his lawn mowed, should he be forbidden to impose it as an obligation binding the singular successors of his neighbour (even in a conveyance to his neighbour of the land next door), so that he is forced into the labour market and has to hire a gardener, or pay the person next door? Does the same apply if he wants to see his neighbour's grass well kept? This is certainly the result of those many modern systems which forbid (at least as a general principle) the running of affirmative duties. The strange result is that this prohibition brings us right back to Rome; and the Roman landowner certainly did not make contracts in the garden-labour market. He bought *things* (lawn-mowers) called slaves.

A reason commonly given for the restriction is that 'every real obligation risks creating an obstacle to the free circulation of things'.[43] Honoré offers a more subtle analysis of the difference between real and personal rights:

> The point of this type of indivestable or not easily divestable right to a thing is to promote security and good management by allowing the holder to count, if he so wishes, on the future use and enjoyment of a particular asset. The point of merely personal rights over property is to give the holder a limited advantage which is compatible with the free circulation of unencumbered property.[44]

Is it the case, then, that property rights are restricted, at the cost of frustrating fancy-fanciers, in order to obtain a benefit in reducing the difficulty, and so the cost, of transactions in general? These costs seem to include those of information, negotiation, and policing.

Information costs These occur in, at least, two ways. The first are at the screening stage; what possible entitlements are available anywhere on the market? The second are incurred after an initial selection has been made and concern the suitability of the particular thing or choice among a range thereof.

[43] S. Ginossar, *Droit réel* (Paris, 1960), No. 58; see also G. Baudry-Lancantinerie and M. Chauveau, *Des Biens* (Paris, 3rd edn., 1905) No. 193; 2 C. Aubry and C. Rau, *Droit civil français* (7th edn., ed. P. Esmein, Paris, 1961), 172 No. 58; Bauer, I. ii. 3 (a) and (b).

[44] Honoré, op. cit. n. 35 above, 468.

At first glance, there seems to be no doubt that the *numerus clausus* reduces screening costs. The potential buyer of a property interest knows that, wherever he looks, he will find less than a dozen. If, say, he wants the entitlement to park his car and wants it to be good against strangers, then he must buy the fee, a life estate, lease, or easement. There is no other possibility. Outside the USA, New Zealand and Israel, the list is even smaller; for the last variety is limited by the non-existence, as property interests, of easements in gross, so he has to look close to home; if he wants durable distant parking, he must buy one of the three possessory entitlements.

Similarly, if we consider it from the position of the buyer of a standard interest (for example, ownership) then he knows that, wherever the immovable is located, he will owe few obligations to people other than the seller. Indeed, the only such obligations will be those falling into the class of servitudes. Here again, outside the USA and Israel, he knows that, in principle, none of them will cost him time or money. All will involve only duties to refrain.

Finally, let us look at it from the point of view of the property owner who wishes to create a fancy real right. He cannot do it simply. He can, however, do it at a cost. He can make routine affirmative obligations run to singular successors by leasing the land. He can make the same run to freeholders if he keeps land nearby and is in the USA or Israel. Perhaps in all systems, even without benefited land and whether or not the duties imposed were purely personal, he could take a lien on the land for performance by his buyer. This would not impose an obligation on singular successors but would make their land liable for its breach. There is no reason whatever why one person's property should not be security for another's obligation, as where I pawn my watch for a loan made to you. In this way, he could in practice exact performance of any fancy. Charges securing a capital indebtedness are, of course, redeemable always and everywhere (outside corporation law). But those securing a non-capital obligation are well known, the common law calls them 'rent-charges' and, in England today, the 'estate rent-charge' is sometimes used to reinforce affirmative obligations. Furthermore, the idea of using security where more straightforward methods will fail is not new. In a system where any lessee had a mere personal right, and so could not prevail over his lessor's singular successors (being left to his action on the contract), we find Bartolus (1313–57) advising his lessee clients to take a lien to secure their lessor's contractual obligation to give quiet possession. Then 'the tenant-farmer can say "I stay in this farm by right of pledge and mortgage for my interest"; for a mortgage is a real right and so good against any successor'.[45]

Transaction costs If we now turn to costs at the transaction stage, we see that the savings effected by the screening process may be outweighed when it comes to acquiring. For although the buyer, at least of a freehold, knows that, in theory, he will not owe many duties to third parties, when he comes to negotiate with a particular seller he may find that, as a matter of *contract*, the seller may seek to impose any number of fancy obligations. Yet there is no *numerus clausus* of contract. On the contrary, freedom of contract means that so long as we stay licit we can have any contractual figure custom-built, not to say boiler-plated. The reason for the absence of restrictions at the contract stage is surely that the acceptance of onerous, expensive, or bizarre obligations will be reflected in a lower price. So why is the same not true of property obligations? If our buyer found that he would be bound, by the fact of his ownership, to do things for strangers, presumably he would pay a price reflecting this.

The purchaser of a lease faces similar problems. He knows that he will be bound to a third party, the landlord, by certain positive obligations; and that these are more or less standardized by the 'touch and concern' of the common law or similar phrases in the civil.[46] Thus he knows already that he cannot be bound by a covenant in the lease to cut the landlord's hair. But he does not know, until he starts to dicker, that there will be no term in the sale obliging him to do this. If there is, he must decide whether or not to accept and, if he does, at what price. Does this possibility impede trade?

It may well be the case, however, that, despite the *numerus apertus* of contract law, the prospective buyer and lessee know that few sellers and lessors are likely to try fancies on them if they cannot feature as standard elements in a deal of that sort. This gives them what they are looking for; ease of access to the good they want, namely, a property in which they can be free not to bother whether what they are doing maximizes wealth or the joint satisfaction with neighbours or landlords.

Land utilization Many commentators are concerned to ensure that the

45 Bartolus ad. D 19.2.25.1. *Qui fundum*, and see ad. C 4.65.9. (In the edition used, *Qui fundum* is numbered 'xxxv': *Bartoli de Saxoferrato, Omnia quae extant opera*, Sexta Editio Iuntarum, Venice, 1590.)

46 e.g. BGB 571 (1)—'aus dem *Mietverhältnis* ergebenden Rechte und Verpflichtigung'.

efficient development of land be not sterilized by 'fancies'. The Romans, and their heirs, are strong on this as is seen from two of their abiding rules on servitudes. Since the burden lessens the utility, and value, of one lot, it will run only if it benefits another: *ius suum deminuit, alterius auxit.*[47] There must therefore be a dominant lot, which must, in fact, be benefited: no easements in gross. Second, the servitude, if it is to run, must not impose an obligation to do things; it thus covers common-law easements and restrictive covenants, but not the American and Israeli affirmative duties.[48] As so often, it is the Argentine CC which spells out the logical consequence:

> 3044. Servitudes which consist of an obligation to do something, even though temporary and for the benefit of an immovable, cannot be established. A servitude so constituted is valid only as a simple obligation for the debtor and his heirs, without affecting the estates nor passing with them to the possessors of the immovables.

Many objections spring to mind. Some positive duties will augment the total value of the two lots, so that the ever-practical Romans allowed support obligations to run. The seller who has imposed a positive duty will see this reflected in the lower price he gets; if it runs, the same will be true of the price paid by singular successors. At any time, dominant and servient owners, who will be neighbours, can get together and cancel the obligation. In the case of numerous lots, the problems of hold-outs and free riders can, if these individuals are thought to be without merit and if this costs less than the value of positive obligations, be solved by a court or tribunal. This happens in many countries already as regards the servitudes they do permit. Finally, the seller who wishes to impose a running affirmative obligation can almost invariably do this everywhere by using some other, more expensive device; by taking a lien as security for performance; or by remaining landlord and selling a long lease.

There may well, however, be a more general case to be made for a restricted list of property entitlements as fostering the most efficient use of land in a market economy. It is interesting here to find that the Scots still allow positive obligations to run in the law of feus, and their courts

[47] Inst 2.3.3: 'no one can have a servitude unless he has land'; D 8.4.1.1; and see D 8.3.5. and 20; D 34.1.14.3. It is found in all modern Civil Codes, but rejected in Israel and New Zealand. See n. 7 above.

[48] Pomponius says (D 8.1.15.1) 'the nature of servitudes is not such that a person be compelled to do something but that he should suffer something, or not do something'. See also Egyptian CC 1015, Louisiana CC 651, Thai CC 1387. The Digest texts give us the high Roman rule; for the confusion in the provinces, see E. Levy, *West Roman Vulgar Law* (Philadelphia, 1951), 55, 58, where he points out that, with the growth of ground rents, 'the rule *servitus in faciendo consistere nequit* had outlived its usefulness'.

accept that certain burdens may be acceptable 'as a condition of a *feudal* grant, as between superior and vassal', but then hold them bad in a modern conveyance of a theatre.[49]

Clearly there are situations where it may increase the efficiency of land if successive owners are obliged to do things: central heating, contribution to upkeep, and the like. What is interesting is not that this is denied but that for over two thousand years (with a pause for 'feudalism') it has been accepted but swallowed only with great difficulty and subjected to many restrictions. As mentioned earlier, even the 1960 Ethiopian Code permits positive servitudes 'only accessorily', and everywhere the background, basic assumption seems to be that there is a closed list of real rights. The Restatement makes much of the argument from land use. An obligation which binds singular successors, says Comment *a* to Number 537, 'creates a burden upon the ownership of land which may have a disadvantageous effect upon its use and development. There is a social interest in the utilization of land [which] is adversely affected ... Unless a burden has some corresponding advantage ... the running of the promise by which it was created is not permitted.'

One difficulty with this type of argument is that different systems have varying views as to the 'corresponding advantage'. The burden of an easement, for all except Americans, New Zealanders, and Israelis, must benefit other land. The same is true of a profit, for all except the English, Swiss, and Germans; and in these latter systems they are fading.[50] Similarly, outside the USA and Israel, the burden of affirmative obligations will not, generally, run with freeholds so as to bind all the assets of each singular successor. In consequence, we find that many apartments in England are disposed of by way of long lease, so the result can be achieved, but not cheaply. Freehold schemes have had to be introduced at no small legislative cost by Strata Titles Acts in the Commonwealth, and England's Law Commission has produced a beautiful, but complex bill. Yet in France, apartments have been separately owned for centuries. The Civil Code's article 664 provided a rough and ready way of making common burdens run until its repeal and refined re-enactment in 1938.[51]

[49] *Aberdeen Varieties Ltd.* v. *James E. Donald (Aberdeen Cinemas) Ltd.* [1939] SC 788, *per* Lord Wark at 796.

[50] BGB 1105 (Reallast); Swiss CC 782 (Grundlast); see Bauer, XXXV. i.

[51] The original art. 664 was simple. When the different storeys of a house belong to different owners and the question by whom repairs and renewals are to be done is not settled by the title-deeds, the same shall be done as follows: the main walls and roof must

The other difficulty has been discussed above: that all those things may be good as contract.

Durability This brings me to the last reason. It is obvious that the relations of property are built to endure; they are inherently static. It is the relations created by the law of obligations which are dynamic, for they exist only to be changed. Contracts are born to die. Perhaps, then, the law confines fancies to the sphere of contract so that each must be negotiated afresh with successive owners of the burdened land. This is Reichman's view: if 'fancies' be permitted as property interests, then 'consensual termination of such rights might not occur because of prohibitive transaction costs' so 'instead of making the transferee negotiate for a release, the aspiring beneficiary will have to reach agreement with each new owner'.[52] Yet, if they were real rights, any singular successor could buy his way out. Epstein makes the point in his rejoinder to Reichman: making them real rights 'only changes the identity of the party who must initiate the transaction. There is no assurance that the number of transactions, and their complexity, will be reduced by placing the burden anew on the original seller.'[53]

It may be, however, that I have been looking at the issue from the wrong end, and the problem is not the creation of real rights, but their termination. Where valid property entitlements such as usufructs, ordinary easements, and restrictive, or positive leasehold, covenants are bought out, there will often be only one seller and one buyer. The bilateral monopoly thus created may be unable to reach a solution, or to do so at small cost. If, as in a development area, the property entitlements and correlative burdens are widely dispersed, there will be hold-out and free-rider difficulties. Perhaps, then, there is sense in limiting the occasions for any of these expensive situations by restricting, ere their birth, the class of real rights. If this be a good reason, it is strange that so little of the standard doctrine and case law spells it out.

Furthermore, bilateral monopolies occur wherever one person has an

be done at their common expense each paying a part proportionate to the value of the storey belonging to him. The owner of each storey repairs the floor on which he walks. The owner of the first storey repairs the staircase leading to it. The owner of the second must repair the staircase leading thereto, beginning from the first floor, and so on. It was repealed and replaced by a law of 28 June 1938, itself replaced by a law of 10 July 1965, amended by a law of 2 Jan. 1979; printed (with relevant Decrees) in *Dalloz Code civil*, at art. 664. The original article survived in Mauritius until its replacement by a condominium regime in the Code Napoleon (Amendment) Act 1978.

52 Reichman, op. cit. n. 28 above, 1233.

53 Epstein, n. 42 above, 1361.

exclusive right against another, and we generally accept that they are free to refuse to behave 'reasonably'. The point was well made by Chancellor Walworth in a New York case of 1832. Having allowed a non-building covenant benefiting one lot to subsist as a real right, good against the singular successor of the burdened lot, and having pointed out that the Romans did the same, he observed regretfully that the owner of the right wanted to stop the perfectly proper, nay laudable, small extension of a Christian church. None the less, he continued,

> however unreasonable I may suppose the complainant to be in this instance, if he has rights, they are guaranteed to him by the constitution and he cannot be deprived of them, even for a public benefit, except by due course of law, and upon receiving a just compensation therefore. The legislature has not deemed it expedient to authorize the taking of private property for such an object; and until they do so, he cannot be deprived of his rights without his consent.[54]

4. CONCLUSION

4.1 *The law*

This essay has tried to demonstrate the pervasiveness of the general rule that we are not free contractually to create more than a handful of entitlements good against strangers, and that everywhere their content is much the same. The problem is compounded by two further factors. First, all that the law of many countries does is to prevent an owner from simply and cheaply creating fancy property interests; he can almost always achieve his aims at some cost by the use of devices (such as long lease or lien) which, when one stands back and contemplates them calmly, appear largely mumbo-jumbo. The latest English example is to be found in the Rentcharges Act 1977 which sets out to get rid of them, but saves the 'estate rent-charge' whose function is to make the burden of positive obligations run. The legislator is, however, forced by his own logic of abolition to stipulate that, in principle, the rent thus charged must not be 'of more than a nominal amount' (s. 2 (5)). Thus, if real, the rent-charge fails; to succeed, it must be a fiction.

Second, many modern systems wish to permit, as property interests, certain regimes involving collaboration by neighbours in the performance of positive acts. Some countries (such as France) with a long tradition of apartment-dwelling developed early a system of 'condominium'. Others seem to find the task extremely difficult, not merely

[54] *Hills* v. *Miller*, 3 Paige Ch 254, 259 (1832).

because of hold-out and free-rider problems where numerous neighbours are involved, but in its basic structure. And all systems restrict their latest creations to a tightly defined *numerous clausus* which is only slightly, if significantly, wider than the old. That this coyness is not confined to one legal tradition may be demonstrated by a glance at the recent scheme of a mixed and sophisticated jurisdiction. Since 1977, the Louisiana Civil Code, by articles 778–9, permits certain affirmative duties to run. These are enforceable by mandatory injunction and so, presumably, by the 'feudal', not to say servile, sanction of contempt of court which makes the singular successor's *body* liable for the performance of positive obligations to which he did not consent. It calls them (emphasis added) building *restrictions*.

4.2 *The economics*

There seems to be a conflict between the law as sketched above and one or other of two economic theories. What is logically the second will be stated first, because it is easy to demonstrate its existence: namely, the view that there is a close correlation between economic analysis and legal rules. Posner tells us that 'many of the doctrines and institutions of the legal system are best understood and explained as efforts to promote the efficient allocation of resources',[55] and the recent literature in the field is said by Veljanovski to establish that 'economic logic can explain the long-term development of property rights'.[56] It is true that the rights and rules scrutinized are those of the common law, but an anglophone economics were strange indeed. If its propositions are true of the common law, they ought to hold good for other systems with similar social and economic infrastructures.

It is much more difficult to find a clear statement of the second theory. The current literature offers no economic explanation of the *numerus clausus*, but seems largely to ignore its existence. Given the authors' concern with the price mechanism, this is strange, because they accept that 'setting prices is itself dependent upon the rights possessed by those who can transfer the rights. In sum, the structure of property rights affects the way prices are determined; fixing prices itself depends upon the rights possessed by those who can transfer the rights.'[57] Instead, the writers make their case for private property (by scenarios in which

[55] R. A. Posner, *Economic Analysis of Law* (Boston and Toronto, 2nd edn., 1977), 16–17.

[56] C. G. Veljanovski, *The New Law-and-Economics* (Oxford, 1982), 69.

[57] Armen A. Alchian, *Pricing and Society* (Occasional Paper No. 17, Institute of Economic Affairs, London, 1967), 15.

Robinson Crusoe and Man Friday play leading roles) and then turn to demonstrate, at greater length, that these rights ought to be cheaply transferable. But the central entitlement assumed to be so traded is simply a 'property right', by which they appear to mean just general exclusive user, good against strangers; and nothing in their work addresses the main concern of the conveyancer, that of defining what is to count as a property right.[58]

To the non-economist, however, the whole thrust of their theories seems to tell against the *numerus clausus*. Judging by the number of times it is cited with approval in later literature, the basic thesis is that advanced by Alchian in a 1967 paper (which, of course, uses the words 'goods' in the economist's, not the common-lawyer's, sense). He says (emphasis added):

> In essence, economics is the study of property rights. Without scarce resources, property rights are pointless. The allocation of scarce resources in a society is the assignment of rights to uses of resources. So the question of economics, or of how prices should be determined, is the question of how property rights should be *defined* and exchanged, and on what terms ... With private property, two persons may exchange rights to goods *on whatever terms they mutually accept*. The exchange ... is unrestricted in the sense that any person who prefers some other mixture ... can ask for it ... *Prices will reflect the variations in preferences* ... In the open market, property rights can be privately *reshuffled* and exchanged ... *the more 'side' conditions asked, the lower price available.* An open market seems to maximise the permissible range of feasible mixtures—the variety of behaviour from which one can choose—perhaps to one's regret.[59]

It is understood, of course, that if total transaction costs exceed the difference in values to each of the two parties, an exchange will not be made.[60] What has been argued in preceding sections is, however, first that transaction costs can be cut by a Landbook system; and it may be worth recalling in passing how the existence of efficient filing under UCC Article 9 has facilitated an extraordinary richness and variety of security interests in movables. Second, there is ample empirical evidence that the benefits are so great that people are prepared to incur the high costs of alternative, 'fictitious' (not to say, preposterous)

[58] See the papers collected in B. A. Ackerman (ed.), *Economic Foundations of Property Law* (Boston, 1975); H. G. Manne (ed.), *The Economics of Legal Relationships* (St Paul, 1975).

[59] Alchian, op. cit. n. 57 above, 6–8.

[60] More formally, it will be inefficient when $G_b - C_s < T_b + T_s$ where G_b is the gain as estimated by the buyer, C_s the opportunity cost as estimated by the seller, and T_b and T_s are their transaction costs.

schemes in order to capture them. While writing the final draft of this essay, I have been buying an apartment in an Oxford house containing only two: I took a 99-year lease 'at a peppercorn rent if demanded', as did my downstairs neighbour; the freehold was transferred to a management company in which each of us is the proud owner of a £1 share. Our costs were heavy.

We have seen that another main argument against unlimited freedom to create property interests is that they endure, while we do not. Alchian, however, points out (his emphasis) that 'it is wise to remember that marketability implies *capitalisation* of future effects on to present values. Thus long-range effects are thrust back to the current owner . . . [who] will heed the long-run effects of current decisions more carefully . . .'.[61] So, although not explicitly, it does appear that the *numerus clausus* will not stand with the Coase theorem: that, while the definition of rights is an essential prelude to market transactions, the ultimate result (which maximizes production) will, through the price mechanism (and absent transaction costs), prove independent of the legal definition.[62] Yet, to say it for the last time, many apparently desirable things, such as claims to share occupation as against, or to have affirmative duties performed by, singular successors, either cannot be traded at all or must live in expensive disguise.

4.3 *The problem*

If all this be, at least in very general terms, correct, the economists are wrong and one of the following four propositions is the case. A world in which all resources are exploited in the economically optimal way would be oppressive to the individual freedom of landowners and householders; or, it is not economically efficient to have freedom in the creation of property rights; or, if it is, the medieval lawyers were superior to the Romans and the moderns; or, if we could be better, no legal system cares to try.

61 Alchian, 12.

62 See Veljanovski, 59.

INDEX